Country Living

AND

Country Thinking

BY

GAIL HAMILTON

BOSTON
TICKNOR AND FIELDS
1864

NINTH EDITION.

UNIVERSITY PRESS:
WELCH, BIGELOW, AND COMPANY,
CAMBRIDGE.

PREFACE.

I KNOW that I can bear censure; I think I could endure neglect: but there is one thing which I will never forgive, and that is, any encroachment upon my personality. Whatever an author puts between the two covers of his book is public property; whatever of himself he does not put there is his private property, as much as if he had never written a word. I do not say, that any information which may be gathered, or any conjecture which may be hazarded, concerning the man or the woman who stands behind the mask of the author, may not be a lawful theme of conversation, if people are interested enough to make it so; but the appearance of any such information or conjecture in any public print, whether in the form of book-notice or news-item, I consider an unpardonable impertinence.

As this seems to me a matter of serious importance in the minor moralities, and one in which this people is verily guilty, I desire to be clearly understood. If any person writes a book or an article, and prefixes his name, he, in a manner, makes an unconditional surrender of himself. The public has perhaps the shadow of a right to ascertain and announce his birth-place, his residence, his wife, the color of his eyes, the length of his beard, the precocity of his childhood, the college at which he was graduated, the hotel in which he is spending the summer months, and similar items — startling, if true — which are so dear to the public. But if he withholds himself, and writes under the signature of Apsby Jones, you, my dear Public, have no right or title to him. That is an indication that he wishes to remain unknown. You should respect his reticence. Though you may have heard from your brother-in-law or your grandmother that Apsby Jones is a Mr. Jonathan Jenkins of Kettleville, refrain scrupulously from printing that report ; for, in the first place, you have probably been misinformed, — Jonathan Jenkins is not the man at all, and is made to feel extremely uncomfortable ; and, in the second place, if he were the man, it would be shamefully impolite in you to rend away the veil in which he chose to drape himself. You may criticise his book to the top of your bent, but don't meddle with him. No matter if he was your schoolmate, no matter if he descended from a French refugee, no matter if he made a speech at your picnic; you be quiet about it, — at least till he is dead. Doubtless he was very glad to have his book published, but doubtless he has insurmountable objections to being published himself.

This is a preface, Public, and you will readily see that I cannot talk as freely as I should like, because it will never do to put you in an ill-humor at the beginning; but you must know, yourself, that you are very much given to illegal gossip. You have a *cacoethes* print*endi*. The moment you get hold, by fair means or foul, of the outermost fibre of the shred of the husk of the semblance of a fact, you go straightway and put it in the newspapers. You are not so much to blame. Your fathers did it before you, and I don't suppose you were ever told that it was ill-bred; but it is. Please not do it again. Be very sure to know whether the name on the title-page is a pen-name or a baptismal name. If it is the former, confine your remarks to the book and its relations; if it is the latter — you cannot do better than follow the same course.

I most eagerly desire, O Public, your good opinion, and especially your friendly feeling. I shall count it one of the greatest happinesses of my life if I succeed in pleasing you, and one of the greatest misfortunes if I do not. But if you commit this sin against me, I will never forgive you! Or, since that may be unscriptural, I will forgive you just enough to save my own soul, but not enough to be of any use to you.

G. H.

NOTE.

It ought perhaps to be mentioned, that portions of this volume have appeared at different times in the National Era, the Congregationalist, and the Atlantic Monthly.

Contents.

Country Living

AND

Country Thinking.

MOVING.

MAN is like an onion. He exists in concentric layers. He is born a bulb, and grows by external accretions. The number and character of his involutions certify to his culture and courtesy. Those of the boor are few and coarse. Those of the gentleman are numerous and fine. But strip off the scales from all, and you come to the same germ. The core of humanity is barbarism. Every man is a latent savage.

You may be startled and shocked; but I am stating fact, not theory. I announce not an invention, but a discovery. You look around you, and because you do not see tomahawks and tattooing you doubt my assertion. But your observation is superficial. You have not penetrated into the secret place where souls abide. You are staring only at the outside layer of your neighbors: just peel them, and see what you will find.

I speak from the highest possible authority, — my own experience. Representing the gentler half of humanity, of respectable birth, tolerable parts, and good education, as tender-hearted as most women, not unfamiliar with the best society, mingling, to some extent, with those who understand and practise the minor moralities, you would at once infer from my circumstances that I was a very fair specimen of the better class of Americans, — and so I am. For one that stands higher than I in the moral, social, and intellectual scale, you will undoubtedly find ten that stand lower. Yet through all these layers gleam the fiery eyes of my savage. I thought I was a Christian. I have endeavored to do my duty to my day and generation; but of a sudden Christianity and civilization leave me in the lurch, and the "old Adam" within me turns out to be just such a fierce Saxon pirate as hurtled down against the white shores of Britain fifteen hundred years ago.

For we have been moving.

People who live in cities and move regularly every year from one good, finished, right-side-up house to another, will think I give a very small reason for a very broad fact; but they do not know what they are talking about. They have fallen into a way of looking upon a house only as an exaggerated trunk, into which they pack themselves annually with as much *nonchalance* as if it were only their preparation for a summer trip to the sea-shore. They don't strike root anywhere. They don't have to tear up anything. A man comes with cart and horses. There is a stir in the one house, — they are gone; — there is a stir in the other house, — they are settled; and everything is wound up and set going to run another year. We do these things differently in the country. We don't build a house by way of experiment, and live in it a few years, then tear it down and build another. We live in a house till it cracks, and then we plaster it over; then it totters, and we prop it up; then it rocks, and we rope it down; then it sprawls, and we clamp it; then it crumbles, and we have a new underpinning, — but keep living in it all the time. To know what moving really means, you must move from just such a rickety-rackety old farm-house, where you have clung and grown like a fungus ever since there was anything to grow; — where your life and luggage have crept into all the crevices and corners, and every wall is festooned with associations thicker than the cobwebs, though the cobwebs are pretty thick; — where the furniture and the pictures and the knick-knacks are so become a part and parcel of the house, so grown with it and into it, that you do not know they are chiefly rubbish till you begin to move them, and they fall to pieces, and don't know it then, but persist in packing them up and carrying them away for the sake of auld lang syne, till, set up again in your new abode, you suddenly find that their sacredness is gone, their dignity has degraded into dinginess, and the faded, patched chintz sofa, that was not only comfortable, but respectable, in the old wainscoted sitting-room, has suddenly turned into "an object," when lang syne goes by the board, and the heirloom is incontinently set adrift. Undertake to move from this tumble-down old house, strewn thick with the *débris* of many generations, into a tumble-up, peaky, perky, plastery, shingly, stary new one, that is not half finished, and never will be, and good enough for it, and you will perhaps comprehend how it is that I find a great crack in my life. On the further side are prosperity, science, literature, philosophy, religion, society, all the refinements, and amenities, and benevolences, and purities of life, — in short, all the arts of peace, and civilization, and Christianity, — and on this side —— moving. You will also understand why that one word comprises, to my thinking, all the discomforts short of absolute physical torture that can be condensed into the human lot. Condensed, did I say? If it were a condensed agony, I could endure it. One great, stunning, overpowering blow is undoubtedly terrible, but you rally all your fortitude to meet and resist it, and when it is over, it is over, and the recuperative forces go to work; but a trouble that worries and baffles and pricks and rasps you, that penetrates into all the ramifications of your life, that fills you with profound disgust, and fires you with irrepressible fury, and makes of you an Ishmaelite indeed, with your hand against every man, and every man's hand against you, — ah! that is the *experimentum crucis.*

Such is moving, in the country, — not an act, but a process, — not a volition, but a fermentation.

We will say that the first of September is the time appointed for the transit. The day approaches. It is the twenty-ninth of August. I prepare to take hold of the matter in earnest. I am nipped in the bud by learning that the woman who was to help about the carpets cannot come, because her baby is taken with the croup. I have not a doubt of it. I never knew a baby yet that did not go and have the croup, or the colic, or the cholera infantum, just when it was imperatively necessary that it should not have them. But there is no help for it. I shudder, and bravely gird myself for the work. I tug at the heavy, bulky, unwieldy carpets, and am covered with dust and abomination. I think carpets are the most untidy, unwholesome nuisances in the whole world. It is impossible to be clean with them under your feet. You may sweep your carpet twenty times, and raise a dust on the twenty-first. I am sure I heard long ago of some new fashion that was to be introduced, — some Italian style, tiles, or mosaic-work, or something of the sort. I should welcome anything that would dispense with these vile rags. I sigh over the good old sanded floors that our grandmothers rejoiced in, — and so, apotheosizing the past and anathematizing the present, I pull away, and the tacks tear my fingers, and the hammer slips and lets me back with a jerk, and the dust fills my hair and nose and eyes and mouth and lungs, and my hands grow red and coarse and ragged and sore and begrimed, and I pull and choke and cough and strangle and pull.

So the carpets all come up, and the curtains all come down. The bureaus march out of the chamber-windows and dance on a tight-rope down into the yard below. The chairs are set at "heads and points." The clothes are packed into the trunks. The flour and meal and sugar, all the wholesale edibles, are carted down to the new house and stored. The forks are wrapped up, and we eat with our fingers, and have nothing to eat at that. Then we are informed that the new house will not be ready short of two weeks at least. Unavoidable delays. The plasterers were hindered; the painters misunderstood orders; the paperers have defalcated, and the universe generally comes to a pause. It is no matter in what faith I was nurtured, I am now a believer in total depravity. Contractors have no conscience; masons are not men of their word; carpenters are tricky; all manner of cunning workmen are bruised reeds. But there is nothing to do but submit and make the best of it, — a horrible kind of mechanism. We go forthwith into a chrysalis state for two weeks. The only sign of life is an occasional lurch towards the new house, just sufficient to keep up the circulation. One day I dreamily carry down a basket of wine-glasses. At another time I listlessly stuff all my slippers into a huge pitcher, and take up the line of march. Again a bucket is filled with tea-cups, or I shoulder the fire-shovel. The two weeks drag themselves away, and the cry is still, "Unfinished!" To prevent petrifying into a fossil remain, or relapsing into primitive barbarism, or degenerating into a dormouse, I rouse my energies and determine to put my own shoulder to the wheel and see if something cannot be accomplished. I rise early in the morning and walk to Dan, to hire a painter who is possessed of "gumption," "faculty." Arrived in Dan, I am told he is in Beersheba. Nothing daunted, I take a short cut across the fields to Beersheba, bearding manifold dangers from rickety stone-walls, strong enough to keep women in, but not strong enough to keep bears, bulls, and other wild beasts out, — toppling enough to play the mischief with draperies, but not toppling enough to topple over when urgently pressed to do so. But I secure my man, and remember no more my sorrow of bulls and stones for joy at my success. From Beersheba I proceed to Padan-aram to buy seven pounds of flour, thence to Galilee of the Gentiles for a pound of cheese, thence to the land of Uz for smoked halibut, thence to the ends of the earth for a lemon to make life tolerable, — and the days hobble on.

"The flying gold of the ruined woodlands drives through the air," the signal is given, and there is no longer quiet on the Potomac. The unnatural calm gives way to an unearthly din. Once more I bring myself to bear on the furniture and the trumpery, and there is a small household whirlpool. All that went before "pales its ineffectual fires." Now comes the strain upon my temper, and my temper bends, and quivers, and creaks, and cracks. Ithuriel touches me with his spear; all the integuments of my conventional, artificial, and acquired gentleness peel off, and I stand revealed a savage. Everything around me sloughs off its usual habitude and becomes savage. Looking-glasses are shivered by the dozen. A bit is nicked out of the best China sugar-bowl. A pin gets under the matting that is wrapped around the centre-table, and jags horrible hieroglyphics over the whole polished surface. The bookcase, that we are trying to move, tilts, and trembles, and goes over, and the old house through all her frame gives signs of woe. A crash detonate on the stairs brings me up from the depths of the closet where I am burrowing. I remember seeing Halicarnassus disappear a moment ago with my lovely and beloved marble Hebe in his arms. I rush rampant to the upper landing in time to see him couchant on the lower. "I have broken my leg," roars Halicarnassus, as if I cared for his leg. A fractured leg is easily mended; but who shall restore me the nose of my nymph, marred into irremediable deformity and dishonor!

Occasionally a gleam of sunshine shoots athwart the darkness to keep me back from rash deeds. Behind the sideboard I find a little cross of dark, bright hair, and gold and pearls, that I lost two years ago and would not be comforted. O happy days woven in with the dark, bright hair! O golden, pearly days, come back to me again! "Never mind your gewgaws," interposes real life; "what is to be done with the things in this drawer?" Lying atop of a heap of old papers in the front-yard waiting the match that is to glorify them into flame, I find a letter that mysteriously disappeared long since, and caused me infinite alarm lest indelicate eyes might see it, and indelicate hands make ignoble use of its honest and honorable meaning. I learn also sundry new and interesting facts in mechanics. I become acquainted for the first time with the *modus operandi* of "roller-cloths." I never understood before how the roller got inside the towel. It was one of those gentle domestic mysteries that repel even while they invite investigation. I shall not give the result of my discovery to the public. If you wish very much to find out, you can move, as I did.

But the rifts of sunshine disappear. The clouds draw together and close in. The savage walks abroad once more, and I go to bed tired of life.

I have scarcely fallen asleep, when I am reluctantly, by short and difficult stages, awakened. A rumbling, grating, strident noise first confuses, then startles me. Is it robbers? Is it an earthquake? Is it the coming of fate? I lie rigid, bathed in a cold perspiration. I hear the tread of banditti on the moaning stairs. I see the flutter of ghostly robes by the uncurtained windows. A chill, uncanny air rushes in and grips at my damp hair. I am nerved by the extremity of my terror. I will die of anything but fright. I jerk off the bedclothes, convulse into an upright posture, and glare into the darkness. Nothing. I rise softly, creep cautiously and swiftly over the floor, that always creaked, but now thunders at every footfall. A light gleams through the open door of the opposite room whence the sound issues. A familiar voice utters an exclamation which I recognize. It is Halicarnassus, the unprincipled scoundrel, who is uncording a bed, dragging remorselessly through innumerable holes the long rope whose doleful wail came near giving me an epilepsy. My savage lets loose the dogs of war. Halicarnassus would fain defend himself by declaring that it is morning. I indignantly deny it. He produces his watch.

A fig for his watch! I stake my consciousness against twenty watches, and go to bed again; but Sleep, angry goddess, once repulsed, returns no more. The dawn comes up the sky, and confirms the scorned watch. The golden daggers of the morning prick in under my eyelids, and Halicarnassus introduces himself upon the scene once more, to announce, that, if I don't wish to be corded up myself, I must abdicate that bed. The threat does not terrify me. Indeed, nothing at the moment seems more inviting than to be corded up and let alone; but duty still binds me to life, and, assuring Halicarnassus that the just law will do that service for him, if he does not mend his ways, I slowly emerge again into the world, — the dreary, chaotic world, — the world that is never at rest.

And there is hurrying to and fro, and a clang of many voices, and the clatter of much crockery, and a lifting and balancing and battering against walls, and curving around corners, and sundry contusions, and a great waste of expletives, and a loading of wagons, and a driving of patient oxen back and forth with me generally on the top of the load, steadying a basket of eggs with one foot, keeping a tin can of something from upsetting with the other, and both arms stretched around a very big and very square picture-frame that knocks against my nose or my chin every time the cart goes over a stone or drops into a rut, and the wind threatening to blow my hat off, and blowing it off, and my "back-hair" tumbling down, — and the old house is at last despoiled. The rooms stand bare and brown and desolate. The sun, a hand-breadth above the horizon, pours in through the unblinking windows. The last load is gone. The last man has departed. I am left alone to lock up the house and walk over the hill to the new home. Then, for the first time, I remember that I am leaving. As I pass through the door of my own room, not regretfully, I turn. I look up and down and through and through the place where I shall never rest again, and I rejoice that it is so. As I stand there, with the red, solid sunshine lying on the floor, lying on the walls, unfamiliar in its new profusion, the silence becomes audible. In the still October evening there is an effort in the air. The dumb house is striving to find a voice. I feel the struggle of its insensate frame. The old timbers quiver with the unusual strain. The strong, blind, vegetable energy agonizes to find expression, and, wrestling like a pinioned giant, the soul of matter throws off the weight of its superincumbent inertia. Slowly, gently, most sorrowfully through the golden air comes a voice that is somewhat a-wail, yet not untuned by love. Inarticulate at first, I catch only the low mournfulness; but it clears, it concentrates, it murmurs into cadence, it syllables into intelligence, and thus the old house speaks: —

"Child, my child, forward to depart, stay for one moment your eager feet. Put off from your brow the crown which the sunset has woven, and linger yet a little longer in the shadow which enshrouds me forever. I remember, in this parting hour, the day of days which the tremulous years bore in their bosom, — a day crimson with the woodbine's happy flush, and glowing with the maple's gold. On that day a tender, tiny life came down, and stately Silence fled before the pelting of baby-laughter. Faint memories of far-off olden time were softly stirred. Blindly thrilled through all my frame a vague, dim sense of swelling buds and singing-birds and summer-gales, — of the purple beauty of violets, the smells of fragrant earth, and the sweetness of summer dews and darks. Many a harvest-moon since then has filled her yellow horn, and queenly Junes crowned with roses have paled before the sternness of Decembers. But Decembers and Junes alike bore royal gifts to you, — gifts to the busy brain and the awakening heart. In dell and copse and meadow and gay green-wood you drank great draughts of life. Yet, even as I watched, your eyes grew wistful. Your lips framed questions for which the Springs found no reply, and the sacred mystery of living brought its sweet, uncertain pain. Then you went away, and a shadow fell. A gleam passed out of the sunshine and a note from the robin's song. The knights that pranced on the household hearth grew faint and still, and died for want of young eyes to mark their splendor. But when your feet, ever and anon, turned homeward, they used a firmer step, and I knew, that, though the path might be rough, you trod it bravely. I saw that you had learned how doing is a nobler thing than dreaming, yet kept the holy fire burning in the holy place. But now you go, and there will be no return. The stars are faded from the sky. The leaves writhe on the greensward. The breezes wail a dirge. The summer rain is pallid like winter snow. And — O bitterest cup of all! — the golden memories of the past have vanished from your heart. I totter down to the grave, while you go on from strength to strength. The Junes that gave you life brought death to me, and you sorrow not. O child of my tender care, look not so coldly on my pain! Breathe one sigh of regret, drop one tear of pity, before we part!"

The mournful murmur ceased. I am not adamant. My savage crouched out of sight among the underbrush. I think something stirred in the back of my eyes. There was even a suspicion of dampness in front. I thrust my hand in my pocket to have my handkerchief ready in case of a catastrophe. It was an unfortunate proceeding. My pocket was crammed full. I had to push my fingers through all manner of rubbish, to get at the required article, and when I got hold of it, I had to pull with all my might to get it out, and when it did come, out with it came a tin box of mustard-seed, a round wooden box of tooth-powder, a ball of twine, a paper of picture-books, and a pair of gloves. Of course, the covers of both the boxes came off. The seed scattered over the floor. The tooth-powder puffed a white cloud into my face. The ball of twine unrolled and trundled to the other side of the room. I gathered up what I could, but, by the time order was restored and my handkerchief ready for use, I had no use for it. The stirring in the back of my eyes had stopped. The dewiness had disappeared. My savage sprang out from the underbrush and brandished his tomahawk. And to the old house I made answer as a Bushman of Caffraria might, or a Sioux of the Præ-Pilgrimic Age:—

"Old House, hush up! Why do you talk stuff? 'Golden memories' indeed! To hear you, one might suppose you were an ivied castle on the Rhine, and I a fair-haired princess, cradled in the depths of regal luxury, feeding on the blossoms of a thousand generations, and heroic from inborn royalty. 'Tender care'! Did you not wake me in the middle of the night, last summer, by trickling down water on my face from a passing shower? and did I not have to get up at that unearthly hour to move the bed, and step splash into a puddle, and come very near being floated away? Did not the water drip, drip, drip upon my writing-desk, and soak the leather, and swell the wood, and stain the ribbon, and spoil the paper inside, and all because you were treacherous at the roof and let it? Have you not made a perfect rattery of yourself, yawning at every possible chink and crumbling at the underpinning, and keeping me awake night after night by the tramp of a whole brigade of the Grand Army that slaughtered Bishop Hatto? Whenever a breeze comes along stout enough to make an aspen-leaf tremble, don't you immediately go into hysterics, and rock, and creak, and groan, as if you were the shell of an earthquake? Don't you shrivel at every window to let in the northeasters and all the snow-storms that walk abroad? Whenever a needle, or a pencil, or a penny drops, don't you open somewhere and take it in? 'Golden memories'! Leaden memories! Wooden memories! Mudden memories!"

My savage gave a war-whoop. I turned scornfully. I swept down the staircase. I banged the front-door. I locked it with an accent, and marched up the hill. A soft sighing breathed past me. I knew it was the old house mourning for her departing child. The sun had disappeared, but the western sky was jubilant in purple and gold. The cool evening calmed me. The echoes of the war-whoop vibrated almost tenderly along the hushed hill-side. I paused on the summit of the hill and looked back. Down in the valley stood the sorrowful house, tasting the first bitterness of perpetual desolation. The maples and the oaks and the beech-trees hung out their flaming banners. The pond lay dark in the shadow of the circling hills. The years called to me,—the happy, sun-ripe years that I had left tangled in the apple-blossoms, and moaning among the pines, and tinkling in the brook, and floating in the cups of the water-lilies. They looked up at me from the orchard, dark and cool. They thrilled across from the hill-tops, glowing still with the glowing sky. I heard their voice by the lilac-bush. They smiled at me under the peach-trees, and where the blackberries had ripened against the southern wall. I felt them once more in the clover-smells and the new-mown hay. They swayed again in the silken tassels of the crisp, rustling corn. They hummed with the bees in the garden-borders. They sang with the robins in the cherry-trees, and their tone was tender and passing sweet. They besought me not to cast away their memory, for despite of the black-browed troop whose vile and sombre robes had mingled in with their silver garments. They prayed me to forget, but not all. They minded me of the sweet counsel we had taken together, when summer came over the hills, and walked by the water-courses. They bade me remember the good tidings of great joy which they had brought me when my eyes were dim with unavailing tears. My lips trembled to their call.

The war-whoop chanted itself into a vesper. A happy calm lifted from my heart and quivered out over the valley, and a comfort settled on the sad old house, as I stretched forth my hands, and from my inmost soul breathed down a *Benedicite!*

The Bank.

WE had much ado to get it, but it was lovely when it was done. The glory of it belongs to me. Halicarnassus, I regret to say, to many amiable qualities does not add executive and comprehensive energy. He occasionally develops very satisfactorily in some one direction, but I have yet to see him become complete master of any situation. He does one thing, but he leaves twenty undone. So it was in keeping with his character to hibernate on the top of a gravel-heap. When I suggested, in the fall, that the gravel-heap be immediately graded and turfed, he replied that there were too many things which *must* be done before winter set in. When winter had set in, and the things were all done, and I repeated my suggestion, there was no turf to be had, — nothing but snow and ice. When the spring sun came and drank up the snow, and the turf sprouted and thickened and matted, and I spoke of the bank, everybody, according to Halicarnassus, was absorbed in ploughing and planting, and could not be lured away to do our work. "Besides," he added, "it is very well as it is. Gravel has more character than grass. Gravel suggests strength. Grass is but a smooth commonplace. Gravel is geological and antiquitous. It carries one back to the drift formation and a wilderness of waters. Grass is a modern arrangement. Gravel is the naked innocence of Earth. Grass is the recourse of sin-born Shame." I let him go on, putting a curb to my lips. If there is anything that tries my temper, it is to have Halicarnassus philosophize. When he confines himself to facts and syllogisms, he is comparatively harmless; but the moment he strikes out into moral reflection he becomes a nuisance. He does not often do it, I allow. A certain blind instinct teaches him to cling to the earth, and not attempt waxen wings. So I only smiled. If I had refuted him, he would have gone on till this time. I knew better. His theory was improvised on the spot to suit his facts, and the facts were culpable indifference and negligence, which no theory could convert into cardinal virtues. I was silent, and recalled to mind my experience in the fall, and the story in the Young Reader. When the farmer announced his intention to reap his field himself, the mother-bird concluded it was time to take her nurslings and go. I determined to see what my own efforts might do towards a bank, and, without consulting Halicarnassus, I walked ten miles one morning, and secured a man. A man is an indispensable thing in the country. He was represented to me as an excellent gardener, if he could be kept sober. He thought he could make the bank in a week, and he promised me faithfully that he would not be drunk once in all the time. Nor was he. You may be sure I plied him with strong coffee and highly-spiced meats, and he did his work in the most beautiful manner. Exultation and admiration filled my heart as I saw the gravel begin to haul, the loam topple over upon it, the turf trundle down upon a wheelbarrow and square itself upon the loam, and a shapely terrace rise slowly from the chaos of *débris*. Halicarnassus enjoyed it too. He enjoys things if he is not forced to originate them. It is the first step which costs him. He would live in a palace with great delight, if he woke one morning and found himself in it; but he would live in a cave many years before he could bring himself to plan and construct even a log-cabin. So he stood by me, and we marked the unsightly gravel-heap transfigured into a sightly bank, and watched the lowering clouds, and hoped it would not rain. Premature rain would wash away the loose turf and loam, and many hopes, and several dollars, and it was already getting late in the season. If it only would keep off just long enough to get the slope finished so that the whole should not be carried away and the work have to be done quite over again! It looked as if it would "pour" every minute. We watched the menacing sky, and the gardener wielded his knife and line and fingers and wheelbarrow, and the slope was finished, and it did not rain, and we breathed again. The next day wore away, and the next, and the next, and the corners were rounded, and the top met the slope in grassy embrace, and it did not rain. How pretty the bank looked; how like the smooth skin veiling and adorning the hideous skeleton was the verdant velvet that soothed away the rough gravel. Then we were ready for the rain. Indeed, we desired rain to cherish the tender little rootlets of the transplanted grass. We longed for rain to keep the turf from cracking and crumbling away. But it did not rain. The green turned gray in patches. The gray struggled for a while, gave up the ghost, and dust reigned in its stead. O, if it would only rain! We talked of warm showers, and the pattering of drops through the cool night, and the new life that would spring under our feet in the morning. But it did not rain. Then we talked of watering-pots, and available light buckets, and we put our shoulders to the wheel, and our hands to the pump, and gave the thirsty and dead and dying grass a thorough drenching. And it did not rain. The evening and the morning came, and it was the third and fourth and fifth day, till we ceased to count, but poured our morning and evening libations with a silent, sad persistence, and there was no rain.

Halicarnassus was very "aggravating." He pretended great solicitude for the bank. I think he would have been sorry to see it relapse into chaos. But did he go to work with all his might to prevent it? Not he. He made every one think he did. He talked, and — that was all. He did not do a penny's-worth of good. He grew tired of pumping and carrying water after the second day. He knew that my interest was too deeply enlisted to permit me to slacken my exertions. He knew that, if he did not work, I would, and he accordingly shirked. "That bank must be watered, or it will die!" he would exclaim, with a great show of efficiency. "Yes," I would answer, "let us go and water it at once." "Very well. But I have my cows to feed just now. Do you begin, and I will presently join you." And that would be the last of him. When it was all over, and I resting on the sofa, he would lounge in and profess great astonishment. "I came to help you, but you had finished," he would say. Generally my sole reply was a steady glance, before which he quailed and retreated, though striving to hide his real feelings under a laugh. Sometimes, by skilful diplomacy, I succeeded in forcing him to draw half a dozen buckets of water, but it was a great deal harder to work him than it was the pump, though that creaked and wheezed and

2

spouted out a stream not much bigger than a knitting-needle, and I presently gave him over as incorrigible. The chief hand he had in the matter was to exacerbate me by talking before friends about *our* efforts to save the bank, and by calling out, as he passed to and fro, "You are putting on more water there than you need," or, "You are leaving this corner quite dry," or, "Here, bring your watering-pot this way." It was bad enough not to have him take hold and help me, but it was intolerable to have him come and order me about. The only satisfaction left was to do the opposite thing to that which he directed. I do not think he minded it at all. He certainly did not issue fewer orders. His only object was to keep up appearances.

As I waved my watering-pot hither and thither, it seemed to me less strange that the old heathen nations should have believed in two Deities, — one of good and the other of evil, — Odin, the All-Father, and Surtur, the black one; I had to bring the faith of eighteen centuries to bear on the point, and even then I was not so patient as I should have been. It might easily seem as if a good being were trying to send rain, that grass might grow for the cattle, and herb for the service of man. It did try very hard to rain. Every sign was favorable. The clouds were black and big. In their bulging bosoms you could almost see the tender grass-blades, and the young peas, and the waving of the asparagus tops, that their scattered treasures were going to bring forth. A night comes and goes leaving the earth thirsty and dewless. That is a sign of rain. Innumerable worms bore up to the surface and throw out little mounds of soil. The fire runs up the outside of the tea-kettle. Everything happens *but* rain, and lo! there it comes! I felt a drop on my chin — I think; and certainly there another fell on my nose. No, the clouds roll off, the worms creep back again, the fire stays in the stove, the sun comes out. The evilly-disposed one is victorious, and there is no rain.

Is there not some malicious sprite who stirs up the wind every night and morning when I want to water the bank? It is work enough at best to draw the water and carry it thirty yards and put it on, but in addition the wind rises. If I stand opposite, it whisks my dress into the water. If I face it, it whisks the water against my dress. In either case I am drenched, and then the dust comes, and I am muddy. Just now a puff wrapped my skirt directly and tightly around the spout from whose fifty orifices the water was pouring, and in a moment I was dripping. Have we not a Surtur among us?

If we could stand off somewhere, and look at creation as a whole, — that is, if we could occupy the stand-point of the Supreme Being, or even, perhaps, of the archangels, we should undoubtedly say no without hesitation. We should see a grandeur in the conception of the universe, a skill in execution, a perfect adaptation of all means to the wisest end, such as could spring only from One Being, and he the perfection of wisdom and of power. We should see everything ministering to a common purpose, circling around a common centre. Innumerable worlds sweep down the sky in their appointed paths, and there is no accident. The music of the spheres has not a jar of discord. Within each world, doubtless, the same harmony prevails. The microcosm is but the macrocosm in miniature. Minuteness, as unerringly as vastness, points to one God. Nothing is done in vain. Nothing does what it was not made to do. What seems destruction is construction. What seems decay is growth. Disturbance is re-arrangement. Death is but the unfolding of a higher life.

But it certainly seems to me that, judging simply from what we see, we should, to say the least, be a very long while in arriving at this truth. We learn from Revelation that there is but one God, and then we take things as they are, and group them around that central truth, and make them "fadge." Revelation laying down the theorem, we press creation into the proof; but the unassisted human mind has always found great difficulty in obtaining the unity of God as the solution of the problem of creation. Without Revelation, that sublime and simple truth seems but blindly written on the sky and the rocks, — seems, I say, — not that it is so written, but our unenlightened eyes would scarcely see more distinctly than did those Christ-anointed eyes of old, to whom men were but as trees walking. We should naturally suppose that, if the universe were the thought of one mind, and the work of one hand, and that mind infinite in wisdom, and that hand infinite in power, there would be everywhere harmony, order, symmetry, finish. There would be no clashing, no incompleteness, no incompatibility, but, as a matter of fact, there are all these. And the theory which we should naturally form would, I should think, be, that there are at least two Deities, one indeed stronger than the other, but not strong enough to hold the other in complete subjection, — not Omnipotent, not therefore God. High and low, there seem to be indications of two powers at work, — one a benevolent, and one a malevolent one. In the sky, the planets and the stars come from the kindly and wise hand of the former. Grave and steadfast, they move on their mighty paths with mathematical accuracy and royal majesty. But of a sudden, from some unexpected quarter, a herd of comets is let loose among them, and the tricksy, capricious sprites go bobbing in here, there, and everywhere, doubling, turning, and pirouetting around the stately monarchs of the sky; irreverent and elfish; now hitting Herschel a box on the ear, now giving Mercury a flap with their tails, and away again before those dignified veterans have recovered from their surprise enough to look about them; now getting entangled with the satellites of Jupiter, and now whirling off on the double-quick through illimitable space; now rushing head-foremost straight into the sun, and now careening over, and right about face again; dashing in helter-skelter among the sober old planets, threatening to hurtle against our own little earth, and turn everything topsy-turvy; curvetting and prancing among the startled worlds; reined in just enough to feel the bit, but not by any means enough to give a sense of security to the well-behaved citizens of the Stellar Republic.

And how came the world that lay between Mars and Jupiter to be broken into inch pieces, each one setting up an orbit, and dashing around on its own account? And who gave a wrong twirl to the moons of Uranus, and sent them spinning furiously backward instead of forward? And whence came the torch that set fire to the star in Cassiopeia? And what is become of the lost Pleiad? And did not the new star that Tycho Brahe found the peasants staring at, run a career that looked very much as if some emulous and jealous power had tried his bungling hand at world-making, and succeeded so far as to set it going, but could neither guide nor stop it, and so it flamed and flared, and staggered, and burned out? And is not some force continually trying to make the moon fall into the earth, and the earth fall into the sun, and things in general crash together and come to grief?

We descend from the splendid, shining heavens to our own homely, dingy, brown little world, and find ourselves plunged at once into a strong and rapid current going one way, with a strong and rapid current in the midst of it going the other, which of course does not make smooth sailing. Everything seems to be conducted on the principle, "If you cannot do as you would, do as you can." It is all defect and compensation. It is as if the powerful and benevolent Being had intended to make everything on a perfect scale, and that the malevolent and less powerful, but still mighty Being, had struck in and marred it all, and then the first Being had made up the deficiency with marvellous skill and kindness, but not so as quite to conceal the deficiency. There is the ostrich that set out to be a bird, but had its wings nipped in the bud, and is only partially compensated for the loss by a most extraordinary pair of legs. There is the kangaroo, with his fore legs too short to signify, and his hind legs as much too long, and who is consequently unable to walk, but manages to get on in the world *per saltum*, — by extensive leaps.

Worse than this is the horrible rapacity, voracity, and violence that crops out everywhere. The whole animal kingdom seems to be impelled by two main motives, — to eat and not to be eaten. The cat lies in wait for the mouse, and the dog falls foul of the cat. The spider catches the fly, and the chicken snaps up the spider, and the hawk swoops away with the chicken. The alligator lays its eggs, and the vulture goes and devours them. The ant-lion decimates a whole colony of ants. The ocean is a scene of constant guerilla warfare. The big fishes eat the little ones, the little ones eat the less, and they all eat each other. The whale gulps down at one mouthful more individuals than there are men, women, and children in Massachusetts.

Everything that is beautiful is veined with something that is not. The country smiles with vineyards and orchards, and an earthquake comes and swallows them up, or a volcano bursts, and blasts and buries them forever. It is a fair land of orange and pomegranate, of gorgeous flowers, brilliant birds, and magnificent beasts, but spiders as big as sparrows, and centipedes whose touch is death. The grand, eternal sea, invaluable for communication, essential to life, soft under the serene sky, sweet with the breath of the spice islands nestling in its bosom, is treacherous and hostile even in its friendship, nursing and nourishing in its hidden depths the whale which shall smite your boat to fragments, and the cuttle-fish that shall drag it down, and the shark that shall swallow you when you get there.

Now it certainly seems to me that, without Revelation, these things would be absolutely incomprehensible, and that the most probable hypothesis would be that which so many pagan creeds set forth, — that there is a Good One and an Evil One, — an hypothesis which is indeed a shadow, perhaps I ought rather to say, a rough likeness, of the facts. It is the God and the Devil of Christianity, dimly revealed by creation, and distorted by man's disturbed medium. We must believe, because Paul affirms it, that God has revealed himself clearly enough to make us without excuse for not glorifying him as God; but, if not from our original constitution, then from our original sin, we did, and do, stand very much in need of this direct verbal revelation to show us that his unity is not trenched upon by the signs of duality that appear in his works, that the good is supreme, and the evil under subjection. With that fact laid down in the Bible, and a general explanation of the apparently antagonistic fact, we can adjust the shreds of facts that come under our observation, and establish harmony. Given this vertebral truth, our little branch truths join on, and there is a plan and a Planner. But without this I fear we should stumble grievously, as most unassisted minds have stumbled. Standing in the very thick of creation, it is difficult for us to take in its great wholeness. Mrs. Browning tells us that, if Mount Athos had been

> "carved, as Persian Xerxes schemed,
> To some colossal statue of a man,
> The peasants, gathering brushwood in his ear,
> Had guessed as little of any human form
> Up there, as would a flock of browsing goats.
> They 'd have, in fact, to travel ten miles off
> Or ere the giant image broke on them
> Full human profile."

So it seems to me that we must have some distant stand-point, furnished by God in the natural course of his providence, or by a verbal revelation, before we can read in the record of His works His absolute omnipotence and unity. Even with revelation, we cannot always reconcile discrepancies. Our fragment of knowledge does not enable us to construct a system free from doubt. The existence of evil is still an unsolved problem. The ultimatum of reason and science is an "if." We fall back on faith, and the reässurance of Divine Love is, "What thou knowest not now, thou shalt know hereafter."

Trusting in that Divine love, we take in all the bafflings and buffetings of life, yet feel in our inmost hearts, and shout with exultant voices: —

The Lord God Omnipotent reigneth. Hallelujah. He giveth and keepeth back. He holds the deep in the hollow of his hand, and giving does not impoverish him, neither does withholding enrich him. He could give us little sprinklings or great rains if he chose. When he does not, there must be some reason for it. Perhaps one object is to show us that we ought to turn our attention to modes of artificial irrigation. We are very ignorant and careless about that, we almost entirely "let time and chance determine." God gives us plenty of water in the course of the year, but it belongs to us to distribute it properly. That is the way God does give us things generally, — not the whole, but the basis. We must work its completion. There is plenty of iron, but we must dig for it, — plenty of salt, but we must separate it from the brine, — plenty of bread, but it does not grow in loaves. I wish people who have inventive genius would bestir themselves. I have n't; but I should like a little rain now and then.

I dare say another reason is to try our patience, and also make it stronger. We have not all of us a bank, but a good many of us have peas, and beans, and lettuce, and morning-glory, and asters, and young apple-trees, in which we feel a tender interest. Can we see them dying of thirst, rolling their tender leaves in parched distress, and yet be quite calm and sweet-tempered, — remember that the Lord has plenty of rain, and yet not be impatient or fret because he does not choose to bestow it? If there is any Achan in the camp whose discontent keeps blessings from us, let him make confession and repent. Let us all be content and glad without rain, if so be the Lord will give us here a little and there a little.

Meanwhile there are many things to be grateful for. Once in a while a heavy dew comes through the drought, and the earth smiles in the early morning. Dew is beautiful in poetry, but more beautiful on banks when there is no rain. How grateful should we be if our wells do not give out, for then not only the grass, but we should suffer, — grateful, too, if our neighbors' wells do not fail, for then they would come to ours, and bank and gardens would stay thirsty. For men and women and little children must be served, even if banks go by the board. Then, too, it is so pleasant to take care of grass. It is so strong and helpful and thankful. Flowers have a languishing, drooping air, as if they would about as soon die as live, if it 's all the same to you; but the grass is sturdy. It makes a desperate struggle for existence. It pulls and tugs away at its little thread of life with a forty-horse power. When it is faint, and almost despairing, give it three drops of water, and it starts up again, and is at it, good as new. Every morning it winks and blinks up at you cheerily, as much as to say, "Here I am. Reckon on me. If I was born to be hay, I 'm determined not to die grass. Just you do your part, and you may be sure I will do mine!"

Dear old grass, I knew you would, though you did look very crisp and bunchy and desperate. I kept faith in you, and you kept faith with me; holding your own till the windows of heaven were opened, and then softening and strengthening into beauty and vigor and velvet verdancy. Now your deft blades cleave the air. Your clover-heads breathe fragrance from their white and purple loveliness. Your saucy buttercups flash back his rays to the summer sun, and through your fairy forests I hear the hum of many a bee.

MY GARDEN.

I CAN speak of it calmly now; but there have been moments when the lightest mention of those words would sway my soul to its profoundest depths.

I am a woman. You may have inferred this before; but I now desire to state it distinctly, because I like to do as I would be done by, when I can just as well as not. It rasps a person of my temperament exceedingly to be deceived. When any one tells a story, we wish to know at the outset whether the story-teller is a man or a woman. The two sexes awaken two entirely distinct sets of feelings, and you would no more use the one for the other than you would put on your tiny teacups at breakfast, or lay the carving-knife by the butter-plate. Consequently it is very exasperating to sit, open-eyed and expectant, watching the removal of the successive swathings which hide from you the dusky glories of an old-time princess, and, when the unrolling is over, to find it is nothing, after all, but a great lubberly boy.

Equally trying is it to feel your interest clustering round a narrator's manhood, all your individuality merging in his, till, of a sudden, by the merest chance, you catch the swell of crinoline, and there you are. Away with such clumsiness! Let us have everybody christened before we begin.

I do, therefore, with Spartan firmness, depose and say that I am a woman. I am aware that I place myself at signal disadvantage by the avowal. I fly in the face of hereditary prejudice. I am thrust at once beyond the pale of masculine sympathy. Men will neither credit my success nor lament my failure, because they will consider me poaching on their manor. If I chronicle a big beet, they will bring forward one twice as large. If I mourn a deceased squash, they will mutter, "Woman's farming!" Shunning Scylla, I shall perforce fall into Charybdis. (*Vide* Classical Dictionary. I have lent mine, but I know one was a rock and the other a whirlpool, though I cannot state, with any definiteness, which was which.) I may be as humble and deprecating as I choose, but it will not avail me. A very agony of self-abasement will be no armor against the poisoned shafts which assumed superiority will hurl against me. Yet I press the arrow to my bleeding heart, and calmly reiterate, I am a woman.

The full magnanimity of which reiteration can be perceived only when I inform you that I could easily deceive you, if I chose. There is about my serious style a vigor of thought, a comprehensiveness of view, a closeness of logic, and a terseness of diction, commonly supposed to pertain only to the stronger sex. Not wanting in a certain fanciful sprightliness which is the peculiar grace of woman, it possesses also, in large measure, that concentrativeness which is deemed the peculiar strength of man. Where an ordinary woman will leave the beaten track, wandering in a thousand little by-ways of her own, — flowery and beautiful, it is true, and leading her airy feet to "sunny spots of greenery" and the gleam of golden apples, but keeping her not less surely from the goal, — I march straight on, turning neither to the right hand nor to the left, beguiled into no side-issues, discussing no collateral question, but with keen eye and strong hand aiming right at the heart of my theme. Judge thus of the stern severity of my virtue. There is no heroism in denying ourselves the pleasures which we cannot compass. It is not self-sacrifice, but self-cherishing, that turns the dyspeptic alderman away from turtle-soup and the *pâté de foie gras* to mush and milk. The hungry newsboy, regaling his nostrils with the scents that come up from a subterranean kitchen, does not always know whether or not he is honest, till the cook turns away for a moment, and a steaming joint is within reach of his yearning fingers. It is no credit to a weak-minded woman not to be strong-minded and write poetry. She could not if she tried; but to feed on locusts and wild honey that the soul may be in better condition to fight the truth's battles, — to go with empty stomach for a clear conscience' sake, — to sacrifice intellectual tastes to womanly duties, when the two conflict, —

> "That 's the true pathos and sublime,
> Of human life."

You will, therefore, no longer withhold your appreciative admiration, when, in full possession of what theologians call the power of contrary choice, I make the unmistakable assertion that I am a woman.

Hope told a flattering tale when, excited and happy, but not sated with the gayeties of a sojourn among urban and urbane friends, I set out on my triumphal march from the city of my visit to the estate of my adoption. Triumphal indeed! My pathway was strewed with roses. Feathery asparagus and the crispness of tender lettuce waved dewy greetings from every railroad-side; green peas crested the racing waves of Long Island Sound, and unnumbered carrots of gold sprang up in the wake of the ploughing steamer; till I was wellnigh drunk with the new wine of my own purple vintage. But I was not ungenerous. In the height of my innocent exultation, I remembered the dwellers in cities who do all their gardening at stalls, and in my heart I determined, when the season should be fully blown, to invite as many as my house could hold to share with me the delight of plucking strawberries from their stems and drinking in foaming health from the balmy-breathed cows. Moreover, in the exuberance of my joy, I determined to go still further, and despatch to those doomed ones who cannot purchase even a furlough from burning pavements baskets of fragrance and sweetness. I pleased myself with pretty conceits. To one who toils early and late in an official Sahara, that the home-atmosphere may always be redolent of perfume, I would send a bunch of long-stemmed white and crimson rose-buds, in the midst of which he should find a dainty note whispering, "Dear Fritz: drink this pure glass of my overflowing June to the health of weans and wife, not forgetting your unforgetful friend." To a pale-browed, sad-eyed woman, who flits from velvet carpets and broidered flounces to the bedside of an invalid mother whom her slender fingers and unslender and most godlike devotion can scarcely keep this side the pearly gates, I would heap a basket of summer-hued peaches smiling up from cool, green leaves into their straitened home, and with eyes, perchance, tear-dimmed, she should read, "My good Maria, the peaches are to go to your lips, the bloom to your cheeks, and the gardener to your heart." Ah me! How much grace and gladness may bud and blossom in one little garden! Only three acres of land, but what a crop of sunny surprises, unexpected tenderness, grateful joys, hopes, loves, and restful memories! — what wells of happiness, what sparkles of mirth, what sweeps of summer in the heart, what glimpses of the Upper Country!

Halicarnassus was there before me (in the garden, I mean, not in the spot last alluded to). It has been the one misfortune of my life that Halicarnassus got the start of me at the outset. With a fair field and no favor I should have been quite adequate to him. As it was, he was born and began, and there was no resource left to me but to be born and follow, which I did as fast as possible; but that one false move could never be redeemed. I know there are shallow thinkers who love to prate of the supremacy of mind over matter, — who assert that circumstances are plastic as clay in the hands of the man who knows how to mould them. They clench their fists, and inflate their lungs, and quote Napoleon's proud boast, — "Circumstances! I *make* circumstances!" Vain babblers! Whither did this Napoleonic idea lead? To a barren rock in a waste of waters. Do we need St. Helena and Sir Hudson Lowe to refute it? Control circumstances! I should like to know if the most important circumstance that can happen to a man is not to be born? and if that is under his control, or in any way affected by his whims and wishes? Would not Louis XVI. have been the son of a goldsmith, if he could have had his way? Would Burns have been born a slaving, starving peasant, if he had been consulted beforehand? Would not the children of vice be the children of virtue, if they could have had their choice? and would not the whole tenor of their lives have been changed thereby? Would a good many of us have been born at all, if we could have helped it? Control circumstances, forsooth! when a mother's sudden terror brings an idiot child into the world, — when the restive eye of his great-grandfather, whom he never saw, looks at you from your two-year-old, and the spirit of that roving ancestor makes the boy also a fugitive and a vagabond on the earth! No, no. We may coax circumstances a little, and shove them about, and make the best of them, but there they are. We may try to get out of their way; but they will trip us up, not once, but many times. We may affect to tread them under foot in the daylight, but in the night-time they will turn again and rend us. All we can do is first to accept them as facts, and then reason from them as premises. We cannot control them, but we can control our own use of them. We can make them a savor of life unto life, or of death unto death.

Application. — If mind could have been supreme over matter, Halicarnassus should, in the first place, have taken the world at second-hand from me, and, in the second place, he should not have stood smiling on the front-door steps when the coach set me down there. As it was, I made the best of the one case by following in his footsteps, — not meekly, not acquiescently, but protesting, yet following, — and of the other, by smiling responsive and asking pleasantly, —

"Are the things planted yet?"

"No," said Halicarnassus.

This was better than I had dared to hope. When I saw him standing there so complacent and serene, I felt certain that a storm was brewing, or rather had brewed, and burst over my garden, and blighted its fair prospects. I was confident that he had gone and planted every square inch of the soil with some hideous absurdity, which would spring up a hundred-fold in perpetual reminders of the one misfortune to which I have alluded.

So his ready answer gave me relief, and yet I could not divest myself of a vague fear, a sense of coming thunder. In spite of my endeavors, that calm, clear face would lift itself to my view as a mere "weather-breeder"; but I ate my supper, unpacked my trunks, took out my papers of precious seeds, and, sitting in the flooding sunlight under the little western porch, I poured them into my lap, and bade Halicarnassus come to me. He came, I am sorry to say, with a pipe in his mouth.

"Do you wish to see my jewels?" I asked, looking as much like Cornelia as a little woman somewhat inclined to dumpiness can.

Halicarnassus nodded assent.

"There," said I, unrolling a paper, "that is *Lychnidea acuminata.* Sometimes it flowers in white masses, pure as a baby's soul. Sometimes it glows in purple, pink, and crimson, intense, but unconsuming, like Horeb's burning bush. The old Greeks knew it well, and they baptized its prismatic loveliness with their sunny symbolism, and called it the Flame-Flower. These very seeds may have sprung centuries ago from the hearts of heroes who sleep at Marathon; and when their tender petals quiver in the sunlight of my garden, I shall see the gleam of Attic armor and the flash of fiery souls. Like heroes, too, it is both beautiful and bold. It does not demand careful cultivation, — no hot-house tenderness —"

"I should rather think not," interrupted Halicarnassus. "Pat Curran has his front-yard full of it."

I collapsed at once, and asked, humbly, —

"Where did he get it?"

"Got it anywhere. It grows wild almost. It 's nothing but phlox. My opinion is, that the old Greeks knew no more about it than that brindled cow."

Nothing further occurring to me to be said on the subject, I waived it, and took up another parcel, on which I spelled out, with some difficulty, "*Delphinium exaltatum.* Its name indicates its nature."

"It 's an exalted dolphin, then, I suppose," said Halicarnassus.

"Yes!" I said, dexterously catching up an *argumentum ad hominem*, "it *is* an exalted dolphin, — an apotheosized dolphin, — a dolphin made glorious. For, as the dolphin catches the sunbeams and sends them back with a thousand added splendors, so this flower opens its quivering bosom and gathers from the vast laboratory of the sky the purple of a monarch's robe, and the ocean's deep, calm blue. In its gracious cup you shall see — "

"A fiddlestick!" jerked out Halicarnassus, profanely. "What are you raving about such a precious bundle of weeds for? There is n't a shoemaker's apprentice in the village that has n't his seven-by-nine garden overrun with them. You might have done better than bring cart-loads of phlox and larkspur a thousand miles. Why did n't you import a few hollyhocks, or a sunflower or two, and perhaps a dainty slip of cabbage? A pumpkin-vine, now, would climb over the front-door deliciously, and a row of burdocks would make a highly entertaining border."

The reader will bear me witness that I had met my first rebuff with humility. It was probably this very humility that emboldened him to a second attack. I determined to change my tactics, and give battle.

"Halicarnassus," said I, severely, "you are a hypocrite. You set up for a Democrat — "

"Not I," interrupted he; "I voted for Harrison in '40, and for Fremont in '56, and—"

"Nonsense!" interrupted I, in turn; "I mean a Democrat etymological, not a Democrat political. You stand by the Declaration of Independence, and believe in liberty, equality, and fraternity, and that all men are of one blood; and here you are, ridiculing these innocent flowers, because their brilliant beauty is not shut up in a conservatory, to exhale its fragrance on a fastidious few, but blooms on all alike, gladdening the home of exile and lightening the burden of labor."

Halicarnassus saw that I had made a point against him, and preserved a discreet silence.

"But you are wrong," I went on, "even if you are right. You may laugh to scorn my floral treasures, because they seem to you common and unclean, but your laughter is premature. It is no ordinary seed that you see before you. It sprang from no profane soil. It came from the — the — some kind of an office at WASHINGTON, sir! It was given me by one whose name stands high on the scroll of fame, — a statesman whose views are as broad as his judgment is sound, — an orator who holds all hearts in his hand, — a man who is always found on the side of the feeble truth against the strong falsehood, — whose sympathy for all that is good, whose hostility to all that is bad, and whose boldness in every righteous cause, make him alike the terror and abhorrence of the oppressor, and the hope and joy and staff of the oppressed."

"What is his name?" said Halicarnassus, phlegmatically.

"And for your miserable pumpkin-vine," I went on, "behold this morning-glory, that shall open its barbaric splendor to the sun and mount heavenward on the sparkling chariots of the dew. I took this from the white hand of a young girl in whose heart poetry and purity have met, grace and virtue have kissed each other, — whose feet have danced over lilies and roses, who has "known no sterner duty than to give caresses," and whose gentle, spontaneous, and ever-active loveliness continually remind me that of such is the kingdom of heaven."

"Courted yet?" asked Halicarnassus, with a show of interest.

I transfixed him with a look, and continued, —

"This *Maurandia*, a climber, it may be common or it may be a king's ransom. I only know that it is rosy-hued, and that I shall look at life through its pleasant medium. Some fantastic trellis, brown and benevolent, shall knot supporting arms around it, and day by day it shall twine daintily up toward my southern window, and whisper softly of the sweet-voiced, tender-eyed woman from whose fairy bower it came in rosy wrappings. And this *Nemophila*, 'blue as my brother's eyes,' — the brave young brother whose heroism and manhood have outstripped his years, and who looks forth from the dark leafiness of far Australia lovingly and longingly over the blue waters, as if, floating above them, he might catch the flutter of white garments and the smile on a sister's lip —"

"What are you going to do with 'em?" put in Halicarnassus again.

I hesitated a moment, undecided whether to be amiable or bellicose under the provocation, but concluded that my ends would stand a better chance of being gained by adopting the former course, and so answered seriously, as if I had not been switched off the track, but was going on with perfect continuity, —

"To-morrow I shall take observations. Then, where the situation seems most favorable, I shall lay out a garden. I shall plant these seeds in it, except the vines and such things, which I wish to put near the house to hide as much as possible its garish white. Then, with every little tender shoot that appears above the ground, there will blossom also a pleasant memory, or a sunny hope, or an admiring thrill."

"What do you expect will be the market-value of that crop?"

"Wealth which an empire could not purchase," I answered, with enthusiasm. "But I shall not confine my attention to flowers. I shall make the useful go with the beautiful. I shall plant vegetables, — lettuce, and asparagus, and — so forth. Our table shall be garnished with the products of our own soil, and our own works shall praise us."

There was a pause of several minutes, during which I fondled the seeds, and Halicarnassus enveloped himself in clouds of smoke. Presently there was a cessation of puffs, a rift in the cloud showed that the oracle was opening his mouth, and directly thereafter he delivered himself of the encouraging remark, —

"If we don't have any vegetables till we raise 'em, we shall be carnivorous for some time to come."

It was said with that provoking indifference more trying to a sensitive mind than downright insult. You know it is based on some hidden obstacle, palpable to your enemy, though hidden from you, — and that he is calm because he knows that the nature of things will work against you, so that he need not interfere. If I had been less interested, I would have revenged myself on him by remaining silent; but I was very much interested, so I strangled my pride and said, —

"Why not?"

"Land is too old for such things. Soil is n't mellow enough."

I had always supposed that the greater part of the main-land of our continent was of equal antiquity, and dated back alike to the alluvial period; but I suppose our little three acres must have been injected through the intervening strata by some physical convulsion, from the drift, or the tertiary formation, perhaps even from the primitive granite.

"What are you going to do?" I ventured to inquire. "I don't suppose the land will grow any younger by keeping."

"Plant it with corn and potatoes for at least two years before there can be anything like a garden."

And Halicarnassus put up his pipe and betook himself to the house, — and I was glad of it, the abominable bore! — to sit there and listen to my glowing schemes, knowing all the while that they were soap-bubbles. "Corn and potatoes," indeed! I did n't believe a word of it. Halicarnassus always had an insane passion for corn and potatoes. Land represented to him so many bushels of the one or the other. Now corn and potatoes are very well in their way, but, like every other innocent indulgence, carried too far, become a vice; and I more than suspected he had planned the stratagem simply to gratify his own weakness. Corn and potatoes, indeed!

But when Halicarnassus entered the lists against me, he found an opponent worthy of his steel. A few more such victories would be his ruin. A grand scheme fired and filled my mind during the silent watches of the night, and sent me forth in the morning, jubilant with high resolve. Alexander might weep that he had no more worlds to conquer; but I would create new. Archimedes might desiderate a place to stand on, before he could bring his lever into play; I would move the world, self-poised. If Halicarnassus fancied that I was cut up, dispersed, and annihilated by one disaster, he should weep tears of blood to see me rise, Phœnix-like, from the ashes of my dead hopes, to a newer and more glorious life. Here, having exhausted my classics, I took a long sweep down to modern times, and vowed in my heart never to give up the ship.

Halicarnassus saw that a fell purpose was working in my mind, but a certain high tragedy in my aspect warned him to silence; so he only dogged me around the corners of the house, eyed me askance from the wood-shed, and peeped through the crevices of the demented little barn. But his vigilance bore no fruit. I but walked moodily "with folded arms and fixed eyes," or struck out new paths at random, so long as there were any vestiges of his creation extant. His time and patience being at length exhausted, he went into the field to immolate himself with ever new devotion on the shrine of corn and potatoes. Then my scheme came to a head at once. In my walking, I had observed a box about three feet long, two broad, and one foot deep, which Halicarnassus, with his usual disregard of the proprieties of life, had used to block up a gateway that was waiting for a gate. It was just what I wanted.

I straightway knocked out the few nails that kept it in place, and, like another Samson, bore it away on my shoulders. It was not an easy thing to manage, as any one may find by trying, — nor would I advise young ladies, as a general thing, to adopt that form of exercise, — but the end, not the means, was my object, and by skilful diplomacy I got it up the back-stairs and through my window, out upon the roof of the porch directly below. I then took the ash-pail and the fire-shovel, and went into the field, carefully keeping the lee-side of Halicarnassus. "Good, rich loam" I had observed all the gardening books to recommend; but wherein the virtue or the richness of loam consisted I did not feel competent to decide, and I scorned to ask. There seemed to be two kinds: one black, damp, and dismal; the other fine, yellow, and good-natured. A little reflection decided me to take the latter. Gold constituted riches, and this was yellow like gold. Moreover, it seemed to have more life in it. Night and darkness belonged to the other, while the very heart of sunshine and summer seemed to be imprisoned in this golden dust. So I plied my shovel and filled my pail again and again, bearing it aloft with joyful labor, eager to be through before Halicarnassus should reappear; but he got on the trail just as I was whisking up-stairs for the last time, and shouted, astonished, —

"What are you doing?"

"Nothing," I answered, with that well-known accent which says, "Everything! and I mean to keep doing it."

I have observed, that, in managing parents, husbands, lovers, brothers, and indeed all classes of inferiors, nothing is so efficacious as to let them know at the outset that you are going to have your own way. They may fret a little at first, and interpose a few puny obstacles, but it will be only a temporary obstruction; whereas, if you parley and hesitate and suggest, they will but gather courage and strength for a formidable resistance. It is the first step that costs. Halicarnassus understood at once from my one small shot that I was in a mood to be let alone, and he let me alone accordingly.

I remembered he had said that the soil was not mellow enough, and I determined that my soil should be mellow, to which end I took it up by handfuls and squeezed it through my fingers, completely pulverizing it. It was not disagreeable work. Things in their right places are very seldom disagreeeble. A spider on your dress is a horror, but a spider out-doors is rather interesting. Besides, the loam had a fine, soft feel that was absolutely pleasant; but a hideous black and yellow reptile with horns and hoofs, that winked up at me from it, was decidedly unpleasant and out of place, and I at once concluded that the soil was sufficiently mellow for my purposes, and smoothed it off directly. Then, with delighted fingers, in sweeping circles, and fantastic whirls, and exact triangles, I planted my seeds with generous profusion, determined, that, if my wilderness did not blossom, it should not be from niggardliness of seed. But even then my box was full before my basket was emptied, and I was very reluctantly compelled to bring down from the garret another box, which had been the property of my great-grandfather. My great-grandfather was, I regret to say, a barber. I would rather never have had any. If there is anything in the world besides worth that I reverence, it is ancestry. My whole life long have I been in search of a pedigree, and though I run well at the beginning, I invariably stop short at the third remove by running my head into a barber's shop. If he had only been a farmer, now, I should not have minded. There is something dignified and antique in land, and no one need trouble himself to ascertain whether "farmer" stood for a close-fisted, narrow-souled clodhopper, or the smiling, benevolent master of broad acres. Farmer means both these, I could have chosen the meaning I liked, and it is not probable that any troublesome facts would have floated down the years to intercept any theory I might have launched. I would rather he had been a shoemaker; it would have been so easy to transform him, after his lamented decease, into a shoe-manufacturer, — and shoe-manufacturers, we all know, are highly respectable people, often become great men, and get sent to Congress. An apothecary might have figured as an M. D. A green-grocer might have been sublimated into a merchant. A dancing-master would flourish on the family records as a professor of the Terpsichorean art. A taker of daguerrotype portraits would never be recognized in " my great-grandfather *the artist.*" But a barber is unmitigated and immitigable. It cannot be shaded off, nor toned down, nor brushed up. Besides, was greatness ever allied to barberity? Shakespeare's father was a wool-driver, Tillotson's a clothier, Barrow's a linen-draper, Defoe's a butcher, Milton's a scrivener, Richardson's a joiner, Burns's a farmer; but did any one ever hear of a barber's having remarkable children? I must say, with all deference to my great-grandfather, that I do wish he would have been considerate enough of his descendants' feelings to have been born in the old days when barbers and doctors were one, or else have chosen some other occupation than barbering. Barber he did, however; in this very box he kept his wigs, and, painful as it was to have continually before my eyes this perpetual reminder of plebeian great-grand-paternity, I consented to it rather than lose my seeds. Then I folded my hands in sweet, though calm satisfaction. I had proved myself equal to the emergency, and that always diffuses a glow of genial complacency through the soul. I had outwitted Halicarnassus.

Exultation number two. He had designed to cheat me out of my garden by a story about land, and here was my garden ready to burst forth into blossom under my eyes. He said little, but I knew he felt deeply. I caught him one day looking out at my window with corroding envy in every lineament. "You might have got some dust out of the road; it would have been nearer." That was all he said. Even that little I did not fully understand.

I watched, and waited, and watered, in silent expectancy, for several days, but nothing came up, and I began to be anxious. Suddenly I thought of my vegetable-seeds, and determined to try those. Of course a hanging kitchen-garden was not to be thought of, and as Halicarnassus was fortunately absent for a few days, I prospected on the farm. A sunny little corner on a southern slope smiled up at me, and seemed to offer itself as a delightful situation for the diminutive garden which mine must be. The soil, too, seemed as fine and mellow as could be desired. I at once captured an Englishman from a neighboring plantation, hurried him into my corner, and bade him dig me and hoe me and plant me a garden as soon as possible. He looked blankly at me for a moment, and I looked blankly at him, wondering what lion he saw in the way.

"Them is planted with potatoes now," he gasped, at length.

"No matter," I returned, with sudden relief to find that nothing but potatoes interfered. "I want it to be unplanted, and planted with vegetables, — lettuce and — asparagus — and such."

He stood hesitating.

"Will the master like it?"

"Yes," said Diplomacy, "he will be delighted."

"No matter whether he likes it or not," codiciled Conscience. "You do it."

"I — don't exactly like — to — take the responsibility," wavered this modern Faint-Heart.

"I don't want you to take the responsibility," I ejaculated, with volcanic vehemence. "I'll take the responsibility. You take the hoe!"

These duty-people do infuriate me. They are so afraid to do anything that is n't laid out in a right-angled triangle. Every path must be graded and turfed before they dare set their scrupulous feet in it. I like conscience, but, like corn and potatoes, carried too far, it becomes a vice. I think I could commit a murder with less hesitation than some people buy a ninepenny calico. And to see that man stand here, balancing probabilities over a piece of ground no bigger than a bed-quilt, as if a nation's fate were at stake, was enough to ruffle a calmer temper than mine. My impetuosity impressed him, however, and he began to lay about him vigorously with hoe and rake and lines, and, in an incredibly short space of time, had a bit of square flatness laid out with wonderful precision.

Meanwhile I had ransacked my vegetable-bag, and, though lettuce and asparagus were not there, plenty of beets and parsnips and squashes, etc. were. I let him take his choice. He took the first two. The rest were left on my hands. But I had gone too far to recede. They burned in my pocket for a few days, and I saw that I must get them into the ground somewhere. I could not sleep with them in the room. They were wandering shades, craving at my hands a burial, and I determined to put them where Banquo's ghost would not go, — down. Down accordingly they went, but not symmetrically nor simultaneously. I faced Halicarnassus on the subject of the beet-bed, and though I cannot say that either of us gained a brilliant victory, yet I can say that I kept possession of the ground; still, I did not care to risk a second encounter. So I kept my seeds about me continually, and dropped them surreptitiously as occasion offered. Consequently, my garden, taken as a whole, was located where the Penobscot Indian was born, — "all along shore." The squashes were scattered among the corn. The beans were tucked under the brushwood, in the fond hope that they would climb up it. Two tomato-plants were lodged in the potato-field, under the protection of some broken apple-branches dragged thither for the purpose. The cucumbers went down on the sheltered side of a wood-pile. The peas took their chances of life under the sink-nose. The sweet-corn was marked off from the rest by a broomstick, — and all took root alike in my heart.

May I ask you now, O friend, who, I would fain believe, have followed me thus far with no hostile eyes, to glide in tranced forgetfulness through the white blooms of May and the roses of June, into the warm breath of July afternoons and the languid pulse of August, perhaps even into the mild haze of September and the "flying gold" of brown October? In narrating to you the fruition of my hopes, I shall endeavor to preserve that calm equanimity which is the birthright of royal minds. I shall endeavor not to be unduly elated by success nor unduly depressed by failure, but to state in simple language the result of my experiments, both for an encouragement and a warning. I shall give the history of the several ventures separately, as nearly as I can recollect in the order in which they grew, beginning with the humbler ministers to our appetites, and soaring gradually into the region of the poetical and the beautiful.

BEETS. — The beets came up, little red-veined leaves, struggling for breath among a tangle of Roman wormwood and garlic; and though they exibited great tenacity of life, they also exibited great irregularity of purpose. In one spot there would be nothing, in an adjacent spot a whorl of beets, big and little, crowding and jostling and elbowing each other, like school-boys round the red-hot stove on a winter's morning. I knew they had been planted in a right line, and I don't even now comprehend why they did not come up in a right line. I weeded them, and though freedom from foreign growth discovered an intention of straightness, the most casual observer could not but see that skewiness had usurped its place. I repaired to my friend the gardener. He said they must be thinned out and transplanted. It went to my heart to pull up the dear things, but I did it, and set them down again tenderly in the vacant spots. It was evening. The next morning I went to them. Flatness has a new meaning to me since that morning. You can hardly conceive that anything could look so utterly forlorn, disconsolate, disheartened, and collapsed. In fact, they exhibited a degree of depression so entirely beyond what the circumstances demanded, that I was enraged. If they had shown any symptoms of trying to live, I could have sighed and forgiven them; but, on the contrary, they had flopped and died without a struggle, and I pulled them up without a pang, comforting myself with the remaining ones, which throve on their companions' graves, and waxed fat and full and crimson-hearted, in their soft, brown beds. So delighted was I with their luxuriant rotundity, that I made an internal resolve that henceforth I would always plant beets. True, I cannot abide beets. Their fragrance and their flavor are alike nauseating; but they come up, and a beet that will come up is better than a cedar of Lebanon that won't. In all the vegetable kingdom I know of no quality better than this, growth, — nor any quality that will atone for its absence.

Parsnips. — They ran the race with an indescribable vehemence that fairly threw the beets into the shade. They trod so delicately at first that I was quite unprepared for such enthusiasm. Lacking the red veining, I could not distinguish them from the weeds with any certainty, and was forced to let both grow together till the harvest. So both grew together, a perfect jungle. But the parsnips got ahead, and rushed up gloriously, magnificently, bacchanalianly, — as the winds come when forests are rended, — as the waves come when navies are stranded. I am, indeed, troubled with a suspicion that their vitality has all run to leaves, and that, when I go down into the depths of the earth for the parsnips, I shall find only bread of emptiness. It is a pleasing reflection that parsnips cannot be eaten till the second year. I am told that they must lie in the ground during the winter. Consequently it cannot be decided whether there are any or not till next spring. I shall in the mean time assume and assert, without hesitation or qualification, that there are as many tubers below the surface as there are leaves above it. I shall thereby enjoy a pleasant consciousness, and the respect of all, for the winter; and if disappointment awaits me in the spring, time will have blunted its keenness for me, and other people will have forgotten the whole subject. You may be sure I shall not remind them of it.

CUCUMBERS. — The cucumbers came up so far, and stuck. It must have been innate depravity, for there was no shadow of reason why they should not keep on as they began. They did not. They stopped growing in the prime of life. Only three cucumbers developed, and they hid under the vines so that I did not see them till they were become ripe, yellow, soft, and worthless. They are an unwholesome fruit at best, and I bore their loss with great fortitude.

TOMATOES. — Both dead. I had been instructed to protect them from the frost by night and from the sun by day. I intended to do so ultimately, but I did not suppose there was any emergency. A frost came the first night and killed them, and a hot sun the next day burned up all there was left. When they were both thoroughly dead, I took great pains to cover them every night and noon. No symptoms of revival appearing to reward my efforts, I left them to shift for themselves. I did not think there was any need of their dying in the first place; and if they would be so absurd as to die without provocation, I did not see the necessity of going into a decline about it. Besides, I never did value plants or animals that have to be nursed, and petted, and coaxed to live. If things want to die, I think they 'd better die. Provoked by my indifference, one of the tomatoes flared up, and took a new start, — put forth leaves, shot out vines, and covered himself with fruit and glory. The chickens picked out the heart of all the tomatoes as soon as they ripened, which was of no consequence, however, as they had wasted so much time in the beginning that the autumn frosts came upon them unawares, and there would n't have been fruit enough ripe to be of any account, if no chicken had ever broken a shell.

SQUASHES. — They appeared above-ground, large-lobed and vigorous. Large and vigorous appeared the bugs, all gleaming in green and gold, like the wolf on the fold, and stopped up all the stomata and ate up all the parenchyma, till my squash-leaves looked as if they had grown for the sole purpose of illustrating net-veined organizations. In consternation I sought again my neighbor the Englishman. He assured me he had 'em on his, too, — lots of 'em. This reconciled me to mine. Bugs are not inherently desirable, but a universal bug does not indicate special want of skill in any one. So I was comforted. But the Englishman said they must be killed. He had killed his. Then I said I would kill mine, too. How should it be done? O, put a shingle near the vine at night, and they would crawl upon it to keep dry, and go out early in the morning and kill 'em. But how to kill them? Why, take 'em right between your thumb and finger and crush 'em!

As soon as I could recover breath, I informed him confidentially, that, if the world were one great squash, I would n't undertake to save it in that way. He smiled a little, but I think he was not overmuch pleased. I asked him why I could n't take a bucket of water and dip the shingle in it and drown them. He said, well, I could try it. I did try it, — first wrapping my hand in a cloth to prevent contact with any stray bug. To my amazement, the moment they touched the water they all spread unseen wings and flew away, safe and sound. I should not have been much more surprised to see Halicarnassus soaring over the ridge-pole. I had not the slightest idea that they could fly. Of course I gave up the design of drowning them. I called a council of war. One said I must put a newspaper over them and fasten it down at the edges; then they could n't get in. I timidly suggested that the squashes could n't get out. Yes, they could, he said, — they 'd grow right through the paper. Another said I must surround them with round boxes with the bottoms broken out; for, though they could fly, they could n't steer, and when they flew up they just dropped down anywhere, and as there was on the whole a good deal more land on the outside of the boxes than on the inside, the chances were in favor of their dropping on the outside. Another said that ashes must be sprinkled on them. A fourth said lime was an infallible remedy. I began with the paper, which I secured with no little difficulty; for the wind — the same wind, strange to say — kept blowing the dirt at me and the paper away from me; but I consoled myself by remembering the numberless rows of squash-pies that should crown my labors, and May took heart from Thanksgiving. The next day I peeped under the paper, and the bugs were a solid phalanx. I reported at head-quarters, and they asked me if I killed the bugs before I put the paper down. I said no, I supposed it would stifle them, — in fact, I did not think anything about it, but if I had thought anything, that was what I thought. I was not pleased to find I had been cultivating the bugs and furnishing them with free lodgings. I went home, and tried all the remedies in succession. I could hardly decide which agreed best with the structure and habits of the bugs, but they throve on all. Then I tried them all at once and all o'er with a mighty uproar. Presently the bugs went away.

I am not sure that they would not have gone just as soon, if I had let them alone. After they were gone, the vines scrambled out and put forth some beautiful, deep-golden blossoms. When they fell off, that was the end of them. Not a squash, — not one, — not a single squash, — not even a pumpkin. They were all false blossoms.

Apples. — The trees swelled into masses of pink and white fragrance. Nothing could exceed their fluttering loveliness or their luxuriant promise. A few days of fairy beauty, and showers of soft petals floated noiselessly down, covering the earth with delicate snow ; but I knew, that, though the first blush of beauty was gone, a mighty work was going on in a million little laboratories, and that the real glory was yet to come. I was surprised to observe, one day, that the trees seemed to be turning red. I remarked to Halicarnassus that that was one of Nature's processes which I did not remember to have seen noticed in any botanical treatise. I thought such a change did not occur till autumn. Halicarnassus curved the thumb and forefinger of his right hand into an arch, the ends of which rested on the wrist of his left coat-sleeve. He then lifted the forefinger high and brought it forward. Then he lifted the thumb and brought it up behind the forefinger, and so made them travel up to his elbow. It seemed to require considerable exertion in the thumb and forefinger, and I watched the progress with interest. Then I asked him what he meant by it.

"That 's the way they walk," he replied.

"Who walk?"

"The little fellows that have squatted on our trees."

"What little fellows do you mean?"

"The canker-worms?"

"How many are there?"

"About twenty-five decillions, I should think, as near as I can count."

"Why! what are they for? What good do they do?"

"O, no end. Keep the children from eating green apples and getting sick."

"How do they do that?"

"Eat 'em themselves."

A frightful idea dawned upon me. I believe I turned a kind of ghastly blue.

"Halicarnassus, do you mean to tell me that the canker-worms are eating up our apples, and that we shan't have any?"

"It looks like that exceedingly."

That was months ago, and it looks a great deal more like it now. I watched those trees with sadness at my heart. Millions of brown, ugly, villanous worms gnawed, gnawed, gnawed, at the poor little tender leaves and buds, — held them in foul embrace, — polluted their sweetness with hateful breath. I could almost feel the shudder of the trees in that slimy clasp, — could almost hear the shrieking and moaning of the young fruit that saw its hope of happy life thus slowly consuming; but I was powerless to save. For weeks that loathsome army preyed upon the unhappy, helpless trees, and then spun loathsomely to the ground, and buried itself in the reluctant, shuddering soil. A few dismal little apples escaped the common fate; but when they rounded into greenness and a suspicion of pulp, a boring worm came and bored them, and they too died. No apple-pies at Thanksgiving. No apple-roasting in winter evenings. No pan-pie with hot brown bread on Sunday mornings.

Cherries. — They rivalled the apple-blooms in snowy profusion, and the branches were covered with tiny balls. The sun mounted warm and high in the heavens, and they blushed under his ardent gaze. I felt an increasing conviction that here there would be no disappointment; but it soon became palpable that another class of depredators had marked our trees for their own. Little brown toes could occasionally be seen peeping from the foliage, and little bare feet left their print on the garden-soil. Humanity had evidently deposited its larva in the vicinity. There was a school-house not very far away, and the children used to draw water from an old well in a distant part of the garden. It was surprising to see how thirsty they all became as the cherries ripened. It was as if the village had simultaneously agreed to breakfast on salt fish. Their wooden bucket might have been the urn of the Danaïdes, judging from the time it took to fill it. The boys were as fleet of foot as young zebras, and presented upon discovery no apology or justification but their heels, — which was a wise stroke in them. A troop of rosy-cheeked, bright-eyed little snips in white pantalets, caught in the act, reasoned with in a semicircle, and cajoled with candy, were as sweet as distilled honey, and promised with all their innocent hearts and hands not to do so any more.

Then the cherries were allowed to hang on the trees and ripen. It took them a great while. If they had been as big as hogsheads, I should think the sun might have got through them sooner than he did. They looked ripe long before they were so; and, as they were very plenty, the trees presented a beautiful appearance. I bought a stack of fantastic little baskets from a travelling Indian tribe, at a fabulous price, for the sake of fulfilling my long-cherished design of sending fruit to my city friends. After long waiting, Halicarnassus came in one morning with a tin pail full, and said that they were ripe at last, for they were turning purple and falling off; and he was going to have them gathered at once. He had brought in the first-fruits for breakfast. I put them in the best preserve-dish, twined it with myrtle, and set it in the centre of the table. It looked charming, — so ruddy and rural and Arcadian. I wished we could breakfast out-doors; but the summer was one of unusual severity, and it was hardly prudent thus to brave its rigor. We had cup-custards at the close of our breakfast that morning, — very vulgar, but very delicious. We reached the cherries at the same moment, and swallowed the first one simultaneously. The effect was instantaneous and electric. Halicarnassus puckered his face into a perfect wheel, with his mouth for the hub. I don't know how I looked, but I felt badly enough.

"It was unfortunate that we had custards this morning," I remarked. "They are so sweet that the cherries seem sour by contrast. We shall soon get the sweet taste out of our mouths, however."

"That's so!" said Halicarnassus, who *will* be coarse.

We tried another. He exhibited a similar pantomime, with improvements. My feelings were also the same, intensified.

"I am not in luck to-day," I said, attempting to smile. "I got hold of a sour cherry this time."

"I got hold of a bitter one," said Halicarnassus.

"Mine was a little bitter, too," I added.

"Mine was a little sour, too," said Halicarnassus.

"We shall have to try again," said I.

We did try again.

"Mine was a good deal of both this time," said Halicarnassus. "But we will give them a fair trial."

"Yes," said I, sepulchrally.

We sat there sacrificing ourselves to abstract right for five minutes. Then I leaned back in my chair, and looked at Halicarnassus. He rested his right elbow on the table, and looked at me.

"Well," said he at last, "how are cherries and things?"

"Halicarnassus," said I, solemnly, "it is my firm conviction that farming is not a lucrative occupation. You have no certain assurance of return, either for labor or capital invested. Look at it. The bugs eat up the squashes. The worms eat up the apples. The cucumbers won't grow at all. The peas have got lost. The cherries are bitter as wormwood and sour as you in your worst moods. Everything that is good for anything won't grow, and everything that grows is n't good for anything."

"My Indian corn, though," began Halicarnassus; but I snapped him up before he was fairly under way. I had no idea of travelling in that direction.

"What am I to do with all those baskets that I bought, I should like to know?" I asked, sharply.

"What did you buy them for?" he asked in return.

"To send cherries to the Hudsons and the Mavericks and Fred Ashley," I replied promptly.

"Why don't you send 'em, then? There's plenty of them, — more than we shall want."

"Because," I answered, "I have not exhausted the pleasures of friendship. Nor do I perceive the benefit that would accrue from turning life-long friends into life-long enemies."

"I'll tell you what we can do," said Halicarnassus. "We can give a party and treat them to cherries. They'll have to eat 'em out of politeness."

"Halicarnassus," said I, "we should be mobbed. We should fall victims to the fury of a disappointed and enraged populace."

"At any rate," said he, "we can offer them to chance visitors."

The suggestion seemed to me a good one, — at any rate, the only one that held out any prospect of relief. Thereafter, whenever friends called singly or in squads, — if the squads were not large enough to be formidable, — we invariably set cherries before them, and with generous hospitality pressed them to partake. The varying phases of emotion which they exhibited were painful to me at first, but I at length came to take a morbid pleasure in noting them. It was a study for a sculptor. By long practice I learned to detect the shadow of each coming change, where a casual observer would see only a serene expanse of placid politeness. I knew just where the radiance, awakened by the luscious, swelling, crimson globes, faded into doubt, settled into certainty, glared into perplexity, fired into rage. I saw the grimace, suppressed as soon as begun, but not less patent to my preternaturally keen eyes. No one deceived me by being suddenly seized with admiration of a view. I knew it was only to relieve his nerves by making faces behind the window-curtains.

I grew to take a fiendish delight in watching the conflict, and the fierce desperation which marked its violence. On the one side were the forces of fusion, a reluctant stomach, an unwilling æsophagus, a loathing palate; on the other, the stern, unconquerable will. A natural philosopher would have gathered new proofs of the unlimited capacity of the human race to adapt itself to circumstances, from the *débris* that strewed our premises after each fresh departure. Cherries were chucked under the sofa, into the table-drawers, behind the books, under the lamp-mats, into the vases, in any and every place where a dexterous hand could dispose of them without detection. Yet their number seemed to suffer no abatement. Like Tityus's liver, they were constantly renewed, though constantly consumed. The small boys seemed to be suffering from a fit of conscience. In vain we closed the blinds and shut ourselves up in the house to give them a fair field. Not a cherry was taken. In vain we went ostentatiously to church all day on Sunday. Not a twig was touched. Finally I dropped all the curtains on that side of the house, and avoided that part of the garden in my walks. The cherries may be hanging there to this day, for aught I know.

But why do I thus linger over the sad recital? "*Ab uno disce omnes.*" (A quotation from Virgil: means, "All of a piece.") There may have been, there probably was, an abundance of sweet-corn, but the broomstick that had marked the spot was lost, and I could in no wise recall either spot or stick. Nor did I ever see or hear of the peas, — or the beans. If our chickens could be brought to the witness-box, they might throw light on the subject. As it is, I drop a natural tear, and pass on to

THE FLOWER-GARDEN. — It appeared very much behind time, — chiefly Roman wormwood. I was grateful even for that. Then two rows of four-o'-clocks became visible to the naked eye. They are cryptogamous, it seems. Botanists have hitherto classed them among the Phænogamia.

A sweet-pea and a china-aster dawdled up just in time to get frost-bitten. "*Et præterea nihil.*" (Virgil: means, "That 's all.") I am sure it was no fault of mine. I tended my seeds with assiduous care. My devotion was unwearied. I was a very slave to their caprices. I planted them just beneath the surface in the first place, so that they might have an easy passage. In two or three days they all seemed to be lying round loose on the top, and I planted them an inch deep. Then I did n't see them at all for so long that I took them up again, and planted them half-way between. It was of no use. You cannot suit people or plants that are determined not to be suited.

Yet, sad as my story is, I cannot regret that I came into the country and attempted a garden. It has been fruitful in lessons, if in nothing else. I have seen how every evil has its compensating good. When I am tempted to repine that my squashes did not grow, I reflect, that, if they had grown, they would probably have all turned into pumpkins, or if they had stayed squashes, they would have been stolen. When it seems a mysterious Providence that kept all my young hopes underground, I reflect how fine an illustration I should otherwise have lost of what Kossuth calls the solidarity of the human race, — what Paul alludes to, when he says, if one member suffer, all the members suffer with it. I recall with grateful tears the sympathy of my neighbors on the right hand and on the left, — expressed not only by words, but by deeds. In my mind's eye, Horatio, I see again the baskets of apples, and pears, and tomatoes, and strawberries, — squashes too heavy to lift, — and corn sweet as the dews of Hymettus, that bore daily witness of human brotherhood. I remember, too, the victory which I gained over my own depraved nature. I saw my neighbor prosper in everything he undertook. *Nihil tetigit quod non crevit.* Fertility found in his soil its congenial home, and spanned it with rainbow hues. Every day I walked by his garden and saw it putting on its strength, its beautiful garments. I had not even the small satisfaction of reflecting that, amid all his splendid success, his life was cold and cheerless, while mine, amid all its failures, was full of warmth, — a reflection which, I have often observed, seems to go a great way towards making a person contented with his lot, — for he had a lovely wife, promising children, and the whole village for his friends. Yet, notwithstanding all these obstacles, I learned to look over his garden-wall with sincere joy.

There is one provocation, however, which I cannot yet bear with equanimity, and which I do not believe I shall ever meet without at least a spasm of wrath, even if my Christian character shall ever become strong enough to preclude absolute tetanus; and I do hereby beseech all persons who would not be guilty of the sin of Jeroboam who made Israel to sin, who do not wish to have on their hands the burden of my ruined temper, to let me go quietly down into the valley of humiliation and oblivion, and not pester me, as they have hitherto done from all parts of the North-American continent, with the infuriating question, "How did you get on with your garden?"

MEN AND WOMEN.

I HAVE read that a stranger, passing through certain portions of New Hampshire, was deeply impressed with the rocky nature of the soil and scenery, and inquired of a laborer whom he met, "What in the world can you raise in a country like this?" "We raise men, sir!" was the prompt reply. I am free to confess that this sounds to me very much like a made-up story; but it will answer my purpose just as well, which is simply to introduce the fact, that, not having found in agricultural pursuits that eminent satisfaction which I had pictured, I occasionally divert myself with speculations touching men and women. After close observation and mature deliberation, I have come to the conclusion that, on the whole, men occupy vantage-ground.

I like women. I love them. I glory in them. What sight can be more impressive than one of those magnificent creations we often read of, and occasionally see, — stately, grand, epic, — with the blackness and beauty of night in the matchless locks that sweep over the calm, still brow, and all the starry splendor of a thousand nights in the eyes that burn beneath? What can be more captivating than the opening life of a gay little blonde, from whose soft curls the flutter never quite dies out, whose dimpling smile is only less sweet than her tender pensiveness? Or, passing from these types of an extinct womanhood, whose departing left but few traces, we see every day pretty, graceful, and elegant women; some neat, simple, and indistinctly limned; some standing out in bold relief, with regal adornings; and in our daily walks we jostle against countless heroines, — self-sacrificing wives, devoted mothers, noble maidens, who bear a hidden grief, who wrestle with a secret foe, who silently, if need be, brave the sneer of the world, who will die and give no sign, — and we cannot choose but admire. Still, narrowing the question down to a point, this is the conclusion of the whole matter, — high or low, rich or poor, bond or free,

There is nothing so splendid as a splendid man!

I need not search the pages of history for facts to confirm my position. I need not point you to Mozart, king in the realms of song; to Napoleon, "wrapped in the solitude of his own originality"; to John Bunyan, standing alone on his Delectable Mountains; to Milton, thrusting his wives behind him when he entered Paradise. They are confessedly unapproached and inapproachable, and therefore would in no wise strengthen my case; for they are unique, not as regards women only, but the whole human race. To be a man does not necessarily imply to be a Milton. Eighteen hundred years furnished but one Napoleon. John Smiths are born, married, and die by the thousand, and nothing apparently can be more commonplace than their lives. What advantage, then, has John Smith over his wife? Precisely this. Commonplace as is the life of John Smith, the life of Mrs. J. S. is still more so. Small as are his advantages and opportunities, hers are incomparably smaller; and so, whether as a man I might have sat in kings' palaces, or ground in the prison-house of poverty, I put on sackcloth and ashes, bewailing my womanhood.

Now don't overwhelm me with a torrent of platitudes about woman's opportunities for self-sacrifice, moral heroism, silent influence, might of love, and all that cut-and-dried woman's sphere-ism; pray don't. I know all about it. I could write an octavo volume on the subject, with dedication, introduction, preface, and appendix; but just go to your window the next rainy day, and notice the first woman who passes. See how she is forced to concentrate all the energies of mind and body on herself and her casings. One delicate hand clings desperately to the unwieldy umbrella; the other is ceaselessly struggling to keep firm hold of the multitudinous draperies; and if book, basket, or bundle claim a share of her attention, her case is pitiable indeed. Down goes one fold upon the wet flagstone, detected only by an ominous flapping against the ankles when the garment has become saturated, — a loosened hold on the umbrella, of which it takes advantage, and immediately sways imminent over the gutter, — a convulsive and random clutch at the petticoats. The umbrella righted, a sudden gust of wind threatens to bear it away, and, one hand not being sufficient to detain it, the other involuntarily comes to the rescue, — sweep go the draperies down on the pavement; then another clutch, another adjustment, — forward! march! — and so on to the dreary, draggled end.

Stalk — stalk — stalk — comes up the man behind her. Stalk — stalk, — he has passed. Stalk — stalk — stalk, — he is out of sight before she has passed a single block.

Of course he is. One sinewy hand lightly poising his umbrella; water-proof overcoat "close buttoned to the chin"; tight-fitting trousers tucked into enormous India-rubber boots. What is the storm to him?

Is this a small matter? Beloved friend, smaller matters than these have swayed the world; and ten thousand such small matters mark the childhood, youth, and maturity of twice ten thousand small men and women.

It is a very small matter for John Smith to take a journey of six or eight hundred miles. He rushes home from his counting-room, office, or workshop, fifteen minutes before the train leaves, bids Mrs. S. put a clean shirt or two in his valise, takes a cold luncheon, kisses the children all round, and perhaps their mother, strides to the station, goes in at one end just as the engine is puffing out at the other, waits leisurely till the last end of the last car is opposite him, throws his valise on the platform, grasps the railing, vaults lightly up the steps, and in half a minute is talking unconcernedly with Mr. Jones, who has probably gone through the same performance, barring the last half-minute.

But if Mrs. John Smith wishes to pay a ten days' visit to her mother, sixty miles away, a fortnight is not too much time to devote to preparations. Her wardrobe is to be thoroughly overhauled; dresses selected, bought, made; a dressmaker consequently to be hunted up and engaged; old skirts adjusted to new basques; collars mended, whitened, and clear-starched; Mr. Smith's shirts, stockings, and handkerchiefs placed where he can lay his hands on them blindfolded, for no Smith ever yet conceived the idea of lifting up one thing to find another under it: the various strata of rocks being tilted, the genus Smith seems to have imbibed the opinion that bureau-drawers should be arranged on the same plan. Then there are the children to be seen to, the marketing to be arranged, Bridget to be admonished, and everything in general wound up to go ten days without stopping or derangement. Consequently, when the appointed morning comes, and with it the appointed coach, Mrs. Smith is not quite ready. With one cheek flushed, and no collar, she gives hurried directions, ties up brown-paper packages with nervous, trembling fingers, which packages no sooner receive the final jerk than they are discovered to be bursting out at both ends; scatters the young folks hither and thither, running down all who are not agile enough to get out of the way, and is only restrained from scolding outright by a dim vision of plunges down embankments, butting against opposing engines, splintered bridges, flying axles, and life-long separation from beloved ones, to which a railroad journey now-a-days renders one so fearfully liable. At length, the last knot is tied, the last kiss given, and Mrs. S., anxiously looking at her watch, stumbles over the hem of her dress into the coach, beseeching the driver to hurry. He politely says "Yes," but persistently drives "No." After what she considers unnecessary delay, she arrives at the station, hurries into the ticket-office, tries to hurry open her portemonnaie, but, as that is governed by the Medo-Persic laws of inertia and attraction, it refuses to be hurried. Hurriedly she asks the ticket-master, "Is the train north gone?" His loud, clear, deliberate, "No, ma'am," startles her, and before she recovers herself, he has gone to the opposite window. She waits her turn again. "How long before it goes?" "Twen-ty — min-utes, — ma'am." With a sigh of mingled relief and weariness she sinks upon a sofa. Time would fail me to follow Mrs. S. on her devious way, — to note her anxious watch over "great box, little box, band-box, and bundle"; her uncertainty as to which train she is to take, and her incessant inquiries of every man who approaches; the intense unrest that looks out of her eyes, quivers on her lips, trembles in her hands, and flutters in every thread of her garments. All these things may only provoke a smile, but Mrs. J. S. is tragically in earnest.

Man, too, is independent. He goes where and when he lists. He need not be rich to gaze upon all the wonders of the New World, all the magnificence of the Old. He can shoulder his knapsack, and traverse the globe. Every spot consecrated by genius, patriotism, suffering, love, is spread out before him. Whatever of beautiful, grand, or glorious is to be found in art or nature, is his. He can people his brain with memories that will never die, adorn it with pictures whose colors will never fade, treasure up untold wealth for his soul to feed on in future years.

If the day's long toil leave him restless, — if throbbing heart or aching head crave a draught of pure elixir, — if the murmur of the waterfall, the glow of the stars, or the ever-new splendor of the moon lure him out into the night, he goes; and the hush and solitude bring him rest and healing; the night sweeps into his soul, and cools the fever in his veins. The world recedes. He stands face to face with God. He receives again the breath of life, and becomes a living soul.

Alas for a woman! She can never do a thing except gregariously. She has no solitude except in the house, which is no solitude at all. She is always at the mercy of others' whims, caprices, tastes, business engagements, or headaches. If she travels, she must partially accommodate her self to somebody's convenience. She must go in the beaten track. Her eyes must look right on, and her eyelids straight before her. There are no wild wanderings at her own sweet will, no experimental deviations from the prescribed route, no hazardous but delightful flying off in a tangent on the spur of the moment. She cannot separate herself from the past, slough off her identity, and become a new being in new scenes. She must take her old associations with her, and they are a robe of oiled silk, effectually excluding the new atmosphere which should penetrate to the very sources of life. She cannot enjoy in quietness and silence. She is one of a party, and must go into a rapture here and an ecstasy there, and give a definite reason for both. She must be wakened from a trance of delight by a lisped "How beautiful!" or a quotation from Byron, by some one whose knowledge of Byron is derived from a gilt volume of "Elegant Extracts," or the "American First-Class Book." It is very appalling.

I remember well the agonizing stupidity of a journey which I once undertook with great expectations. Halicarnassus was obliged to leave me on the road, and I contemplated a solitary completion of my expedition with unbounded delight; but at the very last moment he hunted up an old schoolmate, a planter from the South, and consigned me to him, ready invoiced and labelled! I yielded with a resigned and quiet despair.

He proved to be a very sensible man, and slept most of the time, except when I spoke to him, which I did occasionally for the sake of seeing him jump. He knew that it was not polite for him to sleep, but he cherished the pleasing illusion that I did not know it, but fancied him lost in profound meditation. Bless his dear soul! If he only could have known that it was the most agreeable disposition he could possibly have made of himself, — though, as far as my observation goes, men certainly look better awake than asleep. Slumber is not becoming to the masculine gender. Look at the next man you see asleep in church. What absolute lack of expression; what falling jaws; what idiocy in the bobbing head; what lack-lustre vacancy about the eyes and in the eyes, when they slowly drag themselves open ; how senseless are the fingers, and how, when he awakes, he half looks about, and then suddenly looks straight at the minister for two minutes, and pretends he has been awake all the time, just as if everybody did n't know. It is as good as a pantomime. But I was glad my fellow-traveller slept, for our attempts at conversation were really distressing to a sensitive mind. He had a habit of receiving my most trifling remarks with an air of deep solemnity, which was very provoking. It is bad enough to say foolish things, and to know they are foolish when you say them; but it is a great deal worse to have people think that you think you have said something wise. Then he never would understand what I said the first time; consequently it had to be repeated. Now, when you are putting about in distress for a remark, you do often seize hold of any platitude, and give it audible utterance, despising yourself all the while; but after it has done duty, and you have shoved it from you in disgust, to be forced to stretch out your hand and draw it back once more. Eheu! Our conversation might be daguerrotyped thus:—

I. "This is a fine country."

He. "Ma'âm?"

I. "This is a fine country, I said!"

He. "Yes, a very fine country!" Pause. Profound meditation on both sides.

I. "Is that an eagle?" (with an attempt at animation).

He. "Ma'âm?" (with a start, and wild, bewildered look).

I. "I asked if that was an eagle, but he is gone now!" (Of course he was, — a mile off.)

He. "I don't know, really. I did n't quite see him." Relapse into meditation.

I. "Do we change cars at B——?"

He. "Ma'âm?"

I. "Do you know whether we change cars at B——, sir?"

He. "I don't know, but I think we do. I will ask the conductor!"

I. "O, no! Pray don't, sir! I dare say we shall find out when we get there." Third course of meditation, and so on.

Whenever we did have to change cars, — and it seemed to me as if this occurred at irregular intervals of from ten to twenty miles — [I desire to enter my earnest protest against it. One is scarcely seated comfortably, with valise and satchel on the floor, shawl on the arm, and bundles tucked on the rack, before "Passengers for —— change cars"; and up must come the satchels with a jerk, and down the bundles with a thud, and off we elbow our way through a crowd, across a dusty track, into another car, where the same process is repeated. When people are satisfactorily adjusted, why can't people be let alone?]

As I was saying, whenever we had to change, he was sure to be sound asleep, and I would spare his feelings and not wake him, knowing that the people jostling against him in passing would do that, and suddenly he would rouse, gaze wildly around, and exclaim, "Are you going to get out?" as if all the commotion was caused by me; and I would turn from the window at which I had been steadfastly staring, and answer calmly, and as if I had just thought of it, "Perhaps we would better, sir; the people seem to be getting out!" And so, by constant watchfulness and studied forbearance, I managed to pick up his goods for him, and land him safely at H——, with great respect for his many virtues, and great contempt for his qualifications as guide and protector.

Yet I was currently reported to be travelling *under the care* of Mr. Lakeman of Alabama; as if I could n't take care of myself fifty thousand times better than that respectable stupidity could take care of me.

Men are strong. They do things, and don't mind it. They can open doors in the dampest weather. They can unstrap trunks without breaking a blood-vessel, turn keys in a moment which women have lost their temper and lamed their fingers over for half an hour, look down precipices and not be dizzy, knock each other prostrate and not be stunned. You may strike them with all your might on the chest, and it does n't hurt them in the least (I mean if you are a woman). They never grow nervous and cry. They go up stairs three at a time. They put one hand on a four-rail fence, and leap it without touching. In short, they do everything easily which women try to do and cannot.

Moreover, men are so "easy to get along with." They are good-natured, and conveniently blind and benevolent. Women criticise you, not unjustly, perhaps, but relentlessly. They judge you in detail, men only in the whole. If your dress is neat, well-fitting, and well-toned, men will not notice it, except a few man-milliners, and a few others who ought to be, and to whose opinion we pay no regard. If you will only sit still, hold up your head, and speak when you are spoken to, you can be very comfortable. I do not mean that men cannot and do not appreciate female brilliancy; but if you are a good listener, and in the right receptive mood, you can spend an hour very pleasantly without it. But a woman finds out in the first three minutes that the fringe on your dress is not a match. In four, she has discovered that the silk of your sleeves is frayed at the edge. In five, that the binding of the heel of your boot is worn out. By the sixth, she has satisfactorily ascertained, what she suspected the first moment she "set her eyes on you," that you trimmed your bonnet yourself. The seventh assures her that your collar is only "imitation"; and when you part, at the end of ten minutes, she has calculated with tolerable accuracy the cost of your dress, has levelled her mental eyeglass at all your innocent little subterfuges, and knows to a dead certainty your past history, present circumstances, and future prospects. Well, what harm if she does? None in particular. It is only being stretched on the rack a little while. You have no reason to be ashamed, and you are not ashamed. Your boots are only beginning to be shabby, and we all know the transitory nature of galloon. Your fringe *is* too dark, but you ransacked the city and did your best, "angels could no more." You trimmed your bonnet yourself, and saved two dollars, which was just what you intended to do. "The means were worthy, and the end was won." Your lace is *not* real, according to the cant of the shopkeepers; but it *is* real,—real cotton, real linen, real silk, or whatever the material may be, and you never pretended it was Honiton or point; and if lace is soft and white and fine, and sets off the throat and wrists prettily, I don't see why it may not just as well be made in America for two cents a yard, as in Paris for two dollars, or two hundred. In fact, this whole matter of lace is something entirely beyond my comprehension. Why, I have seen women who, in the ordinary affairs of life, were neat to a fault, just not fall down and worship a bit of dingy, old yellow lace, that looked fit for nothing but the wash-tub; and, when remonstrated with, excuse themselves by saying, "Why, it is fifty or five hundred years old"; which may be a very lucid explanation, but I cannot say I fully understand and appreciate it.

Men can talk "slang." "Dry up" is nowhere forbidden in the Decalogue. Neither the law nor the prophets frown on "a thousand of brick." The Sermon on the Mount does not discountenance "knuckling to"; but between women and these minor immoralities stands an invisible barrier of propriety, — waves an abstract flaming sword in the hand of Mrs. Grundy, — and we must submit to Mrs. Grundy, though the heavens fall. But who can reckon up the loss which we sustain?

"Dry up," — a lyric poem is sealed in that Spartan conciseness. Only have eyes, and you shall see a summer brook murmuring through the greenwood; hushed into stillness where the shadows fall darkly, flashing right merrily where sunlight glints through the mermaiden tresses of the trees; mingling its low song with Nature's many-toned lyre; glassing in frolicsome, ever-changing caricature the damp, soft mosses on its borders; dropping a deeper purple into the cups of bending violets; flinging a roguish little spray against the sober old rocks; cooing small white feet to tempt its limpid depths; frisking with young lambs in loving, cool embrace; curling around smooth-faced pebbles in perpetual overflow; singing, dancing, hurrying, scurrying, grave and gay, till the baleful dog-star rises, the loitering sun treads slowly through the brazen heavens, and the earth lies parched and panting in his fierce, fiery clasp. Then the brook-music dies away. Softly and more softly the ripples sing themselves to sleep. The thirsty lambs go sorrowing. The tender feet turn back mournfully. The white pebbles rise hot and hard. The mosses crisp and wither. The violets faint and fade. The last cool moisture breathes itself to heaven. Sweet life is quenched. The brook is — "dried up."

What equivalent can your drawing-room grammar furnish for such a "sunny spot of greenery"?

It would be easy to go through a long list of tabooed expressions and show how they are informed and vivified with feminine sweetness, brawny vigor, strength of imagination, the play of fancy, and the flash of wit. Translate them into civilized dialect, — make them presentable at your fireside, and immediately the virtue is gone out of them. Can the man who simply rebukes your proceedings compete for a moment with the man who comes down upon you like "a thousand of brick"? Would not myriads of men weakly agree to a compromise, who would start back in horror at the insinuation of knuckling to their opponents?

I should like to call my luggage "traps," and my curiosities "truck and dicker," and my weariness "being knocked up," as well as Halicarnassus, but I might as well rob a bank. Ah! high-handed Mrs. Grundy, little you reck of the sinewy giants that you banish from your table! Little you see the nuggets of gold that lie on the lips of our brown-fisted, shaggy-haired newsboys and cabmen!

But if men, in their strength and courage and independence, are enviable, men in their gentleness are irresistible. You expect it in women. It is their attribute and characteristic. You do not admire its presence so much as you deplore or condemn its absence. But manly tenderness has a peculiar charm. It is the wild ivy shooting over the battlements of some old feudal castle, lending grace to solidity, veiling strength with beauty. And you meet it everywhere, — in the house and by the wayside, in city and country, under broadcloth and homespun. The best seat, the finest stand-point, the warmest corner, is not only offered, but urged upon a woman. You may travel from one end of the country to the other, and meet not only civility, but the most cordial and considerate kindness. You may be as ugly as it is possible for virtue to be, and tired and travel-stained and stupid, and your neighbor of a day will show you all the little attentions you could claim from a father or a brother. He will place his valise for your footstool and his shawl for your pillow, open or close your window-blind at every turn of the road, point out every object of interest, explain everything you don't understand, and do a thousand things to make your journey pleasant. The roughest laborer will step out ankle-deep in the "slosh" to give you a firm footing; and if you have the decency to thank him, his good-natured face will light up with as broad a smile as if you were doing him the greatest favor in the world. When a carpenter drags the heavy old road-gate — which he has just unhinged to mend — half a dozen rods, to lay it across a mud-puddle that a woman, to whom he never spoke before and probably never will again, may pass over dryshod, it is false to say that the age of chivalry is gone. Talk of Sir Walter Raleigh's gallantry! Say rather his shrewdness. Surely his was the most economical use to which cloak was ever put. What wonderful politeness was there in a risking a few yards of plush to win the smile of a sovereign whose smiles were "money and fame and troops of friends"?

I am aware that this universal politeness has passed under the ban of certain of my sex, who are pleased to consider and designate it as "doll-treatment," and resent it accordingly. They ask no favors, despise condescensions, and demand dues. Very well. They are doubtless conscientious. If I thought as they do, I should probably act as they do. Only I do not.

Even if this courtesy were a kind of *quid pro quo*, — a superfluity given for an essential taking away, — a Roland of kindness, thrust upon us for an Oliver of right, fraudulently kept back, — why, I am afraid I must make the ignoble confession that I — believe — I like the Roland better than the Oliver, — that is, if we cannot have both, — if rights preclude courtesy. It is pleasanter, or, as Englishmen would say, "jollier," to sit by the flesh-pots of Egypt, than to starve legally in the promised land. Women would better improve the rights they have, a little more, before going mad after others that they know not of. It seems to me that I have business enough on my hands now to occupy three persons at least; and if men *will* be so good as to do the law-making, and stock-jobbing, and bribing, and quarrelling, and stump-speaking, I will be greatly obliged to them. It will give them employment, and take them off our hands for a good part of the day, which is very convenient. As the big man said, when asked why he let his little wife beat him, "It amuses her, and it don't hurt me."

This is not at all heroic, I know; and I suppose, if there was the least probability that anything would ever come of it, I could work myself up to the proper pitch of indignation, and prefer a crust of bread and the right of suffrage to enjoying the pleasures of slavery for a season. But Plato says it is an awful gift of the gods that we can become used to things; and I have become so used to this, that, notwithstanding an occasional spasm, really I am — pretty well, thank you, *but* —

I do not believe that the stream of kindness, which flows so continually from men to usward, has any such polluted source. It is not underhand, as some would have us believe, nor sinister. Men do not systematically oppress us. They mean well, only they are a little thick-headed. As soon as they see their way clear, they will walk in it. Meanwhile comes in this involuntary outgushing, this innate nobility of soul, this germ of the possible angel, which I pray God may spring up, and bud and blossom into glorious fruitage. Am I enthusiastic? I have a right to be. A nation of men loyal, not to grace, beauty, magnificence, but to womanhood, to the highest impulses of fallen human nature, to the love element of the universe, is a thing to be enthusiastic about. "I will indulge my sacred fury."

I have somewhere read that, in a part of the Jewish worship, the men say, "I thank thee, O God, that thou hast not made me a woman"; and the women devoutly and meekly follow, "I thank thee, O God, that thou hast made me as it pleased thee." The first is the language of nature, the second of grace. The first is physiology, and impracticable to us; the second, philosophy, and attainable. Let us take courage.

From the confession of faith which I have

made, it will readily be inferred that I have no petty spite to gratify, but that I speak more in sorrow than in anger when I say that men do sometimes act like downright — persons devoid of sense (dictionary definition of a word which I refrain from using for courteous reasons), and it really is necessary to fall back on undisputed proofs of their common sense in other matters, to convince ourselves that this is only a *mono stultitia.*

I do not blame men for not understanding women. It is, perhaps, not in the nature of things. Two organisms so delicate, yet so distinct, — so often parallel, yet so entirely integral, — can perhaps never be thoroughly understood objectively. But I do blame them for obstinately persisting in the belief that they do when they don't. Instead of going quietly on their way, and letting us go quietly on ours, giving and receiving help when it is needed, and standing kindly aloof when it is not, they are continually projecting themselves into our sphere, putting their officious shoulders to our wheels, poking their prurient fingers into our pies. They seem to have no idea that there is any corner of our hearts so hidden that their halfpenny tallow-candles cannot illuminate it; and, at the first symptom of doubt, the tallow-candles are accordingly produced. Assuming that they are entirely conversant with woman's nature, conscious with all their stolidity that there is friction somewhere, and perfectly confident that they can tinker us up "as good as new," with the best of motives and the clumsiest of hands, they begin forthwith to hammer away, right and left, on the delicate wheels and springs, till we are forced to cry out, "Dear souls, we know you are good and honest and sincere. You would die for us; but your fingers are all thumbs. Let us alone!" Do you think they will? Not they. Undaunted by their want of success, apparently even unconscious of it, they ding on doggedly, and if continuity, persistence, inflexibility, and a continual harping on the same string, could have reformed us, we should have been reformed into the seventh heaven long ago. But God works by means. Water does not spontaneously run up hill. No combination of numbers can make two and two equal five. The strength of Samson would not enable a man to lift himself to the stars, by pulling at the strap of his boots. So the Conflict of Ages goes on.

O, if those who are at such infinite pains to teach woman her duties, and make her contented with her lot, would but stop a moment to take their reckonings, and compare notes! "Go to, brothers; we don't seem to get on very fast. There must be a screw loose somewhere. Let us investigate."

Do I flatter myself that what I may say will

have the slightest tendency to modify the views or the practice of any one of my masculine readers, should I be so fortunate as to have any? Not in the least. Though I speak with the tongues of men and of angels, yet, of six men who should do me the honor to read me, half a dozen, invited to deliver an address at the anniversary of a female boarding-school, would rise slowly in their places, smile down a bland and benignant compliment on the white-robed beauty before them, and glide gracefully into an oily eulogium upon woman's influence, her humanizing and elevating mission, promulgating the novel and startling theory that her power is in her heart, not in her arm; that she judges by intuition rather than induction; that her sphere is not on the rostrum, but by the fireside; that she is to rule by love, not by fear; — interspersing some venerable fling at woman's-rights conventions and their strong-minded leaders, quoting with unutterable pathos,

> "I called her angel, but he called her wife," —

(Query: what right has any man to be calling another man's wife angel?) — and winding up gloriously in a metaphoric convulsion.

Do you ask me, then, why I write? Because I know that I shall be read by girls, and, as we have been told nine hundred and ninety-nine times, the girls of this generation are to be the mothers of the next, and I hope and believe that the few crumbs I cast upon the waters will be returned to me or mine after many days.

Boarding-school anniversaries are becoming a part of our institutions, and the above outline is no fancy sketch. I once heard a lecturer on such an occasion introduce such an address with the remark that he was left no choice. The subject was forced upon him by the nature of the case; and having thus apologized at the outset, he immediately struck the trail, and came in at the death handsomely. His voice was melodious, his accentuation perfect, his language elegant, his manner refined. He did in the best possible style what needed not to be done at all. And he knew that it needed not to be done. The very fact that he did apologize indicated that he saw the necessity of apologizing. It was as if he had said, "My dear girls, I know you are bored to death with people's telling you what your sphere is, but I must give the screw one more twist. I pray you try to bear it; for what the mischief is a man to talk about, if not this?" This would not have been dignified, but it would have been frank.

But I take issue on the fact. There is a choice of subjects. A man is not confined to this stupid treadmill. Girls can understand and appreciate a broader sweep of thought. One of the finest public addresses I ever heard was on such an occasion. I have forgotten the definite theme, but it treated of the cultivation of the beautiful, and, strange to relate, there was not in it, as far as I recollect, a single injunction to women to mind their own business. Truth obliges me to confess that, though all the good people admired it as very beautiful, they all added, " but not appropriate." In my opinion, however, it was appropriate. Instead of telling us to stop doing nothing, and refrain from doing the wrong thing, he showed us how to do a right thing; and no matter if people do find fault with a good lecture. It only proves that their taste is weakened by long disuse, and must be educated up to a higher level.

That villanous old woman-hater, Alexander Pope, avenged himself for the unpardonable superiority of Lady Mary Wortley Montagu's wit to his own, and her scornful and merry refusal of his proffered love, — one shrinks from profaning the sacred word by applying it to such mockery of the divine passion, — by pattering rhymes against the whole sex, as

> " Matter too soft a lasting mark to bear,
> And best distinguished by black, brown, or fair."

The men of to-day, with all their boasted progress, seem to have gone but a step farther. They do indeed give us sufficient consistency to bear whatever impress themselves shall stamp, but acknowledge no inborn power of self-development. Singularly enough, there is a wonderful sameness in all their stamps. If we were what men have tried to make us, and only that, *a man* ⋈ *his mark* would be set upon us with the uniformity of the red cross on a flock of sheep. Now, if there were in our seminaries only one class of girls, and that a class reared in luxurious homes, and tempted by mere surfeit of idleness into forbidden paths, there would be more excuse for the monotone, though it would still be utterly ineffectual; but, collected as our New England schools are, — and I am speaking now of these particularly, — there is many and many a girl in them who has come from a home of poverty, some perhaps of ignorance, a few, alas! of vice. He who should be the stay and honor of his family is its weakness and shame. A frail girl, with a strong heart and a clear brain, throws herself in the breach. She studies with energy, purpose, and effect. She stands on the threshold of womanhood, and turns to take a last look at her girlish days. All the luring pictures spread out by a poetical speaker her woman's heart has already portrayed, and she knows that she must resolutely shut her eyes, and turn away from them. Maiden hopes, wifely trust, mother's love, are not for her. The sacred privacy and dear delights of home,

> "The graces and the loves that make
> The music of the march of life,"

she gazes upon with tear-dimmed eyes and pale lips; for between them and her rises a sad vision,

— a care-worn mother tottering graveward, brothers and sisters who will rush into rude, ignorant and immature maturity but for her. Her path lies straight, but very rough. Duty points with stern finger, "This is the way, walk ye in it," and with silent heroism she presses the thorn to her heart, and gathers up her womanly robes, trembling, but unwavering. Have you no word for her? You roll out musical periods, exhorting her companions to be content with the love that waits to receive them with open arms: can you not speak a word of comfort to her for whom no arms shall ever be outstretched? Must she feel herself exiled from man's sympathy, because a man's sin forces her to assume a man's duty? The poor ye have always with you, — the orphaned, the unfriended, the faint-hearted. They stand alone, and see the jostling, eager, selfish crowds go by, and draw back, shrinking and shuddering, but have no sanctuary from the throng. Speak to *them*. Give them your sympathy. Show them the dignity of self-respect. From your wiser years and your larger experience, assure them that a crown of thorns nobly worn shall become a crown of rejoicing, to be cast before the Lord. Strengthen the weak hands and confirm the feeble knees, by telling them how duty is greater than pleasure, integrity better than happiness, and he alone rich who is "dowered with the hate of hate, the scorn of scorn, the love of love."

O men, O brothers, you talk of woman's influence, but you do not know your own. You cannot suspect how much a woman dreads your sarcasm, who will yet, if need be, brave it unflinchingly,—how priceless is your sympathy and approbation to the heart that will yet throb just as highly without it. Cease to exhaust yourselves on those whose every step is watched and guarded by home affection, who face no sterner "duty than to give caresses," who neither need nor heed your injunctions, and turn to those whose weakness must be consolidated into strength, and to whom your appreciation would be as the breath of life.

Even those whom you do address are not benefited thereby. Upon the young girl about to leave school for her home of comfort and peace and plenty, you inculcate the duty of making home happy, because you think it is the most appropriate thing you can do. Very well, if you will only tell her how to do it. But you do not. You utter glittering and sounding generalities. You are definite in your directions only where her way is straight ahead. You bid her minister to the wants of her parents, to rock the cradle of their declining years gently, to tend the couch of sickness, to supply the wants of the poor, and be a useful member of society. To what end? All these things she is forward to do. She dusts the parlor, sees that the guest-chamber is aired, supplies the breakfast-table with flowers, reads to the one or two poor old women of the village, tends her garden, teaches in the Sunday school, and — what then? Half her time remains on her hands. Her soul is full of the nebulæ of great thoughts, lofty purposes. Can you help her resolve them into perfect, self-radiant, and radiating suns? From the chaos, as yet without form and void, will you teach her to evoke a world of symmetry and beauty, which God the Judge on the Last Day shall pronounce to be very good? You have a pleasant voice, and play well on an instrument, but "How shall I make my life noble?" is her eager cry. "How shall I wrest from every day the heroism that it holds? What shall I do with my Monday, and Tuesday, and Wednesday, — with my June and September?" Can you answer her these questions? Can you even mark off a section of the heavens, that she may sweep with her telescope, to find the answer? If you cannot, your words are as idle tales. You might just as well repeat your lecture as gay nuns do their prayers, — "Our Father, which art in heaven, &c., &c., &c., Amen." Of what conceivable use is it to tell her that a woman's place is the

> "Sweet, safe corner by the household fire,
> Behind the heads of children,"

when the very clay of which the bricks are to be made, with which the hearth is to be built, on which the fire is to be kindled, around which the children are to gather, behind whose heads she is to hide, is not yet dug! This mode of talking is all wrong,—to some useless, to others absolutely hurtful. I have not observed that American girls are generally too coy. They do not, to the best of my knowledge, evince any conventual epidemic, any unnatural repugnance to the society of men, any accountable reluctance to assume the duties of wife and mother. A respectable middle-aged gentleman, of rare intellectual endowment and excellent moral character, tells them, sonorously and seriously, that they will probably be married one day, and they would better be getting ready for it. He evidently thinks the sweet little innocents never heard or thought of such a thing before, and would go on burying their curly heads in books, and sicklying their rosy faces with "the pale cast of thought" till the end of time, if he did not stir up their pure minds by way of remembrance. My dear sir, a good many of your artless hearers think of nothing else from morning till night. They talk of their wedding-ring long before they can give you a definition of the circle which is its form. They are firm believers in the truth of the principle, that it is better to be ready and not go, than to go and not be ready; and they have already decided to be married in church with the Episcopal form, because it is so much more impressive. To us who are behind the scenes, and know all this, your exhortations sound, to say the least, rather funny; and we cannot avoid the faintest *soupçon* of a suspicion that you are carrying coals to Newcastle.

"Of all the blind fanatics in this perverse world," says one writer, "your professed hater of fanaticism is the most inveterate and conspicuous; of all agitators, your determined foe to agitation is the most pestilent and effective. Many an excitement has been kept up long after it would have died a natural death, by the wrong-headed hostility of those who had determined and proclaimed that it should be suppressed *instanter*." These men have profound faith in the *vis inertiæ*. Like the dog Noble, they believe that a squirrel once in a hole cannot by any possibility have got out again. If women are ever caught doing a foolish thing, men evidently fancy that they must be keeping up a steady doing it. Many years ago, women compressed themselves suicidally in steel and whalebone, and, though the custom is dead and buried beyond all hope of resurrection, there are men not a few who will go down to their graves in the firm belief that women are killing themselves off by thousands with tight lacing Here and there a foolish girl is said to have been found on damp pavements with thin shoes. Corollary: no end of homilies on the folly and wickedness of sacrificing health to beauty. A handful of women have occasionally amused themselves by thrusting a long stick into the mud-puddle of society, and forthwith what a hubbub among the animalculæ! Fie! fie! Do men really believe that the mass of women are possessed with an insane and insatiable desire to distinguish themselves before the world? Nothing is farther from the truth. A decade of years may perhaps produce as many women who see fairer pictures than in the household fire, who find sweeter music than the lisping voice of childhood, but such cases are very rare. On the contrary, women need to be roused rather than repressed. They are far too apt to be content with small attainments and ignoble ends. This woman's rights agitation is but the natural reaction from frivolity, aimlessness, inanity. It is only a move too far in the right direction, or rather an injudicious means to compass worthy ends. I can far more readily sympathize with those who are, blindly and blunderingly it may be, but honestly, endeavoring to right the wrong, than with those who weakly acquiesce. When such things as these happen without comment, — that a school for boys and girls is changed into one for girls only, the boys being removed with their "excellent and efficient Principal" to another, and the girls remaining behind with their female assistant, who receives less than half the salary of her male predecessor, — when a father on his death-bed is allowed by law to bequeath the only child of his wife to strangers, and that child is torn from her widowed bosom, and all her prayers and tears and agony of love are of no avail, — do you wonder that a woman can help thinking, if she has any think in her? And if she be a woman of energy, accustomed to act as well as think, and if the men around her be stupid or indifferent, is it strange that, with her burning sense of wrong, her woman's intense hatred of injustice and sympathy with the oppressed, she should herself strive to redress the grievance? And if so be the reins shall slacken in her unwonted hand, — if her feeble fingers essay in vain to stay her steed of heaven, — if, on the sharp thorns or jagged rocks of some untrodden mountain-side, you shall see her womanhood lie, bleeding, shattered, formless, — you may weep and wail, but — mock, if you dare!

They, therefore, are right — right in their premises, though wrong in their conclusions — who dolefully affirm our Female Conventions and things of that kind to be the sad results of our free society. They *are* the results of free society; just as the smoke and soot and cinders belched forth by George Stephenson's first locomotive engine were the results of the practical application of a great principle, — the might of matter quelled by the might of mind. But just as the more perfect elucidation of that principle converted this very smoke and soot into a motive power, so will free society, when it has learned wisdom, turn all this surplus activity into its proper channels, and make all things work together for good, — which is God

Newspaper readers will perhaps remember a statement, originating, I am sorry to say, in Massachusetts, but copied by our enlightened free press as accurately, extensively, and intelligently as a flock of sheep follow their leader over the gap in a stone fence. I am sorry that I cannot give the paragraph exactly; the writer seemed to have bounced suddenly against the fact, that there are not so many marriages in the country as there used to be, and ought to be. Being greatly exercised thereby, he casts about for a cause and a remedy for this deplorable state of things. In a frenzy of haste, he seizes his cudgel, and bangs away at whatever comes within his reach; and, as he could not walk up and down the fine old high street of his native city without seeing troops of handsomely-dressed women, he "falls to" upon female extravagance. "I have found it! I have found it!" he cries with ill-concealed exultation; and his sorrow for the fact is for a moment overpowered by rapture at his own sagacity in discovering it. "It costs so much to support a wife, that is the reason why the young men don't marry. They feel that they must wait till their income is enough to maintain a wife in the style to which she has been accustomed. Girls think they must begin where their mothers leave off," &c. The mother, too, receives her share of the blame, and generally the lion's share; for it somehow happens in almost all these jeremiades, that the father comes off scot-free. Then statistics are duly produced to show the quantity of silks, laces, velvets, and feathers yearly imported, and the whole ends with a dismal groan over the degeneracy of the nineteenth century, and a prolonged howl for the melancholy prospects of the twentieth, in case there should be any twentieth.

Now this is an elevated way of treating the subject, is it not? Are we not placed in a dignified position? They come to us with a silk in one hand, and a husband in the other, — "Which will you choose? You can't have both. Come, now, there 's a dear, wear calico, and it shall have a nice little husband, so it shall." Girls, don't do it! There are thousands more women than men in New England, and the chances are that you lose both husband and dress. The husband is very well, but at any rate make sure of the silk. It is your duty to dress as well and look as pretty as you can, consistently with your other duties. You are to be guided by what is right, not by what a rabble of men may like. And, above all things, don't retrench because men threaten not to marry you unless you do. Just let them try it, and see who will hold out the longest.

But, as a matter of fact, the statement is false, — at least to this extent, that women are, if anything, less extravagant than men. They dress up, not down, to their fathers', and brothers', and husbands' wishes. I do not believe there is one woman in five hundred in New England, who, if frankly informed of the sources and amount of her husband's income, would not cheerfully and handsomely bring her expenses within it. Women do undoubtedly spend a great deal of money; but if their fathers or husbands give it to them to spend, why should they be blamed? How many failures, I beg to know, have been laid on the shoulders of women the last few years? But when the numbers are counted up and handed in, will the statistician be so good as to tell us in how many cases the husband had been in the habit of making his wife conversant with the state of his affairs, — how many times the wife knew, or had any means of knowing, what the amount of her expenses for the year ought to be.

There are very few men who are capable of telling whether a woman is extravagant or not. It is very dangerous to attempt to judge the cost of her dress from its appearance. It is not the most showy things that cost the most, nor the most simple that cost the least. It is not the most elegantly, not even the most richly-dressed woman, who runs up the highest bill. I know women who tread royally in satin and velvet, who entertain magnificently, and give generously, who yet can economically, and do merrily, spend hour after hour in making mosquito-bars, covering ottomans, putting locks on doors, upholstering old chairs quite "as weel's the new," mending sewing-machines, and by thousands of ingenious and happy devices saving money from animal wants, to spend it in generous, intellectual, and social pleasures. If your lady-love's dress does not offend your taste, my fine fellow, never trouble yourself about its price; for the flounces which make you so uneasy are seven years old, and redeemed from a dress which her mother cast off when she went into mourning; — the velvet basque, which you must allow to be very becoming, is the joint product of two worn-out cloaks of her sisters; — the bonnet was made by herself from a lace veil that has been in the family for years, and all the while she was pricking her soft fingers over it, she smiled unconsciously at the thought of pleasing your eyes; and this is all the thanks she gets for it. Insensate! Look at her face. Is it blank? To her conversation. Is it stale, flat, and unprofitable? Find out the stuff of which she is made, — the texture of her soul. If there is a jewel, wear it on your brow and in your heart, though the casket be gold. If there is a treasure, make it yours, though the vessel be rarest Sevres China. If she does not love you enough to prefer poverty with you to wealth without you, her love is little worth. The fault is not that her purse is full, but that her heart is empty. You insult not womanhood merely, but human nature, by supposing that the incidents of life are more valuable than life itself.

You discover innate meanness in that you can conceive of a love influenced by dollars and cents. What kind of affection, pray, is that which counts the cost, and coolly compares chances? If you are a true man and she is a true woman, you will so enfold her life, so fill her heart and her eyes, that she will have no power to perceive any lack. If you are not true, you have no right to marry her or any one else. Begone!

"But," moans our editor, "a man who finds he has married a wardrobe and a piano, and not a living, loving woman, is most egregiously taken in." Of course he is, and deserves to be. Why did he marry the wardrobe? Whose fault is it? The world was all before him. What right has any man to marry a woman before he knows whether she is a wardrobe or not, — where her dress ends and her soul begins? He has every opportunity for knowing; and if he does not choose to take the trouble, let him not complain. He at least has no cause to cry foul play. The game was not even, inasmuch as his superiority gave him the advantage; and if a man finds himself checkmated by a wardrobe, more shame to him, but don't let him come whimpering to us for pity and sympathy. I for one feel very much as did the old woman witnessing, with arms akimbo, the conflict between her husband and a bear, "Go it, husband! Go it, bear! *I don't care which beats!*"

"O, if parents in educating their daughters

would but insist upon their having a reasonable notion of what it is to be a wife, rather than upon a smattering of French, and a little thrumming upon the piano, there would be such a revolution," continues our disconsolate author. (I should like first privately to put the question, whether any man ever wrote upon any subject connected with woman, without being sure, somewhere in the course of his article, to trot out that unflagging piano. I have heard many musical performances in my day, but I never was so tired of hearing any girl thrum upon a rosewood instrument, as I am of hearing men thrum on this imaginary one.) But what do you mean, you talkers and writers, in saying that girls should be educated to be wives and mothers? Is not a wife a woman? Is there any special course of instruction to be followed? Is not that education the best which most fully develops every power, — moral, mental, and physical? Womanhood is greater than wifehood. It comprehends and embraces it. The best woman will make the best wife. If the mind of a woman is dwarfed, and her faculties weakened by disuse, she will be an inefficient wife, because she is an inefficient woman. If, on the other hand, her mind is trained, her judgment cultivated, her powers developed, she will be adequate to any emergency as woman or wife. Soul is stronger than circumstance. If a girl is a fool in silks, will she be any the less a fool in calico?

Does a feeble, frivolous nature grow strong and self-reliant, by being transferred from a palace to a cottage. What folly is this? Let girls be taught to make the most of themselves. Let them fulfil present duties, and the future will take care of itself. She who walks grandly as a woman will not walk unworthily as a wife. She who stands upright alone, will not drag her husband downward. She who guides her own life wisely and well, will not rule her household with an erring hand. Familiarity with the details of domestic management will be a help, but want of familiarity will not be an insurmountable obstacle.

I lay this down as a self-evident proposition: a woman of sense, married to the right man, can do anything.

But you, O maidens and matrons beloved, you are greatly to be blamed for this style of acting and tone of thinking. You care too little to be, and too much to seem. You must command, not ask, respect. You must not complain of contempt, so long as you are contemptible. There is no power to keep you permanently below or above your proper level. In this great rolling sea of society, you will sink or swim according to your specific gravity. If you are stupid and heavy, plump you will go to the bottom where you belong. If you are light and empty, — no cargo, no ballast, no rudder, — you will be tossed about by every eddy, aimless and useless, except as the toy of an hour. You must be well proportioned, well provisioned, with adequate machinery in good working order, if you would ride the waves proudly and make your haven successfully. Remember this. Whatever is done for you must be done by you. All real improvement must work from within outward. Woman's incapacity is the only real barrier to woman's progress. Whenever women show themselves able, men will show themselves willing. This is what you need, — strength, calibre. You do not set half enough value on muscular power. Æsthetic young lady-writers and sentimental penny-a-liners have imbibed and propagated the idea, that feebleness and fragility are womanly and fascinating. The result is, a legion of languid headaches, an interesting inability to walk half a dozen consecutive miles, a delicate horror of open windows, northwest wind, and wholesome rain-storms. There is no computing the amount of charming invalidism following in the wake of such a line as

> "There is a sweetness in woman's decay," —

a lengthened sweetness long drawn out by some compliant and imitative females. I do not, of course, refer to real invalids, who have inherited feeble constitutions, and, by unavoidable and often unselfish and unceasing wear and tear, have exhausted their small capital, and to whom life is become one long scene of weariness and pain. Heaven help them bear the burden; and they do bear it nobly, often accomplishing what ought to make their ruddy and robust sisters blush for shame at their own inefficiency. I mean women who have every opportunity to be healthy, but who are not healthy, — who are sick when it is their duty to be well. A woman of twenty, in comfortable circumstances, ought to be as much ashamed of being dyspeptic as of being drunk. Fathers and mothers, burdened with cares and anxieties, may neglect physiological laws without impugning their moral character; but for a girl, care-free, to confess such an impeachment, is presumptive evidence of gluttony, laziness, or ignorance, and generally all three. This is not elegant language, I know; but when we have learned to call things by their right names, we shall have taken one step towards the millennium; and it is an indisputable fact, that a great majority of ailments arise from over-eating and under-exercising. The innumerable hosts of nervous diseases with which our women are afflicted are always aggravated, and often caused, by these indulgences. Women do not know this, and if they did, it would be of little use, so long as they consider illness one of the charms of beauty. Let the idea once get firm hold, that illness is stupid and vulgar, and a generation or two — nay, even a year or two — would show a marked change. If a woman is ill, let her take it for granted that it is her first business to get well, and let her forthwith set about it. A good stout will, a resolute purpose, would work wonders. "Few persons like sick people," says Charles Lamb; "as for me, I candidly confess I hate them." Whatever poetasters sing, you may depend upon it, a good digestion is "an excellent thing in a woman."

Health once re-established, let women next divest themselves of the idea that moral weakness is an essential attribute of a well-developed character. It is a pandering to masculine prejudices with which I have no patience. If there is anything more disagreeable than your strong-minded women, it is she who denounces them to ingratiate herself with men, — who obtrudes herself as not being one of them. Whenever prominent women are made the subject of conversation by men, if there is a possible peg in their character or course on which a commendation can be hung, be sure you hang it. Scold them or spurn them privately as much as you think they deserve, but defend them publicly as much as you can. Scorn the meanness of striving to attract men's admiration by affecting little weaknesses. "I dislike to travel alone," said a young lady; "I always feel as dependent as a child." Dependent on what? Whom? How? It is exceedingly disagreeable to be obliged to sit on the same seat with a person who evidently does not believe that man is an amphibious animal. It is not pleasant to elbow your way through a mob of vociferous hackmen. You feel safer and far more comfortable to be under the care of a good traveller; but that the necessity of independent and intelligent action should produce a feeling of dependence, indicates an unsoundness somewhere which should be looked after at once. I know no risks in ordinary travelling so great that one should prefer an indifferent companion to one's own society. I do not believe men apotheosize this amiable incapacity to the extent supposed; but what if they do? God does not. He gave every muscle and nerve, every power and faculty, to be used. He never intended that we should effervesce in a sigh, or collapse to a shadow. If men think so, it only shows that they need, as the Brahmin said, "to have a little more intellect put into them."

The old oak quivers through all its tremulous leaves at the passing of the softest summer breeze; but deep hidden in the heart of its greenness flows its sap of life; and away down under the ground spread out its roots of strength; and it stands the storms of a hundred years; nor does it murmur out a less delicious music in June, because the skirring blasts of December have no power to destroy. They make a great mistake, who think a strong, brave, self-poised woman is unwomanly. The stronger she is, the truer she is to her womanly instincts,—the more unswervingly does she point to the mysterious pole-star of her womanhood. A feeble soul loves, hates, wills, feebly It is only those who have borne the burden and heat of the day who know the blessedness of the evening-tide. It is only those who have walked well, unsustained, who fully appreciate the unutterable happiness of leaning on a stronger arm. Love is like the cholera, dysentery, and other acute diseases. An emaciated, sickly nature takes it lightly, and recovers quickly; but with your generous, hearty, healthy, robust, vigorous souls, it goes hard. Ten to one if they ever recover; and when they do, they bear the scars for life. Do not, therefore, fear to be too strong. Be not afraid to grapple with the higher mathematics, lest you should be called strong-minded. "Sir!" thundered the rhinoceros-hided Ursa Major of the eighteenth century, "what harm does it do a man to call him Holofernes?" What harm, indeed, in being called strong-minded? It is better than weak-minded. Do whatever you think, on mature deliberation, you ought to do. "Be sure you are right, and then go ahead." Never mind what men think about it. I do not mean that you are not to try or to wish to please them. It is both natural and proper. But do it honestly and openly. Have a benevolent desire to give pleasure, and it is very probable that the innocent desire to please will be gratified. If you cannot please without being false to yourself, you would better displease. Admiration gained by slurring over your convictions, or refraining from having any, is dearly bought. Best of all, take no thought of pleasing. Have no anxiety about it. Make yourself worthy of love, admiration, reverence, and you will always hold trumps.

"Woman's devotion" is another theme which has been run into the ground. Orators extol it. Editors paragraph it. Poets rhyme it, and women exemplify the old proverb, "Give a dog a bad name, and kill him." But devotion, of itself, has no moral character. It is simply stickiness, shared in common, and to a far greater degree, by oysters, molasses, blood-suckers, court-plaster, and office-seekers. Intelligent, voluntary devotion — devotion to a great principle endangered, to justice though obscured, to nobility though persecuted — is good. But a discerning public utters devout moral reflections over a wife's devotion to her scamp of a husband. He commits theft, and is thrown into prison; he is unkind and brutal in his treatment of her; or he is coolly indifferent to her happiness, and alive to the charms of other women, — but still she clings to him with all a woman's devotion.

Now I beg to ask this question. When a woman marries, what does she marry? Is it a coat, moustache, and umbrella? If it is, then so long as the coat, moustache, and umbrella are extant, she does well to devote herself to them with constancy and fervor. But if, as is popularly supposed, she marries a soul, a heart, a character, then, when she discovers that the soul rung false, the heart is not there, and the character assumed, I do not see what there is to cling to, nor where is the merit in clinging. You love what you think a man is, not necessarily what he is. You cherish reverently a lock of hair, because it once shaded the brow of an absent friend; but when you find that you have been deceived, and that it is only from the head of Tom, Dick, or Harry, who happened to be tonsured at the same time and place, you cast it from you in disgust. We admire Satan, appearing to us as an angel of light; but when the horns protrude, shall we still cling to them with woman's devotion? Heaven forbid! Do I then aver that a woman may break away from her marriage vows so soon as she becomes dissatisfied with her husband? No more than I would advise you to burn down your house because it is not built according to contract. You may alter it if you can, and if not, you must make the best of it as it is. But you need not admire and extol it, just as it would have been right for you to do if it really were what you wished and planned it to be. A woman judges wrong in the chief incident of her life. She makes a mistake, whose consequences are far-reaching, and very deplorable, but she must bear them. Her husband's neglect or refusal to fulfil his part of the contract does not justify her non-fulfilment any further than is necessary. I say *than is necessary*, for the promise is of such a nature that I do not see how it is in her power to keep the whole of it, and, consequently, what is the possible use of making it. She vows to love, honor, and obey; but love and honor do not depend on the will. You cannot love a man if he has not the qualities which inspire love, nor honor him when he ceases to be honorable. God, it is true, commands us to love him; but his character is such that it needs only to be considered to be adored. Man is a long way from Divinity, and our feelings towards him cannot be bespoken beforehand. They are entirely contingent on his deserts, which are variable. Therefore, a woman promises to do what is quite beyond the sphere of her volition, and she can neither keep nor break her promise. But for her own soul's sake she must maintain her integrity. She must be faithful and just and gentle and blameless. If she does more than this, — if she is so unfortunately constituted that she still prostrates herself before the fragments of her broken and debased idol, — she is to be pitied. She is not to be praised.

For a grand nature in ruins we may have a mournful and tender reverence. For a nature which we thought grand, but which proved to be petty, we have only contempt.

This idea of devotion is sometimes carried to a most unreasonable, unjust, and mischievous extent.

John Jones and Sarah Smith played together when they were little children, and took sleigh-rides together when they had become great children. He has given her innumerable ribbons and flowers and candies, and she has worked him a watch-case, a guard-chain, and a pair of slippers. Of course, they are "engaged." So says the world of Onionville, and so, very likely, they think themselves. At least, they have as yet formed no higher ideas of happiness than to gather flowers and work watch-cases for each other all their lives long. Presently John's father removes to the city, and John goes to school, and subsequently to college, and then to a theological seminary. All this while he cherishes a beautiful and fragrant memory, and looks forward with a young man's ardor to the time when boyish and girlish fancy shall be moulded into mature and undying love. In the mean time his mind becomes cultivated by reading and study, his manners polished by mingling with beauty and refinement. He visits his early home, and rushes into the presence of Sarah Smith. What? Is *that* Sarah Smith? Is that girl in a green and blue broad-striped de laine dress, with a bright plaid ribbon pinned round her neck, and a silver watch, — is that the fair dream he has borne in his heart these years? To be sure there are rosy cheeks and bright eyes and a buxom lass; but — but — alas! poor John. He has shrined her in the secret chambers of his soul so long, but his soul-love grew with his growth and strengthened with his strength, and Sarah Smith did not. Walking alone by the river-side where he so often walked with her, "What shall I do?" is the question that ever and ever recurs. He is disappointed and miserable. Like too many of us, he finds his idol is but common clay, — very common. His happiness is turned to cinders, ashes, and dust. Is *she* to be the "angel of the house"? Is hers the delicate ethereal nature which is to bear him on the white wings of love up beyond his lower level? Will she help him to be true to himself, to his country, to his God? Aside from himself, can he make her happy? Will she not see enough of the disparity between them to be discontented and uneasy? Will she not be entirely out of her sphere in the circle of his educated and accomplished friends? The thought makes him hot and nervous. He becomes restless, dissatisfied, and cannot sleep o' nights. Finally, after much debating and many struggles, he decides that their future paths must diverge, and he tells her so very gently and tenderly. She has felt the same thing all along. She knows there is something in him to which she cannot respond. She feels that a change has been going on during the years of their separation, and that they cannot make each other happy. They part friends. She reverences his superiority. He respects her good sense. When he is gone, she goes to her own room, has a "good cry," almost wishes she were safe in heaven, but finally thinks she would, on the whole, prefer to wait till her little brothers are grown up, and on the strength of this postponement goes to bed and to sleep, — is paler than usual for a while, but her voice soon recovers its tone, her cheek its color, her step its elasticity, and anon she is as merry as before.

Well, what of it? Nothing, if you would only let them alone; nothing whatever. But you won't, — busy, prying, inquisitive, meddlesome, mischief-making neighbor that you are. You think John left town rather suddenly, and you fancy Sarah is a little low-spirited; and because Satan can find nothing else for your idle hands to do, you put this and that together, and saunter over to Mr. Smith's, determined to ferret out the whole matter. You find Mrs. Smith alone. You talk indifferently on indifferent topics. Sarah comes in. You say, smilingly and carelessly, (your look is a lie, for you are intensely interested, and you want her to think you are not,) "Well, Sarah, I suppose that handsome young minister is going to carry you off pretty soon, according to all appearances." (On the contrary, the only reason why you came was that, according to all appearances, you suppose no such thing.) Sarah blushes, laughs an embarrassed little laugh, hesitates a moment, and leaves the room. Her mother says, quietly, "That is all given up." "There I, thought so!" leaps to your lips, but you do not say it. You exclaim, "Do tell!" as if you never were so surprised in your life; and though you do not succeed in extracting the details of the occurrence, you have in the simple fact sufficient capital to do a flourishing business; so you blazon it abroad in Onionville; and Onionville, nothing loath, takes it up, and at every sewing-circle and tea-party where the Smiths happen not to be present, you discuss it in all its bearings. Poor John Jones! Every virtue is torn from him piecemeal, till he stands before you a mere skeleton of vices; while Sarah Smith, in your transforming hands, becomes an angel of light. "To keep company with her when he was nobody, and cast her off when he got his learning!" indignantly exclaims one. "Yes," chimes in a second, "he feels very grand now, — too proud to take a woman who knows how to work. He must have a city lady, with her flowers and her flounces." "Well, let him have her," says a third, "there 'll no good come of it, mark my word. He 'll come to some bad end. Never knew it to fail. There 's Captain David, dismissed Lucy Perkins, and married Squire Willis's daughter. What with her boarding-school airs and high-flown notions, her pianos and her gold chains, and her new cloak every year, she soon found the bottom of the Captain's purse. And there 's their sons now, what are they good for? You 'll see" ; — and the good woman shakes her head ominously. Now, kind-hearted people, I respect your sympathy, but what is the matter? Why are you making all this ado? Do you really mean that you would have him marry her? Marry her in the gloom of that cloud which darkened his being? Marry her, when between his soul and hers there could be no real communion? It is true, that, before he was able to read his or her inner history, he deemed her all-sufficient; but, discovering his mistake, he would do her irreparable wrong if he should allow her to go on, unknowing and unsuspecting the discovery, — irreparable wrong, to fulfil his promise to the letter, when he cannot to the spirit, — irreparable wrong, to stand up before God and man, and solemnly promise love till death, knowing that at the very moment the life of love is gone. Alas! you would consign her to a fate compared to which the prospect of death is but a pleasing hope, — to the cheerless, dreary, desolate doom of an unloved and unloving wife. He is not to be blamed. The fault, if fault there be, is hers, not his. She knew that he was devoting himself to study, and rising above his former rank, and she might have done the same. The way was open to her, as to him. But she preferred to go to huskings and quiltings, to take care of the children, and do the dairy work; — all very well, and quite proper, only she must abide by the consequences.

But, in fact, what harm is done? Her happiness is not destroyed. This little incident is but a pebble against the tide. In a year's time, the rosy cheeks, the muscular arm, the lithe figure, and the strong, elastic spirit, will bless the heart and cheer the home of some thriving young farmer; and a President and all his Cabinet may yet be chosen from the healthy, ruddy faces that will gather every morning round her wholesome and plentiful table. Spare your pity. Of this happy home she will be the centre and light and stay. In this, her appropriate position, her faculties will be brought into full play, her abilities shown to the best advantage. Her many and active duties will develop vigor of mind and of body. Keen intellects and iron nerves, for many generations, will rise up and call her blessed. Joined to one whom she could not appreciate, nor by whom be appreciated, — placed in a sphere for which she was unfitted, and which she could not adorn, her joyous, bounding, buoyant life would be checked, and the poor country minister's wife, harassed, careworn, pale, and meek, would go no pleasure tour so swiftly as her own pathway to the tomb.

I am aware that this is only the bright side of the picture. Every woman does not take the matter so easily. It does not follow, however, that the gentleman is any more at fault, or that the lady is any more aggrieved. She may be only less sensible and humble. Instead of doing with all her might whatsoever her hand finds to do, the rich and petted Ida, after parting from her equally rich and petted Mortimer, grows languid and languishing, weeps much, seems to have lost all interest in affairs of the world, listens attentively to discourses turning upon the instability of all earthly friendships, but turns a deaf ear to music, except of the *Il Penseroso* key. Doting friends mourn over the crushed affections and broken heart of the dear girl.

I know I am naturally cruel. Having no superfluity of heart myself, I am apt to make too little allowance for an excess of it in others. But, with all sincerity and kindness, I do believe that in nine cases out of ten it is the pride that is mortified, rather than the heart that is broken. Ida knows that, to all intents and purposes, she has been weighed in the balance, and found wanting. There may be no real justice in her feeling so. She may be vastly superior to her lover. Women generally are. But however that may be, she knows that she stands before the world as one who has given her all, and the gift has been rejected. Barkis is *not* willin'.

Now if scorn and disdain were her style, you would hear nothing of sighing and moanings ; but she is not of that calibre, so she becomes gentle, pensive, and interesting. I do not blame her for her sorrow. I do, indeed, think it would be better for her to consider that the man who, after six months or a year of acquaintance, is not profoundly impressed with a sense of her superiority, cannot be a man whose name she will be honored in assuming, and his memory, therefore, is unworthy a regret. Still, if she choose to look at it objectively rather than subjectively, from the world's point of view rather than her own, very well. I only insist that *she* shall *not* insist upon our taking her wounded self-love for a broken heart, — her disappointment in not becoming the jewelled mistress of a brown-stone palace, an army of negro servants, and a coach and six, for the agony of misplaced affections. For look you. Ida's anxious parents, in view of her faltering tread and drooping form, call a family council. The decree goes forth that she must travel, and anon they bear her hither and thither; dip her in the surf at Newport; nauseate her with the waters at Saratoga; deafen her with the roar of Niagara; enervate her with the voluptuous airs of the South; tone her up with the breezes of the Alleghanies. After undergoing these sundry processes of resuscitation, the whole business is "done up" in the twinkling of an eye, by the sudden entrance upon the stage of a rich, handsome, mustachioed cavalier, who is smitten by the "most musical, most melancholy charms" of the fair sufferer, and not disenchanted by the excellent name that papa bears on Wall Street. Mirth and gayety are reinstated, a bridal veil closes the scene, and the cracked heart is just as good as new.

You see I have little faith in dying for love. I have, however, great faith in moping one's self to death out of spite, or stubbornness, or false shame. If I am wrong, I am sorry — or glad; perhaps I ought to be glad. At any rate, I am in just that state of mind in which I ought to be under the circumstances. If I have injured any one's feelings by my unbelief, I most humbly beg pardon. I dare say I shall die of unrequited love myself some day. It would be no more than strict poetic justice. "Doubtless God might have made a better berry than a strawberry, but doubtless God never did." Doubtless there might be such a thing as dying for love, but doubtless there never (or seldom) was. In point of fact, there is not a great deal of marrying for love. Not that I suppose all marriages are mercenary. Far from it. But people marry for a thousand things, — money not only, but a home, beauty, genius, because others do, because it is respectable, convenient, &c. Some of these motives are objectionable, some perhaps not. When a poor girl, after laying the worn-out bodies of her father and mother in the grave, sees no prospect before her but unremitting toil, loneliness, poverty, and death in the dreary end, and marries the kind old physician who has tended her parents without prospect of reward; who has been the witness of her assiduity, watchfulness, generosity, good cheerful sense, and real worth, and feels that she would shed upon his widowed hearth something of the light of other days, I am far from blaming her. She is not false to her noblest nature, although perhaps, in the dreams of her early and happy girlhood, his was not the arm she looked to lean on. He will love her with a fatherly love; she will return it with grateful affection, and therefore her walk in life will be higher, her ends nobler, her benevolence more expansive, her womanhood better developed. Though the ecstatic glow that flushed her morning sky, when

> "Life went a-Maying,
> With Youth and Hope and Poesy,"

may have faded; yet a calm serenity — "the sober certainty of home-felt bliss" — will enwrap her in a holy atmosphere, soft, hazy, and warm-tinted, as the beautiful Indian-summer.

When a young man is captivated by the fall of a graceful shoulder, or the twirl of a tiny toe, and on the strength of it marches straightway to church, and there promises to love and cherish, I shall not forbid the banns:

> "Honored well are charms to sell,
> If priests the selling do"; —

or, if more practical, and with an eye to the windward, he notes that the pretty silk is not new, but simply colored, turned upside down, wrong side out, with new fringe and trimmings, and new waist and sleeves, and bethinks himself how, under such management, his narrow cottage walls would stretch away into stately halls, — if he can secure the fair artisan he is doubtless lucky. I do not object. Their talk will be of bread and butter, the baby's teething, and the price of turnips; but let them marry. I do say, however, — and am I not right? — this is not that resistless tide, which, gathering to itself the thousand streams that ripple through the quiet meadows of life, sweeps suddenly over the heart, bearing down all the old landmarks of pride and prejudice; not that raging and quenchless fire which consumes the dross of selfishness, and fuses into a glowing devotion every power, thought, faculty, and purpose; not that great, deep, absorbing, passionate, deathless love, which, having once passed into a soul, can go no more out forever.

I could wish that women were happier. This may appear a needless wish to those who look only on the surface; but below the smoothly-flowing surface there is an undercurrent which the world knoweth not of. There is a restlessness, an unuttered discontent, a vague longing, which frets and wears away the cheerfulness and happiness of life, particularly in the young. It is involuntary, unsought, resisted, but all-powerful. Ah! the capacity for suffering that there is in girls, — the capacity, too, for enjoying and for acting. It is weighed and measured by those who are armed for the conflict, girded for the race, but for whom no conflict and no race ever wait. It is the slow wasting away of powers that have nothing to grasp; the silent, subtle corrosion of a heart turned in upon itself. O girls, everywhere waiting and watching for a day that never comes, I have seen you. I know you. I have followed you through the dreary days that dragged their slow length along. I know how the tramp of the monotonous years seems to you the dead march of your young aspirations, — how the pulse of your heart grows fainter and fainter, beneath the swelling fountain of tears.

> "My heart, and hope, and prayers, and tears,
> Are all with you, are all with you,"

and therefore I have a right to bid you take heart and hope, for this very unrest is a sign. It is the beating of your soul against its prison-bars. It is a token from above, — a voice from the unseen world, bidding you come up higher. It tells you of a level you have not yet reached; of energies not yet developed; of a life not yet rounded off to full perfection. Your soul is unconsciously sending out feelers, and they find nothing to grasp. The world is six thousand years old, but it has not yet learned to use its resources. It knows not what to do with you, and you know not what to do with yourselves. Your pastors and teachers exhort you to fear God and keep his commandments; and you try to do it. But that does not fill the void, does not stop the aching, nor soothe the unrest. No, and it never will. People may talk as much as they choose about the power of religion, but it will not satisfy your hungry heart, any more than it will your hungry stomach. God has given to every appetite its appropriate food, to every emotion its corresponding object. He has given us means and ends, but we blindly work at cross-purposes, and take wrong means for right ones, making his word of none effect by our traditions. When we ask him for bread, he gives us bread; his children, in all kindness, but ignorantly, give us oftentimes a stone. Do not reproach or think meanly of yourselves for not being happy. If you were absorbed in dress, visiting, pleasure-seeking, you would have no discontent; but would it be better so? If you were identified with any great work, anything which could enlist your whole being, you feel that it would be different; but women seldom have a great work to do. Their work is great only in its results, in the spirit with which it is done. It is a vast conglomeration of little things. You are where God has placed you, or suffered you to be placed, and for our purposes now it is all the same. If, in truth as in poetry, love could take up the harp of life, and smite on all the chords with might, then this chord of self would, trembling, pass in music out of sight, and this would be better. This self-abnegation is perhaps indispensable to womanly completeness. Until this chord has been touched, there is no diapason. The depths of the soul are unstirred. There is a power lying waste, a fountain sealed. No character can be perfect which is not symmetrical. You may, you ought to love Christ with an overmastering love, but the two are entirely distinct. One cannot take the place of the other. Every earthly affection should indeed be baptized in the heavenly, — but only baptized, not transmuted. I do not think God ever intended it should be.

Have I found you a remedy? No, certainly. I have only pointed out what would be a remedy if found, but no searching will ever bring it. It comes unsought, if it comes at all. What good have I done you, then? None at all so far; but here is the point where I wish to utter a note of warning. Here is where you are in danger of mistaking the seeming for the real. Faint and famishing, you will eagerly pluck the fair-looking apple, and it will turn to dust and ashes in your mouth. You would better have died of starvation. Because God has made you so that love is your life and breath, and you pant and gasp without it, you are not to inhale a foul malaria, under the mistaken impression that it is mountain air. If it be pure, the more you breathe of it the better, only be sure it is pure. Therefore do not love indiscriminately. An over-ripe apple falls at the first gust, whether into lily-white hands or on the unheeding ground. Do not you so; nor be content with a slight preference, — a pale, nerveless, flickering, uncertain emotion, that brings as many misgivings as heart-throbs. I have heard of girls pausing on the threshold of an engagement, "at a stand to know what to do"! Never allow yourself to be in such a position. If you don't know what to do, it is the very strongest of all providential indications that you are to do nothing. By all means, give yourself the benefit of the doubt. "Friendship with all, entangling alliances with none," is a good motto for women as well as for nations. Faithfully adhered to, it will keep you free from those little attachments which insensibly but surely fritter away your power to form a lasting and noble one; while it will no more prevent your soul from going out to meet its lord and king, when his trumpet sounds, than the seven green withes had power to restrain the Hebrew athlete when his spirit returned to him, after its ignoble sleep on a treacherous bosom.

Do not affect a motive in love. It is not a question of motive, but of fact. I have no faith in marrying to do good. The end does not sanctify the means. If you do all the good you can with your own individuality, I do not believe God will hold you responsible for anything more. Nor, in my opinion, does the respectability of the sinner diminish the enormity of the sin. I have known missionaries, excellent men, bury their poor wives in Hindoo jungles, and return to America to replace them, just as madam sends for a China teacup to replace the one broken by a careless servant. Men and women combine with Nature to abhor a vacuum, and the missionary's loss is often far more easily made up than madam the housekeeper's. Mysterious wheels, wires, and pulleys are set in motion by a clique of mothers in Israel behind the scenes, the result of which is, that some unoffending, benevolent, and practical Miss Brown finds herself suddenly precipitated, *nolens volens*, (generally *volens*,) into the arms of the good missionary; — he congratulating himself on the success of his business transaction; she consoling herself that she has gained an excellent husband, and done God service, thereby killing two birds with one stone; and the mothers aforesaid rejoicing in their skilful matrimonial diplomacy. Now I affirm that it is miserable business the whole of it. It may be good manœuvring, where all manœuvring is out of place. It is an unholy traffic, though all the traffickers be members of an orthodox church in good and regular standing. It is transferring to the head what comes under the jurisdiction of the heart. The parties concerned may "live happily ever after," but they have no right to expect it. Of course, if a woman marries a missionary because she loves him, even though her love sprang up on his first Transatlantic appearance as a widower, and goes to Boorioboola Gha with him, because she would rather do it than stay at home without him, there is not the slightest objection; she is quite right; only let her say so honestly, if she feel called upon to say anything. But when she explains her marriage by enlarging on her sense of duty, the poor little children who stand in such pressing need of a mother's care, the heathen who are perishing for lack of knowledge, why then, I say, if these really are her motives, she is wrong,—just as truly, though not perhaps as greatly, wrong as she who follows the glitter of gold. Let her take a lesson from Jane Eyre and St. John, since she has failed to learn it from her Bible. If the claims of the heathen urge her so irresistibly, let her go to them untrammelled. The cause of God is not so desperate that it needs to be propped up by a falsehood.

Nor do I believe in marrying because, as I have frequently heard alleged, a woman's nature is such that she "must love somebody." In the first place, the implied fact is a convenient little fiction. There is no sort of necessity for your "loving somebody." It may be very pleasant to do so; it may be very distressing not to do so; but it is not immediately fatal. Even if it were, never mind. Remember Pompey's sublime words, "It is necessary for me to go; it is not necessary for me to live." Death comes to all, and the world does not need your bodily presence so much as it needs your moral heroism. If you die rather than live falsely, you will enrich it by one great example. Moreover, granting that you "must love somebody," does it inevitably follow that you "must love" a grown man in possession of a respectable yearly income? Look abroad at the orphans, thousands upon thousands, fatherless, motherless, to whom your love would be as the dew of Hermon. Christ's little ones are all around you, — the ignorant, the uncared-for, the outcast. Lavish on them your irrepressible affection. The sunshine of love might melt the ice in which their better nature is incrusted, and warm into healthy, vigorous growth the wasting germ of many a virtue. The idea, girls, the *idea* of sacrificing your whole life to a so-so sort of person, for the sake of having "somebody to love," in a world so full of children that the most excruciating hand-organ will in two minutes block up the sidewalk in any portion of any city with admiring throngs of white-headed urchins!

To marry for a home or for happiness is little better. A home purchased by the sale of yourself is a dear bargain, and happiness is the most uncertain shadow you can pursue. It is incidental. It comes upon us unexpectedly; but if we set out determinately and definitely in pursuit of it, it generally leads us into bogs and quagmires, and leaves us there.

If, instead of promising to love and honor in

the future, custom enjoined a woman, on her marriage-day, solemnly to aver that she did at that moment love and honor, I verily believe there would be fewer mock unions. I think it would be safer to let the future build itself, taking care to secure in the present a firm foundation, than to take the foundation for granted, and proceed prematurely to the superstructure. Many women, conscientious, but vague, unaccustomed to make distinctions, to know clearly the difference between one thing and another, after long hesitating and vacillating, do finally zigzag their way to church, and make the most tremendous promises, with a misty kind of belief that they shall be able to keep them when the indefinitely distant trial comes, — who, if the plain question were put to them point-blank, "Do you now love and honor this man?" could not find it in their hearts, and therefore not in their consciences, to say "Yes," and would thereby be saved from a lifetime of suffering, perhaps of sin. Yet, I have heard a Christian woman seriously advise her young friend to accept a marriage proposal, because *she* "*would not be likely to do better. A superior woman must not expect to marry her superior.*" I have known a gentleman write, "I advise you, if an intelligent, truly Christian man, who really loves you, wants you to marry him, to do so." And a highly moral and religious community does not cease to warn contumacious maidens of the danger of "going through the woods, and picking up a crooked stick at last."

There certainly are occasions on which, if you cannot do as you would, it is quite proper to do as you can. Nothing can equal a good sweet-potato, yet you would be very foolish to throw away mashed Irish ones, because the frost has destroyed the more saccharine tuber. In default of mashed Irish, roasted will have no mean flavor. If the potato crop fails, "Boston brown bread," fresh from the oven, will enable you to bear the loss with philosophical resignation, and even boiled rice, the most unpretending of all edibles, is better than starvation. But a husband is not a potato, and if you select him on the same principle, be not surprised if you find him extremely indigestible.

> ". . . . . as the dove, to far Palmyra flying,
> From where her native founts of Antioch beam,
> Weary, exhausted, longing, panting, sighing,
> Lights sadly at the desert's bitter stream";

(Perfectly right in the dove.)

> "So many a soul, o'er life's drear desert faring, —
> Love's pure, congenial spring unfound, unquaffed, —
> Suffers, recoils, then, thirsty and despairing
> Of what it would, descends, and sips the nearest draught,"

and is refreshed and strengthened, just as the shipwrecked sailor is refreshed by the mocking salt sea-water, which he bears in frenzy to his fever-parched lips.

Do you now, seeing that I have dealt chiefly

in negatives, ask me what shall be the token? My dear child, how can I tell? By just as many girl's hearts as are throbbing this wide world over by just so many ways will love enter in and take possession. Keep your eye single and your heart pure, and you will not fail to recognize the heavenly visitant. The molecule of oxygen roams lonely through the vast universe, yearning for its mate, and finding no rest, till of a sudden it meets the molecule of hydrogen in a quiet nook, when lo! a rush, an embrace, and there is no more either oxygen or hydrogen, but a diamond drop of dew sparkling on the white bosom of the lily. So, I suppose, will it be with you, when you meet your destiny. A flash, and it is all over. Your heart is gone, your power is gone; power over your blood, that plays mad pranks in your cheeks, — over your thoughts, that hover continually about one spot, — over your memories that wake to music only one string, — over yourself henceforth forevermore, to be held in solution by a stronger nature than your own. Unless your love comes upon you thus, like a strong man armed, do not believe in it. If you, in cold blood, give up your name, your independence, your individuality, for a consideration, whatever that consideration be, you will be a wife only in name. Priestly blessing cannot sanctify unholy contract. If you have parted with your birthright, what matter whether it was for a mess of pottage or a stalled ox?

I know, therefore, of no reason why a woman should marry, except because she cannot help it,— because "the spirit of life which dwelleth in the most secret chambers of the soul, all trembling, speaks these words: 'Behold a god more powerful than I.'"

If your love raises and exalts you, if it helps you on your heavenward way, if it brings you nearer to God, if it strengthens you to brave endurance, stimulates you to heroic action, and makes all greatness possible; if, in one word, it possesses itself of you, and sweeps you up and out from the finite to the infinite, as a wave bears seaward the strong swimmer, powerless,—you are safe.

If anything less than this satisfies you, if you content yourself with a feeble, sickly sentiment, that wilts in the sun and breaks in the storm, your soul will surely suffer. An inferior nature may waken feeling enough to blind you for a little while. The cares and pleasures of a busy life may twine their rank growth so closely as to hide from you for a season the real barrenness of the soil beneath. But from the one, twenty, forty years that lie before you, shall be born a day on which you will awake to know that you cannot give without receiving back full measure, life for life. And when your dream is dreamed out, you will exclaim, more bitterly than the old dame of the ballad,—

"Yesterday I was the Lady of Linn,
And now I'm but John o' the Scales' wife."

Your demon of discontent, cast out for a while, will return, with seven other spirits more wicked than himself, and your last state shall be worse than your first.

Better, a thousand times better, go wandering all your life, than bring your household gods under an unworthy roof-tree.

There is, then, a way that seemeth good, but the end thereof are the ways of death. With this you have nothing to do.

But settle the point clearly. Know just where you stand. Have the boundary-lines accurately defined. Be able to give a reason for the hope and faith that are in you. Missing the crowning glory of womanhood, do not childishly depreciate it. Do not try to persuade yourself or others that you are at the utmost bound of the everlasting hills, quite in the promised land, when in fact you only see it through a glass darkly. Meet the fact boldly. Courage does not consist in feeling no fear, but in conquering fear. There is no heroism in marching blindfold through a thousand dangers. He is the hero who, seeing the lions on either side, goes straight on, because there his duty lies. Acknowledge to yourself, "I am not happy. I do not like my life. I must be capable of better things. I am uneasy, restless, discontented." Then, knowing exactly the state of your case, apply to yourself comfort and healing. Remember first that God reigns. Infinite power is wielded by infinite love. The fatherly eye that sees the sparrows as they fall, will not let you walk in a random path. Life is a chain of sequences. From the cradle to the grave — ay! and beyond it — stretch the series of cause and effect; and what thou knowest not now, thou shalt know hereafter.

You are in a school carefully graded. When you have passed your examination satisfactorily, you will be promoted. Just as soon as you have got all the discipline which your present circumstances have for you, you will be surrounded by new. Just as soon as you are fitted for a higher career, the gates will be flung wide open to you. You can know exactly what is best for you only by observing what is. You think you could do something better, something greater. Do you perfectly accomplish everything that you undertake? Until you perform in the best possible manner everything which it is at present your duty to do, you have no right to complain of your contracted sphere. Why reach out among the stars for a treasure that lies at your feet? Be faithful over a few things, before you repine at not being made ruler over many things. You may talk of opposing friends, unfavoring circumstances, adverse fate; but circumstances are full of Divinity, planning and directing. We are not the children of Fate,

but the children of our Father in Heaven ; a. ,
when the Heaven-appointed hour is come, fate,
friend, and circumstance will swell the tide that shall bear us out triumphantly to the bosom of the boundless sea.

Another thing remember. Threescore years and ten are not the whole of life. We say that we know it, but we act as if we knew it not. With our lips we affirm ; but with our lives we deny. Blind and eager, we grasp for all our good things now. We weep and moan and faint, because for a moment we are hungry and thirsty. We forget that God has not put us in this world to be happy, but to be trained. It is true that there is a great deal of happiness thrown in ; and we find it so delightful, that we are apt to substitute it for the real end of life, and mourn that we cannot accomplish it ; which is as if children, having feasted on their Christmas candy, should cry to be fed on it all the year round. Life is one combined and continuous process and proof. Riches, poverty, happiness, misery, education, ignorance, are so many chisels to form and touchstones to try our characters. One substance stands fire, another water. If you reverse the trial, it is fruitless. One soul must be purified by prosperity, another by adversity; one in society, another in solitude. Who dare be so presumptuous as to say, " This is not the right kind of test for me. My character would be better developed and ascertained in such and such circumstances." "Shall not the Judge of all the earth do right?" You pant for activity and exertion. You are ingenious, constructive, fertile in devices, skilful in combination, rapid in execution. You want a subject, a field, a career. Very well. Find one or make one, if you can. Exert yourself to the utmost. Move heaven and earth; but, having done all without success, decide conclusively that your lesson is to be learned in another school, and reflect peacefully that "they also serve who only stand and wait." Bring this principle in prematurely, and you will be an indolent, inefficient cumberer of the ground. Leave it out of view entirely, and you will be a pricking, irritating thorn in all sensible and sensitive flesh. Apply it just at the right time, and the world will be better for your having lived in it.

As for a little happiness, more or less, never mind it. Be content to put it off. When the Shekinah dwelt in the Holy of Holies, did the high-priest note in passing that the porch of the temple was shrouded in twilight? Believe what you say you believe, that there is a life beyond death. Weeping may endure for a night, but joy cometh in the morning. It is only for a little while. Can you not for a little while be brave to bear and to do? The fulness of joy, the perfection of being, belong to another world. The secret of contentment is not the gratification nor the crucifixion of every right desire, but faith in their ultimate fulfilment.

> "He who sees the future sure,
> The baffling present may endure."

If God has happiness in store for you here, it will surely come; you need not stir to find it. If he has not, all effort is vain; no movement of yours will bring it. Therefore be calm.

Now, if you suppose that I wish to sublimate you into an airy nothing, — a cross between the patient Griselda and a Romish saint, I have only to inform you that you are entirely mistaken. Though I would have you depend chiefly for your happiness on the next world, I would also have you, by all means, make the most of this. It is very certain that there is a heaven, but earth is also a fixed fact. It may be very pleasant to die, but for the present your especial business is to live; and if you can't be as happy as you would like to be, be as happy as you can. Because you can't get what you want, don't throw away what you can get. Squeeze out of the world all the juice there is in it. It is a mistake to suppose that you must be either at the brow or at the foot of the hill. There are many steps between, some of which command a charming view, and all a new horizon. Because you are not particularly happy, don't condemn yourself to particular misery. It is possible to sleep soundly, eat heartily, and be on the whole very comfortable, without being in a rapturous frame of mind. Only, when you are simply comfortable, don't pretend that you are tremendously happy. There is nothing to be gained by the deception; and if there were anything, you don't want to gain it. Do with your might whatsoever your hand finds to do. Sympathize largely. Don't merely try to feel, but feel. Associate with children, not to harass them by continually setting them right, — which is of no use, since they will inevitably and immediately fall back into their original sin, — but make yourself one with them. Nothing pays so well. I think it is the easiest of all ways to amuse yourself and benefit others. But don't confine yourself to any one class. Whenever anybody's orbit intersects yours, make something come of it. Sink a shaft wherever there is the least probability of water. Find out the secret place where abideth the soul of your Irish "girl." See if there may not be something in common between you and your washerwoman, your seamstress, your chambermaid, your cook. If there is a single plank in their platform on which you can stand, join hands thereon, and give one throb to the heart of humanity. Do not wait supinely for opportunity, but go out and seek her in the highways and hedges. Be alive at every pore. Make your soul great with unceasing benevolence. Make common cause with virtue against temptation, with goodness against wickedness, with right against might. If truth is solvent in falsehood, precipitate the truth, and cast out the false. Do not be intimidated because human nature is not every inch a saint, nor cajoled because it is not every inch a satan. This great world is a powerful diluent. Accustom yourself to analyze, and, having decided deliberately, maintain stoutly. However weak, unpopular, or ridiculed the just cause may be, let it find in you an unflinching and impartial supporter; — impartial, for women are too apt, having once espoused a cause, to cling to it "with woman's devotion," right or wrong; or, having rejected it, to fancy no good thing can come therefrom. If you approve one thing and condemn another, both of which Mrs. Grundy alike condemns, don't abstain from saying so for fear of being called inconsistent. If to-day you approve any measure which yesterday you condemned, don't be afraid to say so for fear of being deemed fickle. Is it not Ruskin who says that he has little faith in an opinion till he has changed it three times? Pope asks what changing the mind is, but saying we are wiser to-day than we were yesterday. And Ruskin again bids us say what we think to-day in words as hard as cannon-balls, and say what we think to-morrow in words just as hard, no matter if one assertion flatly contradict the other. Consistency is the bugbear of small, inactive minds. A living soul, grappling with the great truths of the present, has no leisure to go digging among last year's ruins to see whether the two sets dovetail exactly. Let bygones be bygones. Let the dead past bury its dead. A sincere and honest life will arrange itself. All opinions and beliefs, intelligently and conscientiously adopted, will group themselves into a beautiful mosaic, which you cannot now see because you are too near, and must behold one at a time; but when a stand-point in the other world gives you the proper focal distance, you will behold, with wonder and admiration, how the most diverse and the most similar were alike necessary to form a perfect and artistic whole.

There are sorrows that spring from other sources, — hope deferred, love wasted, expectation disappointed, ambition crushed, — noiseless grief that saps the foundation, eats into the very penetralia of life, of which the whited walls without give no sign, though Death riot within, — anguish that sweeps over the soul like the desert Simoom, blasting every green thing, drinking up every fresh fountain, leaving in its wake only blackness and blankness, — troubles that come naturally, and troubles that seem to have been wrenched from their places to assail some doomed life, — troubles that no wisdom could have averted, and troubles wantonly and wickedly self-inflicted, yet all alike sore evils, and of long continuance. There is in woman a power of acute suffering, from causes which scarcely affect the sterner nature of man. Repulsive but merciful necessity bears down upon his sorrow, smothering it with rude, relentless hand, indeed, but smothering it. Her quieter, more monotonous life fans the flames, but gently, so that though the bush is burning a long time, yet is it not consumed. There are many, I see them every day, whose garden of lilies and roses is become a howling wilderness. The poetry and sprightliness and spring of life are gone forever. They walk, perhaps, with downcast, introverted eyes. They are called reserved, haughty, cold, stupid. Mere thoughtlessness would fain see if there is blood beneath the marble, and, drawing her bow at venture, sends an arrow quivering into the heart of hearts, and goes on her smiling way.

But all this can and must be borne. The hand that metes out the measure to us all never yet held false balance. Every pain is instinct with good, if you will but have the wisdom to discern it. From every bitter, pluck its soul of sweetness. The conflict may be fierce, but who fight for God in the fighting grow strong. You may leave the battle-field with rent and blood-streaked robes, but with a nervous right arm. "*Ce n'est pas la victoire qui fait le bonheur des nobles cœurs; c'est la combat,*" — (Not the victory, but the struggle, makes the happiness of noble hearts), — says a French writer; but upon you, if you will, wait both struggle and victory. Strength which a placid life can never give may be yours. Heights which unruffled souls never attain you can climb if your feet are willing; and from those mountain-tops you will gaze on such visions as never met the eye of dwellers in the valley.

> "Behold yon grotto where the dropping tears
> Are crystallized to columns by long years;
> So shall thy sorrows, child of mighty grief,
> Bear up like pillars for thy soul's relief."

But if your sorrow is to be thus converted into strength, yourself must work the change. It has not, as many seem to suppose, an innate, self-developing, elevating power. Whether the sculptor's chisel carve from Parian marble the purity and grace of an ideal womanhood, or the grim visage of a churchyard Death, depends on the hand that holds it. The April rain falls alike on the gray rock and the brown earth. But the one, unmindful of the treasure, yields it up to the first ray of sunshine, the first breath of the west wind, and anon is as gray as before. The other takes the soft visitor to her kindly bosom, and down out of sight the little messenger goes to where young life is stirring in the darkness, and there works a miracle. So your grief will be to you a savor of life unto life, or of death unto death, according as you use it. If you nurse it, and cherish it, and brood over it, and talk about it, it will wax greater and greater, filling your vision, shutting out from you all sunshine, concentrating upon itself all your thoughts, and clinging to you, a huge excrescence, instead of entering into your blood and nerves and sinews, softening, refining, Christianizing. Grief, it is truly said, is sacred; but grief brought forward promiscuously, harped upon, condoled over, made the staple of conversation, becomes rapidly profane. Grief is a bond of union between men who, however dissimilar in other respects, are alike liable to its attacks; but the great world rushes on, and cannot loiter long. You must not pull the string too hard, or it will break. If you have a sympathizing friend to whom it would be a relief to unbosom yourself, do so; but, even then, be careful that you do not dwell too long upon, or recur too often to, your skeleton. Your friend will grieve with you sincerely for a while, but will presently outgrow you. Does this seem harsh? I trust not. Far be it from me to wound those whom God hath smitten. I only say what I believe to be true, and what, if true, it behooves you to know. It is, moreover, best for yourself that your eyes should not always be turned inward. To bring happiness to others is the surest way to bring it to yourself. Apply healing to other minds diseased, and you will not fail to heal your own. The law of impenetrability obtains in mind as well as in matter. Sorrow cannot wholly fill the heart that is occupied with others' welfare. Constant melancholy, furthermore, is constant rebellion. If you will only square yourself to God's will, you will command a cheerful equanimity. To drag along a miserable, fretful, repining, or desponding existence, is not resignation; but she who turns away from the mound beneath which her first-born lies, back to a world which brings only an aching sense of void, shrinking from no duty, smiling through eyes that will ever and anon turn wistfully heavenward, showing her sorrow only in the softer footfall, the added tenderness of voice, the gentler sympathy, the warmer pity with which she binds up the broken-hearted, — ah! she is the true victor. On her brow shall the crown be set.

In the old days, when our fathers were a handful of men in a great land, and foe, famine, and pestilence threatened destruction to their lessening ranks, they nightly laid their dead to rest, levelled the frequent graves with surrounding earth, and planted in the sacred soil their corn and grain, that they might conceal their weakness from a wary and watchful foe.

So, bury your griefs out of sight, deep, deep, where the eye of the world cannot pierce, and over them sow with a bountiful hand the seed of Christian virtues, and from the ashes of your dead hopes shall spring up a living growth of Faith, and Patience, and Charity, and Love, beneath whose waving shadow your soul shall calmly sit in the evening-tide of a serene life, waiting the voice of the Lord.

But unhappiness cannot be prevented or exterminated by a "whereas, be it resolved" alone. Action is not more the chief part of an orator than of every other human being. It is the necessity of every noble nature. Change is the essence of life, and action is continuous change, — wise action, continuous advancement. Whether grief be real or imaginary, — and imaginary grief *is* real, — employment is an excellent specific. Ah! that is the very thing you want, — something definite to do. Well, there is the school-house, which ninety-nine girls in a hundred enter, not because they feel that they have any particular call that way, but because it seems to open the only loop-hole of escape from inanity. That you have no taste for the work is the smallest possible objection. Good, honest people, reasoning *a priori*, affirm that no one can be a good teacher unless he loves teaching. Educational conventions and professional periodicals reiterate the statement, till they perhaps come to believe it themselves; but it is only a popular fallacy. In all my life, I have known but one woman who really loved teaching for its own sake. Some of the best teachers — the most respected and the most beloved — have adopted it because it was the only work that offered; and, hating it most heartily, have accomplished it most successfully. But it is far more probable that, being young and inexperienced, you fancy teaching will be the "*open sesame*" to Paradise, — or a triple coat of mail against all the ills that flesh is heir to; but you may as well undeceive yourself at once. You think it will give you the great desideratum, — employment, occupation, something to think about.

Yes, it will, indeed; so much, that, if you do all that you see standing in need of doing, you will require the strength of Hercules and the days of the planet Jupiter. If you are strong and healthy, you will have the satisfaction of spending five or six of the best years of your life in a school, and at the expiration of that time be allowed to leave with honor, a pale face, disordered nerves, tired brain, and shattered constitution. The labor required in ordinary schools of the higher class is such, that I think a woman of average physical strength cannot spend more than four consecutive years in them without breaking down. The draughts on the vital energy are so unceasing, that the supply cannot equal the demand, and the fountain is exhausted. Of course I refer only to teachers of conscience and character. An inefficient, commonplace routinist can drone on in the same rut, *ad infinitum*, and perhaps give complete satisfaction to an astute public. So, if you have been tenderly nursed and nurtured, if you have indulged an appetite for sick headaches, if you have been trained in the belief that rest should follow labor, and that the best work can be performed by the best-conditioned animal, engage to "wash for the ladies" at sixpence an hour, or enter a bookbindery and be paid by the job, or dig clams on the sea-shore and sell them in the shell, (which I always fancied must be a delightful occupation,) or hire yourself out as nursery-maid to nine small children, but don't enter a public school, — and a private school is no better, and a great deal worse, since the former only devours you piecemeal, but the latter swallows you whole, body and soul.

But you think it will be so delightful, so *juvenescent*, to be surrounded by happy, joyous, bounding children. You can quote reams of poetry on the subject, —

> "A beautiful, and happy girl," —
>
> "Child amid the flowers at play," —
>
> "A simple child,
> That lightly draws its breath," —
>
> "A baby in a house is a well-spring of pleasure," etc., —

all of which I am not prepared to contradict; but a hundred and fifty babies in a house, together, representing every stage of infancy, from the bread and molasses of three years old, to the nuts and apple coquetry of thirteen, will make larger draughts on your patience than on your poetry, and exercise your judgment more than your imagination. You must divest yourself, as soon as possible, of the idea that all children are little white-winged angels, with golden curls and rose-bud lips. You must prepare yourself for diamonds in the rough, and sometimes for the rough without the diamond. Even where there is a diamond, you must not expect to polish it in the twinkling of an eye. Perhaps it will not flash its full lustre till the hand that first made way for its gleaming has crumbled into dust. We have all read any number of stories about hordes of ferocious boys, who have organized successful and successive rebellions, and ejected a long line of male dynasties from the professional chair, but who have suddenly been brought to roar you as gently as any sucking dove, by the apparition of a sweet-faced, low-voiced woman. Now, I know that calmness and gentleness and firmness will work wonders, where passion and violence and storm have been only abbots of misrule, — and of the whole circle of things that may happen to you, this may happen; but I would not advise you to set your heart upon it. If you begin with the practical, at least, if not theological belief, that the children of men are deceitful and desperately wicked, prone to evil as the sparks are to fly upward, you will be happily disappointed, if you are disappointed at all. Expect to meet wormwood, senna, and Epsom salts; and if you do find the land overflowing with milk and honey, you will be doubly delighted. Be prepared to employ sternness of tone, severity of manner, and anything else that may be necessary; and if a fair trial convince you that music has charms enough to soothe the savages, why then all you will have to do will be to sing with all your might and main.

I hope you will not be shocked, and think I recommend you to turn into a kind of ogress, with the appetite of the Wantley dragon, whose ordinary dessert was

> "Poor children three,
> That could not with him grapple,
> But at one sup he ate them up,
> As one would eat an apple";

nor into a modern Medusa, with power to transform the trembling urchins to stone by a look. I only wish to give you a hint of unpleasant possibilities, so that, if your Spanish castle should fall, it may not bury you in the ruins. As the Cat observed to the Ugly Duckling, "I say disagreeable things, but it is for your good." I take it for granted that your own hearts will teach you enough of love, and the spirit of meekness; that your woman's nature makes it incumbent on one to exhort you to let justice temper mercy, rather than mercy temper justice.

There are other stones of stumbling, against which you may as well be forewarned. Every community that has emerged from a state of barbarism is infested with excellent and exemplary individuals, leaning to the "goody — good," accustomed to take things on trust, who will embrace every opportunity to speak a word, in season and out of season, especially out of season, on the fearful and weighty responsibilities of your position. I advise you, as a friend, not to listen to them. The comparative amount of your responsibility and mine, his, hers, or its, is a thing not cognizable by human eyes.

It is not necessarily the man who comes in contact with the largest number of people who exercises the most influence. It may be so, but it does not follow, and we do not know whether it is or not. When John Bunyan was cast into Bedford jail, there were doubtless many pious souls who mourned that the zeal and power of his best years should be thus wasted; yet through those prison-walls there streams a light which will grow brighter and brighter, till lost in the glory of the Celestial City. Every person is responsible for all the good within the scope of his abilities, and for no more, — and none can tell whose sphere is the largest. A mother, tending her child in the quiet seclusion of a Virginian home, sees no foreshadowing of a mighty destiny, yet there comes a day when an empire's fate trembles in the tiny hand now clasping hers. It is therefore impertinent to assume that the responsibility of teachers, or of any one class of people, is greater than that of any other. The only difference is, that one influences at first hand, another at second or third. At every footfall, we set in motion a chord whose trembling thrills ten thousand more, and will quiver on eternally. Every thought and word and deed of every human being is followed by its inevitable consequence; for the one we are responsible; with the other we have nothing to do.

You will also probably encounter a great many

deprecatory remarks, concerning superficial knowledge, a smattering of the sciences, &c. Fond mammas will think they are making a display of great and judicious wisdom, in exhorting you to render their infants thorough masters of whatever study they pursue. Now I think superficial knowledge is a very good thing; and, for my own part, I should be only too glad to be well-smattered. In the first place, complete mastery by school-children of any one study is a moral impossibility; not only from the organization of our school system, but from the very structure of the human mind. Take geography, one of the earliest and perhaps the simplest studies attempted. Childish capacity cannot seize it in all its bearings, nor is the attempt to present them wise. Many things are taught to children which it would be far better for them to find out themselves. Let them grow up to their difficulties naturally, instead of having difficulties thrust upon them from without. If you lead them tenderly up to a fact, they will quite probably be indifferent, or but partially interested; but if they run against it, they will not leave it till they have found whence it came, and why it is there. School life should be considered only a preparatory course. It is a means, not an end. It is what you work out of their minds, and not what you put in, that is of importance. If a boy, at the end of his school days, has learned how to study, if he has acquired mental, moral, and physicaı self-control, his career is a success, no matter how many or how few *things* he knows. Of all the knowledge learned, he may have forgotten the greater part; but the wisdom which that learning brought him is his inalienable estate. You must be content to lodge the seed, for April rain and May sunshine and June warmth are necessary to bring it to perfect fruitage. You may drive the nail, but time alone can clinch it.

This charge of superficial knowledge is so often brought up against women, that I may be pardoned for pursuing it a little further, and asking how many *men* there are in America whose knowledge of things generally extends far beyond a smattering? I have something more than a suspicion that, if the principle should obtain that we are to know nothing of a science unless we know that science thoroughly, the sphere of our knowledge would suffer a sudden collapse. Is it indeed desirable that we should be entirely ignorant of the history of Greece, unless we can become imbued with the spirit of her golden age, — entirely conversant with her literature, her antiquities, her topography, her climate, her Fauna and Flora, — know precisely what tide of religious emotion it was that swept over her, bearing on its crested wave the Parthenon, — what silent influence of sun and shade and dew and rain centred on the germ that sprung up into that magnificent outgrowth of national eloquence, whose fruit was Demosthenes and his immortal compeers? Shall we not trace the long wanderings of the heroic Ten Thousand, and share their madness of delight, when, from the heights of the Sacred Mountain, their eyes beheld the sparkle and glow of the Euxine Sea, or watch "Idalian Aphrodite beautiful" flush from the ocean foam, to live in marble forever; or dream in the shadow of Olympus, to the music of that harp whose strings have not yet ceased to quiver, — because, forsooth, we do not know in what city Homer was born, or even whether there was any Homer at all; what force of nature the poetic mind of early Greece symbolized in the Cytherean myth; what wire-pullers, lobby-members, or Hellenic Maintenon moved the lever that thrust the Persians and the Greeks in each others' faces? Nay, verily. The world grew nearly six thousand years before it flowered in Linnæus, yet every child in our village school-houses will listen with appreciative eagerness while you point out to them the different parts of a common pea-blossom, stamen, pistil, keel, wings, and banner; every eye will sparkle, and every little listener become a practical botanist, and bring you specimens from every kitchen garden in the neighborhood. The Old World of his birth and the New World of his adoption alike contend for Agassiz; but on shady Saturdays in May, every brook in New England is fringed with ichthyologists in jackets, who will tell you the habitat, the breathing apparatus, the locomotive power, of trout and roach and shiner and sucker for miles around. A lifetime is not too much to spend in the investigation of the structure of the earth; but in three months an intelligent boy can learn enough of "rock and tree and flowing water" to give a new interest and beauty to every landscape on which his manhood's eye may rest. Many men have a specialty, something towards which they are drawn by an irresistible impulse, and to which they devote themselves with eager and delighted zest. Shall they therefore be ignorant of everything else? Many more have no specialty. They have an accumulative, analytic, and critical power, and roam at large through many fields. They make no new discoveries, and establish no new generalizations, but they are delightful companions, the appreciative welcomers and true interpreters of the Master Spirit when he comes. None, so far as I know, are thoroughly versed in all branches of knowledge; few, in any one; but many, very many, are sufficiently conversant with a large variety to realize the words of the poet,

> "My mind to me a kingdom is."

I have by no means exhausted the possible exasperations which society in general will give you, if you decide to teach. The man who makes your shoes thinks it incumbent upon him to learn the trade; the woman who trims your bonnets finds it necessary to serve an apprenticeship ; but the world at large, collectively and individually, considers itself abundantly qualified to make suggestions, offer opinions, and pass judgment on so simple and easy a matter as teaching; nor will any motive of delicacy prevent its doing so. You will also have the satisfaction of knowing that you, devoting the prime of your life, are receiving from one to three fourths as much money as a boy preparing for his junior examination would receive in the same situation ; or a graduate, laying up money for his medical or theological lectures. The subject grows too rapidly under my hand, and I believe I shall have to devote a separate treatise to its discussion ; but I must show you a few gleams from the "Sunny Side," before I pass on.

In the first place, if you wish to love and to be loved, it offers you delightful opportunity. You will bind fresh young hearts to your own, with a tie that time only strengthens and hallows. They are too far removed from you to see your faults, and they will leave you before they have acquired discernment enough to do so. Consequently, you will be enshrined in their memories, haloed with a glory that is less of your deserts than of their imaginings. They will see what you aim to be, rather than what you are. They will mark your standard, and not your inability to reach it. You will be associated with their purest thoughts and ambitions, their most innocent joys and simplest pleasures, — with all that in after days they will sigh to remember, — with the dew and freshness of their morning. You will also be doing godlike work, — moulding mind, fashioning material which is indestructible. You will see your influence, as you go on from day to day, in the awakening interest, the brightening eye, the more thoughtful brow, the kinder hand, and warmer heart; and below the surface, below all that you can see, the train you have set in motion is going noiselessly on. Without sound of hammer or axe, there is rising a beautiful temple, meet residence for the indwelling of the Holy Spirit. A lovely, gentle woman, who went to heaven long ago, probably never dreaming of the work she had done, perhaps weeping that she had been but an unprofitable servant, changed the current of at least one life, turning it from the valley of the Shadow of Death, through the pleasant land of Beulah; and now, years after, a young man, her pupil, writes thus tenderly of her: "She has a place in my soul, a little inner room, where once dwelt passion, gloom, and chaos; but when she opened it, she gently arranged it, dispelled the gloom that obscured the window, and till I fall asleep her face shall ever meet me there, with all I hold most dear."

To be thus treasured up, not in one soul, but in many souls; to live, not your own life only, but hundreds and hundreds of other lives, perhaps wiser, purer, or happier than yours; to be woven in with the warp and woof of boyhood's strong, firm web; to gleam and flash through the finer, subtler texture of girlhood; — this is your "exceeding great reward."

Girls generally have more or less taste for writing. If we could believe critics on the subject, they take to poetry as naturally as ducks to water; but we do not believe critics, because they write from theory, not from observation, and know little about the inner life of girls, — actual, everyday girlhood. Of all those who are unfitted by their organization for a life of inactivity, by their moral sense for frivolity, by their position, possessions, or taste for manual labor, by far the larger part will turn to the school-room rather than to the pen. Still there are, in the aggregate, many who cast wistful and furtive glances towards authorship. It is to them a

"Summer isle of Eden, lying in dark purple spheres of Sea," —

a Land of Promise, wreathed in golden mist, indistinctly limned, but wondrous fair. To the high-spirited and finely-strung it proffers mental work and pleasurable excitement behind an impenetrable veil. To the poor and struggling it is a mystic Aladdin's lamp, flashing before their dazzled eyes the gleam of gold, paving their way to happiness with pearls and diamonds.

Undoubtedly these castles in the air are not

"the baseless fabric of a vision," but, like our thrilling novels, are founded on fact, perhaps on just about as large a proportion of fact. There is a charm about writing. I can conceive of few things more delightful than to see one's self right-angled off in oblong form, on fine white paper, with broad margins, clear type, Russian calf, and illustrations by Darley.

If your cistern is over-full, a newspaper is a very convenient faucet, if you can unscrew it. I know that editors complain bitterly of the multitudinous pipes directed to their sanctums, and the "weak, washy, everlasting flood" with which they are inundated; but I would not hold back on that account. What is the use of having newspapers, pray, if you cannot write for them? Do dry-goods clerks complain because their counters are continually strewed with silks and muslins, — because they are constantly obliged to arrange, and derange, and rearrange? Why, it is their business. It is a sign of prosperity. A shop whose shelves were always in order would be apt to close business in a month, and a newspaper which is not sufficiently alive and active to draw into its vortex a host of spirits from the vasty deep around it, will soon stagnate into decay and death. Besides, how small a portion of the whole suffering is borne by the editor. It is absolutely appalling to think of the hopes and fears, the aspirations and dreams, the anxieties, tears, and heart-throbs, the watching, waiting, and disappointment, shut up in the "dark drawers" of editorial tables, — those terrible Black Holes of literature. And the worst of it is, that in the great majority of cases the execution is merited. I suppose it does sometimes happen that wheat and chaff are alike condemned. In fact, I know it does. If you should be impertinent, and ask me how I know, I should follow the example of the Autocrat of the Breakfast Table, and simply say, "*Nullum tui negotii.*" Still, as I was remarking, if your poem is not printed, there is a presumption, at least, that it was not worth printing.

Men talk as if it were a sin to write, unless the writing be of the very highest order. But are all preachers Pauls? all soldiers Bonapartes? all actors Garricks? all statesmen Washingtons? Shall a woman not dance unless she have the heels of an Ellsler, or sing without the voice of a Lind, or paint without the pencil of an Angelo? Would it even be better so? Is there not many a man whose pulses thrill to the notes of "Yankee Doodle," who would sit calm and impassive under "Casta Diva"?

A certain reviewer said of a certain writer, that her poems had done positive harm, — they had weakened the English language and perverted the English taste; that it would really be better if she had never taken a pen in her hand; and then he pronounced an anathema on the whole race of feminine rhymers. Nonsense, again! Is the English language more important than the English heart? Is the marble statue which the skilful artist carves with his chisel of greater moment than the living soul which he is to shape, "not for an age, but for all time," — ay, and for all eternity? All over the green fields of England, and under the blue skies of America, hearts have throbbed and eyes have filled with tears at a woman's simple songs. Of what use is it, then, for a critic to rise up in his self-conceit and say, "This is not poetry; this is all sentiment; it ought not to be written; it is not Miltonian nor Spenserian nor Virgilian nor Dantesque; it is not written according to the rules of high art."

You may tell a mother that her child's features are not Grecian, that his skin is browned and freckled by sun and wind, that his hair is coarse and his form ungainly; but will she clasp him to her bosom with any the less tenderness, or will she thenceforth cease to whisper his name in her morning and evening prayer? The object of poetry is to please— and whom? Not the elegant, the cultivated, the delicately-nurtured, merely; but the poor, the homely, the ignorant, as well. It is to polish the rough, to refine the vulgar, to ennoble the commonplace, to scatter pearls before those who find the path to heaven among the untrodden ways of life. Go to now, fools, and slow of heart to believe! There must be vessels of honor and vessels of dishonor. All stars have not the same glory; but one star differeth from another star in glory. Homer wrote the Iliad, and Florilla Flowerdale writes a Sonnet to a Dew-drop; and though the soul of the one be the basin of an ocean, and that of the other a gill dipper, they are both full. There is but one Chinese wall, but there are many stone fences; and they are entirely effectual in keeping the cows from the meadow and the sheep from the corn. There are but few St. Paul's Cathedrals, but white spires peer heavenward from every valley; and way-worn feet tread cheerily thitherward, and many souls are refreshed and gladdened. The nightingale is the sweetest of all birds, but we could ill spare from our woodland chorus the notes of the robin, the hum of the bee.

No little confusion of ideas prevails as to what constitutes useless and useful, light and heavy literature. There are many who open their damp *Gazettes*, *Journals*, *Chronicles*, *Couriers*, and plod through miles of dry, dusty, dreary political editorials, going to show that the country will sink to remediless ruin if Jenkins is elected town-clerk, but will rise to untold heights of glory should the spotless Muggins radiate his splendor from that lofty station; and they fancy themselves patriotic, absorbed in noble themes, interested only in what is excellent and of good report. Or they plunge into the foreign news column, litter their brain with the grand dinner given by the Legation on somebody's birthday, or the astute prophecies of some mercantile agent, whose historical knowledge is bound up in Whelpley's Compend, concerning the ultimate fate of Italy, the far-reaching designs of Louis Napoleon, and the balance of power in Europe; and don't *think*, probably, but have a kind of pleasant, unconscious *feeling*, that they are employing their vast intellect on abstruse and weighty matters. Or they watch the light-heeled Blondin on his tight rope, admire the financial operations of enterprising scoundrels, marvel at the manifold and ingenious crimes brought to light in New York, and call this "intelligent," "well-informed," — "keeping up with the times"; while they pass over the stories, the essays, the poetry, to their wives and daughters, as light reading, quite too small for the attention of their stupendous minds.

But a story or a poem may comprehend the whole duty of man. I have read such a one. I recollect "Herman, or Young Knighthood," which contained not only more wit, but more wisdom, — not only more beauty, but more grandeur, — not only more play of fancy, more power of imagination, more directness of purpose, more felicity of expression, and more elegance of diction, but more knowledge of human nature, more soundness of judgment, grander conceptions of human aspirations and human capacity to love and to suffer, to enjoy, to act, to die, and to rise again, — a vaster sweep of thought, broader generalization, more comprehensive views, more logical and accurate reasoning, nicer analysis, and a higher standard of Christian manhood, — than you will find in a column of your "solid reading" that would reach from Maine to Georgia?

People *must* live their life, one way or another, — on battle-field or quarter-deck; in cabinet, laboratory, pulpit, or nursery. Boys expend theirs on Virgil and bandy; men, on farm and ledger, with a small surplus that goes to liquidate the claims of Smith and Jones to the suffrages of an enlightened community. Girls read Lalla Rookh, crochet lamp-mats, write interminable letters to immortal female friendship, and so manage to drain off their spare life, till, in the course of human events, it runs naturally to housekeeping and babies, and takes the whole force to keep the mill a-going.

But sometimes the farm and nursery and workshop do *not* use up all the fluid; then, according as it makes for itself a channel, or is pent up in too narrow bounds, you have Shakespeare chaining the ages to his triumphal car, or Chatterton flinging down life at sixteen years as a burden too heavy to be borne. You have Raleigh, leaving the apple-orchards of beautiful Devon for an unknown Land of Faery, a new Jason, wandering world-wide for a golden fleece; Spenser, walking with Genii in enchanted woods, and weaving a mightier spell than they; Burns, upheaving not only the soil with his plough, but the land with his song; Browning, voicing on her many-stringed lyre the "Cry of the Children" who pass through the fire to Moloch; Brontë, chained to her desolate rock, and eating her own heart out with a sharper than Promethean torture; Stowe, throwing open to the shuddering day a sepulchre full of dead men's bones, and all uncleanness; Sappho, harping her own requiem on the Leucadian cliff; Socrates, calmly quenching with hemlock the life that would no otherwise be stayed; Dante, gazing in rapt beatific vision on the glorified face of Beatrice; Galileo, spinning the world around in spite of the pious dunces who sat on it in solemn conclave to hold it down; Kane, walking in silence with the Spirit of Storms; Paul, transported with a holy ardor, denouncing woe to himself if he rein in the fiery words that leap to his lips; David, the stripling, ruddy, and of a beautiful countenance, changed by the spear-touch of an heroic purpose from the dreaming shepherd-boy to the champion of Israel; and William of Orange, and Alfred the Great, and Milton, and Tasso, and Napoleon, and Homer, and Mozart.

Corollary 1. Everybody has just so much life to live, and if it is dammed up in one direction it will overflow in another.

Corollary 2. Greatness, heroism, glory, spring

from what is left over and above necessity. That is, some people have just soul enough for salt. You cannot conceive a further diminution of their mental endowments unattended by immediate physical decomposition. Of course they have nothing to spare for fame. But the highest must have body as well as the lowest intellect. The body is the strong cord which keeps the "animula vagula blandula" from flying off in a tangent. They cannot live in a state of pure mind, any more than the others can live in a state of pure matter. Consequently, there is a plane on which they both meet, and that plane is bread and butter. But the one never soars above it, while the other never remains upon it. Herein consists the difference between the two. It is from the latter, roaming about in the empyrean, that we get our grandeur and sublimity, our pathos and poetry.

Corollary 3. Female authorship, instead of being deprecated, ought to be encouraged as the great safety-valve of society; and those who ridicule and oppose it show themselves far behind the age in endeavoring to put down such an army with no better weapon than that wherewith Samson slew a thousand Philistines fifty centuries ago.

Many a woman with no pretensions to genius walks her daily round, fulfils all wifely duties, seems contented and happy in her home of peace and plenty, who is nevertheless sometimes lonely and dispirited. There are glimmerings of somewhat higher; shadowy remembrances of girlish aspirations and heroic purposes; a sad and eager questioning — "Is *this* all?" — to the heart that vouchsafes no reply. This feeling can find no vent like poetry or music. If from the keys of her piano or the strings of her harp her troubled spirit, Saul-like, shall find rest, it is well; but if she have no spell to evoke the genius of song, why should you forbid her to give expression by rhythmic cadence to the feeling which, unvoiced, will be crushed back into the soil whence it sprang, to moulder and decay, and cast a mildew and blight on all the graces, virtues, and affections which should adorn and beautify life? The little poem may be simple in thought and rugged in outline; it may be at once consigned to the silence of a secret drawer; but the longing is gratified, the pent-up mind has found an outlet, and the weary woman goes on her way rejoicing. Years afterward, when the hand that wrote it is cold in the grave, a daughter's eyes, it may be, will fall upon it, and a page of that mother's history, hitherto all unrevealed, be suddenly illuminated; and between the daughter on earth and the mother in heaven there will be another and a golden link, which the world knoweth not of.

Girls, do not be deceived. Write. Write poetry, — write in rhyme, — if it is only

"One, two,
Buckle my shoe;
Three, four,
Open the door."

Form the habit. It is often convenient. It is a refuge from ennui. It may do good. Any one of you who refrains from writing for fear of ridicule, is a coward. Don't be a coward. There is not much to a woman at best. She is not expected to have physical courage; but if she has not moral, pray, what has she? The more a man tells you not to write, the more do you write. By this I do not mean to say that you must immediately publish a volume of "Something, and other Poems," though even that I advise you to do, if you feel disposed and can afford it. It is better than to be talking scandal or making flounces. Would-be critics lament pathetically or satirize mercilessly this "rushing into print." It is mere selfishness on their part. You might rush elbow deep into a batter pudding, or bury heart and soul and mind, beyond all hope of disinterment, beneath a confused rubbish of unmended stockings, or by a letter of recommendation become the fifth wife of some hard-worked, hard-working, broken-down, and worn-out missionary, and they would not lift a finger to prevent. No, girls; no. If your heart is stirred within you to write, write! If you can find an editor or publisher who is willing to print for you, print! Somewhere in the world, a heart-string may tremble to your feeble and unsteady touch, with a strange bliss. I do not suppose a line of poetry was ever written, from the New Hampshire bard's

> "The beauties of nature, I positive declare
> The beauties of nature are very rich and rare,"

to the stately hexameters of Britain's sturdy old Republican, which did not bear a message of joy or consolation to some of God's children, — whose coming was not watched for, perhaps, by many loving eyes, and gazed at with untiring satisfaction. Never be concerned about readers. You will, at all events, read it yourself, and, better than all, you will appreciate it. Your darling Arabella will read, admire, and very probably cut it out and place it in her scrap-book. What is fame, more than this?

If you are a little inclined to egotism, and tolerably imaginative, you can trick yourself out in all sorts of Protean shapes; serve yourself up in as many different disguises as a French cook does a *ragout;* and, at the same time, preserve the most rigid reticence; because no one knows how much is memory and how much is imagination. Or if you have acquired the habit of entertaining views of things, it gives you an excellent opportunity to exhibit them; and of the many comfortable things in the world, one of the most comfortable is to give your views. It is so agreeable to say things, when you have things to say. Your opinions may not be very striking, or original, or important; still it is a relief to express them. No matter if they have been said fifty times before; you never said them. They were but bulky bullion. They must go through the mint of your brain in order to become your current coin. The stream may have meandered down the mountains of life a thousand years, and heaped together priceless diamonds and ingots of gold, and yet fail in that fertilizing power more valuable than all, till it sweeps along the rich alluvial deposits that lie in the green meadows of your own soul. It does not satisfy your craving for the "delicacies of the season," to know that salmon and peas have been eaten since the world began.

In so far as literature seems to you a royal road to fame and fortune, let me entreat you not to be deceived. If you have been put through Watts's "Sixteen Rules for Gaining Knowledge and Mental Improvement" as thoroughly as I, I shall not need to say, "Be not so weak as to imagine that a life of learning is a life of laziness and ease." But, besides good Dr. Watts's exhortations, the testimony of the great mass of writers proclaims,

> "Hard the labor, small the gain,
> Is in making bread from brain."

I have seen, in several modern American novels, certain counter statements. Brilliant but obscure young women are represented as having surreptitiously sprung a book upon an unsuspecting public, and being summarily overwhelmed with money, and fame, and troops of distinguished friends and patrons. I know that charming Fanny Burney did really smuggle her Eveline into the world without even the complicity of "Daddy Crisp," and that there presently fell upon her listening, straining, but scarcely expectant ear, a rustling among the mulberry-trees; coaches blocked up the way to the circulating libraries; Burke sat up all night to watch the adventures of a young lady upon her first entrance into the world; fops levelled their glasses; women of fashion patronized the shrinking authoress; and the brutal, benevolent "Great Cham" coiled his huge arm thrice about her slender waist, and bound her to him forever. Nor have I any doubt that, notwithstanding Campbell's savage toast, publishers are often honest, upright, excellent men, many of whom would gladly bind up the wounds and bruises which their own hands have been forced to inflict. There are individuals among them — several I know — who are perfect pinks of disinterested kindness, full of good works and alms-deeds. Still, I think I do not err in affirming that, as a class, they are not largely addicted to sending huge rolls of spontaneous bank-bills to anonymous correspondents. When you hear of men's receiving twenty, forty, or a hundred dollars a page, and twenty and forty thousand for a volume of history or romance or science, don't think of the forty dollars simply, but of the forty years of daily and nightly toil, research, study, thought, contrivance, experiment, disappointment, discouragement, vexation, and heartache that have preceded them.

> "The crowd, they only see the crown,
> They only hear the hymn;
> They mark not that the cheek is pale,
> And that the eye is dim."

Do you prize the crown so highly, that you will bear the cross? To be purified by the poet's fire, will you endure the anguish of the burning? Do you worship the goddess with so true a faith, that you will offer up yourself at her shrine?

There are obstacles without as well as within. A certain prejudice against female writers "still lives." It is fine, subtle, impalpable, but real. It is like the great ocean of air that wraps us round. A little of it cannot be seen; it is only in mass that it becomes visible. It is like a far-off star; look straight at it, and it is not there; look askance, and it twinkles and winks at you again. It is like the Indian in warfare; it never meets you face to face, and takes fair aim, but, darting behind shelter, sends a shot obliquely. It is also like the Devil; resist it, and it will flee from you. It is indeed vanishing every day; and as woman gravitates to her proper place, and the elements cease to be agitated, it will entirely disappear. Like other fashions founded on whim, caprice, or injustice, and not on the eternal fitness of things, it will go from master to man, from man to scullion, from scullion to the dogs. It has already begun its downward progress. Large-hearted and large-brained men, the monarchs of thought, have flung it clean off. The ranks below them, men of small capacities but unbounded ambition, who see in women their own rivals, — who fear, and justly, too, that a fair field and no favor would oust them from seats they have questionable claim to fill and infinite difficulty to hold, — have caught the flimsy, floating thing, and see but darkly through its tremulous shimmer; and, with limbs tangled in its fine, strong, invisible meshes, walk stumbling and uncertain. So long as you will lend yourself to the amusement of these men, — be witty, playful, piquant, affectionate, and saucy; dance and sparkle along their ascending pathway; circle, as brilliant a satellite as you please, round themselves, the central, acknowledged sun, — they will shine down on you the most benignant and complacent condescension. But once undertake to set up for yourself; get the troublesome idea into your head, that that head was given you for something more than a series of fireworks; tell them seriously that you have been thinking whether all play may not make Gill a mere toy, just as it does Jack, and whether there may not be something in the world for you to do, — whether the purling, singing, happy brook, that now only freshens the violets on its banks, may not, by widening and deepening the channel, be made subservient to nobler and not less pure uses, — whether the same vivacity, compactness, and power that enliven the social circle, and fling a charm around a few favored lives, may not gleam on a broader sphere with no diminished lustre, soften the harsh outline of some unwelcome truth into grace and loveliness, light up some sombre picture with golden tints, polish some hidden blade — rusty, disused, and rusty because disused — into Damascene gleaming, suppleness, and sharpness, and restore it once more to the armory of God, — and lo! our respected friend, who, whilom, found no words so sweet as fitly could express his love, complacence, interest in your weal, admiration of your character, and pride in your reputation, cools suddenly down to zero, leans leisurely back in his comfortable study-chair, strokes caressingly his black moustache, and, with eyes turned contemplatively ceiling-ward, and infinite and pitying forbearance of voice and manner: "Yes" (with an inflection indicative of mental and subjective interrogation), — "yes" (falling inflection; interrogation not satisfactorily answered). "You may be able to effect something. There are very respectable authors among women." (Magnanimous concession!) "There is no doubt that the thing is overdone. Still —" and here, or a minute after, at furthest, he will cut an intellectual pirouette, and, with a most frank, arch, and engaging smile, inform you that, after all, he would "rather see a ring on your third finger than an ink-spot on your first." Stupid!

You will often see the outcropping of this feeling in the criticisms of women's books; not that just and generous criticism which discriminates between the evil and the good, condemns the one without rancor, and applauds the other without servility, but that half-flattering, half-contemptuous, and wholly contemptible notice, whose compassionate blame and condescending praise are alike insulting. Such was the revenge of some of our sleek, respectable, self-admiring male writers, when Aurora Leigh dashed in upon their fancied security, and shivered her most knightly yet right womanly lance against their time-honored commonplaces. What a shaking of the dry bones there must have been, indeed, under the hoofs of her high-mettled steed! But as soon as their spirits returned to them again, they fell a-babbling of Socialism, and Fourierism, and Chartism, and "all the others that end in" ism; and there was poetry in the book, *but* there was a deal of obscurity; and there was felicity of expression, *but* there was occasional awkwardness; and there were a great many things, *but* there were also a great many others; and, on the whole, Aurora Leigh must be pronounced a failure. Self-blinded! If Aurora Leigh be a woman's failure, what would a woman's success be?

Sometimes this prejudice takes the form of disinterested counsel, paternal and affectionate advice; but through the lion's skin, the long ears reveal indubitably the true nature of the animal. "Aspiring sisters," says the domestic brute before alluded to, "why is the tone of your lucubrations always so mournful? If you must write, write cheerfully. Don't let every song be a dirge. We want to be amused when we read" (there is the ear again); "consume in private your private griefs." Not a doubt of it. Beyond cavil, it would be vastly agreeable to our private Neros, — Heaven be praised that they are few, I know that there are some, — who harry the life out of wife and child, who are tyrants without the fear of assassination, because their victims are too good, or of public opinion, because the thing is done in a corner, or of the law, because it takes no cognizance of soul-murder, — doubtless it would be vastly agreeable to them, that women should endure uncomplainingly. No voice louder than theirs in praise of her sweet self-abnegation and silent fortitude, or in deprecation of publicly-displayed sorrow, when, in song or story, the minor key of sadness, the outburst of long-pent-up anguish, or the unmistakable wail of a broken heart, sends home to their own breasts the prophet's stern charge, "Thou art the man." Consume in private your private griefs! No. Take them in a bundle, and bear them to the highest mountain-top; ring the church-bells, hoist the flags, beat the drums, and let the whole world see the bonfire; and if the flame scorches our sensitive friends, let them stand back. Why should they flutter about it, if they don't want their wings singed?

Do all or any of these things move you? Do you fear to launch your bark on so unquiet a sea? Do you shrink from the lion without, lest you should be slain in the street? Then by all means remain within doors, and hold your peace. Do not fancy that you would achieve immortality, if you only had the chance, — that you would soar sunward, if your wings were not pinioned. Genius is expansive, irresistible, and irresistibly expansive. If it is in you, no cords can confine it. A good book will get itself written. Authorship is not a thing to be quietly chosen, as circumstance may determine. It chooses you; you do not choose it. Did Mrs. Browning sit down in her little back parlor, and wonder whether she would better fashion a song, or devote herself exclusively to Robert's shirts and stockings? And, observing that she had facility in language, familiarity with the classics, knowledge of human nature, and abundant leisure, did she forthwith seize her pen, and tell us

> "how a fairy bride from Italy,
> With smells of oleander in her hair,
> Was coming through the vines"?

I trow not. I rather believe that her spirit groaned, being burdened, – that she was but an unwilling Sibyl, lashed on, foaming, by a fierce Apollo. Currer Bell trod in agony the desolate heaths of Haworth, till the consuming fire burned deep scars in her tortured soul, before Jane Eyre leaped, full armed, not from her throbbing brain alone, but from her riven heart.

If prejudice, ignorance, or sloth pile a Hill Difficulty which you hesitate to scale; if indifference, neglect, or rebuff quench your spirit's flow; if encouragement and appreciation must be the Aaron and Hur on either side, without whose aid your failing hands droop, nerveless; if you fear to speak out boldly your convictions lest you forfeit approbation; if peace and smiles and sunshine seem to you more desirable than truth; if you are not in and of yourself sufficient to yourself; if a mind conscious of rectitude, of upright intentions, and honorable performance, is not to you a sufficient guerdon, — you may be

> "A perfect woman, nobly planned,
> To warn, to comfort, and command,"

but lyre and tripod are not for you. The world awards its meed of praise to no uncertain claimant. Only to him that hath shall be given. You go out on a mission of high emprise, with scrip and staff and "sandal shoon," and there are few to say, "God bless you." You return in purple and scarlet and fine linen, with gilded chariot and horse of Arabia, and the world comes out to meet you, with timbrels and dancing, and ministers unto you a triumphal entrance. I do not say that this is wrong; only that it *is*. You must conquer Fate, before Fate will bow the knee. You must prove your royal blood, before you can wear the royal crown; and that perhaps so late that it will only press, cold and heavy, on aching brows.

Watchman! What of the night? The morning cometh.

It is not for the generation among whom Elizabeth Browning has sung, and Charlotte Brontë spoken, and Harriet Hosmer chiselled, and Rosa Bonheur painted, and Mary Lyon taught, and Florence Nightingale lived, to despair of woman's achievement of her highest destiny. In whatever direction you choose to walk, you will find that a firm footfall has preceded yours; that a strong hand has hewed down the giant trees, and cleared away the tangled undergrowth, so that the forest which once required all a man's strength and a woman's fortitude, a child may thrid unharmed. Thus do the strong bear the burdens of the weak. Thus have noble women made straight, in the desert, a highway for our God. "Inasmuch as ye have done it unto one of the least of these my brethren, ye have done it unto me." The costly step has been taken.

But let us not suppose that generous ends can be attained only on the mountain-top. To but few is strength given to climb its rugged sides, and clearness and breadth of vision to take in the broad sweep of its low-lying landscape. Down in the valley there is work to be done, — humble, yet divine; small in the germ, yet great in the unfolding. However simple or however difficult, however obscure or however prominent the work may be, matters not, provided it be God's appointed work. It is better to rule a household well, than a kingdom ill.

"Who sweeps a room as to God's law,
Makes that and th' action fine."

The ring on a child's finger is as perfect a circle as the zone of this round world. The Dairyman's Daughter "just knew, and knew no more, her Bible true," lived out her brief and simple life, and was not, for God took her. But from her humble island home her voice still speaks comfort and hope to the ends of the earth.

Here and there, both in the beaten paths and the untrodden ways, on the lowlands and the uplands of life, I meet an angel, — not in white robes, garlanded with roses, and winged for Heaven, but plain in calico, it may be, or grand in velvet. I recall now the face of one whose life is to me a constant gospel. A slight, pale girl, orphaned, homeless, neglected by those who should have watched her young years tenderly, she yet seems to have drawn to herself, by some magnetic power, all the good of all the persons by whom she has been surrounded, and to have fed her own soul thereon. She went to school, bearing in her mean and scanty dress, her thin cheeks, and hard hands, the marks of poverty and toil; and wild, thoughtless, elegantly-dressed, and carefully-nurtured girls hushed their heedless sarcasm, softened their merry voices, and spoke to her with love, and of her with tears. Shrinkingly sensitive to their opinions, tremblingly alive to her own disadvantages, conscious as she must have been that she served a hard taskmaster, no word of complaint ever passed her lips. Always cheerful, modest, happy, willing to be pleased, grateful for kindness, and patient of any chance neglect, you might have supposed her entirely insensible to the motives and feelings that influence ordinary girls, were it not for the occasional quiver of the lip, the quick, nervous gesture, the moistened eye, and faltering tone. She left school with disease lurking in her system, slowly and surely undermining the citadel of life; but she kept up her courage. She had no idea of dying till her hour should come, and, as long as she should live, she determined that her living should bring forth fruit. She earned money enough to transport herself to a climate which was pronounced favorable to her health; there, in wild backwoods, among a rough people, who had forgotten, if they ever knew, the common refinements of life, she opened a school. From her rude home she wrote merry letters, describing her adventures and her circumstances. There was no talk of self-denial, the greatness of sacrifice, the hardship of missionary life. Over all the harsh outline, and the harsher filling in, she threw the veil of her playful fancy, and few heard the mournful undertone that thrilled through the gay, sprightly song. The new scenes and the softer air did not have the desired effect, and a short time since she wrote to a friend: "I have moved from a small, quiet school to a large, rollicking, frolicking, fun-loving one. I am happy; I think I ought to be. Every one is kind. But I am quite puzzled. I don't know just what to do. If I am to teach much longer, it would be better for me to return to New England, and go to school awhile. I have earned enough to keep me at school a year or so, and I do believe I am willing to exert myself to the utmost to improve. But, then, this cough increases. It may not be long before it will have an end. If I go to New England, I may spend all the life left me in *acquiring* knowledge, and so lose the opportunity for usefulness that I might have if I remained here. Now the question is, Which will bring the largest pile of wood, — the dull axe for six hours, or the sharp one for two?"

This is what I mean by heroism. This young girl standing at bay, watching what she believes to be the approach of inevitable death, asking for no rest from toil, no indulgence for weakness and weariness, no sympathy in loneliness, but only striving to know how the little life that remains may be turned to the best account. Brave heart! on the wings of this soft south-wind, that murmurs of violets in the ear of winter, I send you greeting. In your far-off home my voice may never reach you; but if by any chance your eyes should fall upon these words, know that my soul does willing homage to yours, and forgive these few sentences, for the love and reverence that prompted them.

"None but thou and I shall know."

I remember another, a stranger in a strange land; an exile from the home of her fathers; a fair-haired and blue-eyed girl, a warm-hearted and whole-souled woman; of exquisite sensibility, refined taste, and elegant culture; a lover of song and grace and beauty in any guise; a man in strength, a martyr in endurance; performing a father's duty to children not her own; fighting the battle single-handed, and no holiday contest, but a life-and-death struggle with the wolf at the door; welcoming the cold embrace of Duty as smilingly as if it were the warm clasp of Love; eager eyes and ears wide open to the green fields, the upspringing daisies, the note of bee and bird, yet swerving not a hair's breadth from the rocky path which her aching feet most resolutely tread; and where I see her footprints, I know it is holy ground.

And yet another face shines on me through the night, — a face over which the Angel of Sorrow has swept his wing in passing, and saddened into a beauty that is not of the earth. You, looking, see only dark eyes that flash laughter, love, or tears; a delicate cheek, that pales and flushes at your words; red lips, whence drop rare gems of wit and wisdom. These are there, and I see them; but beyond these, and deeper than these, I see a soul that has been weighed in the balance and not found wanting; a heart that has been wrung by sorest anguish, and only grown more pitying and tender; a hand that has touched every note from highest to lowest, and learned to strike from earthly chords most heavenly harmonies; a woman who has said to wealth and station and ease, "Get thee behind me!" and, mailed in her own integrity, has dared opposing fate. It is these, and such as these, that

> "show us how divine a thing
> A woman may be made."

They redeem their sex from the charge of frivolity, inanity, and feebleness, revealing to us the capacities that lie hidden in her heart of hearts; and it is because I have witnessed such noble living, such "extraordinary, generous seeking," that I believe in woman; and when I see life going to waste, — when I see a woman's soul bent on ignoble ends, frittered away on trifling toys, finding content and happiness in things that perish with the using, — I feel, not contempt, not anger, but sadness and sore regret: —

> "The pity of it, Iago, the pity of it."

I mourn for gold grown dim, and fine gold changed, — for fields white to harvest, and the reapers disporting among flowers, — for a world lying in ignorance and wickedness, and the power that should raise and redeem it, and fit it once more for the footsteps of its Lord, spending its strength for naught.

O, if this latent power could be aroused! If woman would shake off this slumber, and put on her strength, her beautiful garments, how would she go forth conquering and to conquer, — how would the mountains break forth into singing, and the trees of the field clap their hands, — how would our sin-stained earth arise and shine, her light being come, and the glory of the Lord being risen upon her!

One cannot do the world's work; but one can do one's work. You may not be able to turn the world from iniquity, but you can at least keep the dust and rust from gathering on your own soul. If you cannot be directly and actively engaged in fighting the battle, you can at least polish your armor and sharpen your weapons, to strike an effective blow when the hour comes. You can stanch the blood of him who has been wounded in the fray, — bear a cup of cold water to the thirsty and fainting, — give help to the conquered and smiles to the victor. You can gather from the past and the present stores of wisdom, so that, when the future demands it, you may bring forth from your treasures things new and old. Whatever of bliss the Divinity that shapes our ends may see fit to withhold from you, you are but very little lower than the angels so long as you have the

> "Godlike power to do, — the godlike aim to know."

You can be forming habits of self-reliance, sound judgment, perseverance, and endurance, which may one day stand you in good stead. You can so train yourself to right thinking and right acting, that uprightness shall be your nature, truth your impulse. His head is seldom far wrong whose heart is always right. We bow down to mental greatness, intellectual strength, and they are Divine gifts; but moral rectitude is stronger than they. It is irresistible, — always in the end triumphant. There is in goodness a penetrative power that nothing can withstand. Cunning and malice melt away before its mild, open, steady glance. Not alone on the fields where chivalry charges for laurels, with helmet and breastplate and lance in rest, can the true knight exultantly exclaim,

> "My strength is as the strength of ten,
> Because my heart is pure,"

but wherever man meets man, wherever there is

a prize to be won, a goal to be reached. Wealth and rank and beauty may form a brilliant setting to the diamond, but they only expose more nakedly the false glare of the paste. Only when the king's daughter is all glorious within, is it fitting and proper that her clothing should be of wrought gold.

From the great and the good of all ages rings out the same monotone. The high-priest of nature, the calm-eyed poet who laid his heart so close to hers that they seemed to throb in one pulsation, yet whose ear was always open to the "still sad music of humanity," has given us the promise of his life-long wisdom in these grand words: —

> "True dignity abides with him alone
> Who, in the silent hour of inward thought,
> Can still suspect and still revere himself."

Through the din of twenty rolling centuries pierces the sharp, stern voice of the brave old Greek: "Let every man, when he is about to do a wicked action, above all things in the world stand in awe of himself, and dread the witness within him." All greatness and all glory, all that earth has to give, all that heaven can proffer, lies within the reach of the lowliest as well as the highest; for He who spake as never man spake has said that the very "kingdom of God is within you."

Born to such an inheritance, will you wantonly

cast it away? With such a goal in prospect, will you suffer yourself to be turned aside by the sheen and shimmer of tinsel fruit? With earth in possession and heaven in reversion, will you go sorrowing and downcast, because here and there a pearl or ruby fails you? Nay, rather, forgetting those things which are behind, and reaching forth unto those which are before, press forward. Discontent and murmuring are insidious foes; trample them under your feet. Utter no complaint, whatever betide; for complaining is a sign of weakness. If your trouble can be helped, help it; if not, bear it. You can be whatever you will to be. Therefore, form and accomplish worthy purposes. If you walk alone, let it be with no faltering tread. Show to an incredulous world

> "How grand may be Life's might,
> Without Love's circling crown."

Or if the golden thread of love shine athwart the dusky warp of duty, if other hearts depend on yours for sustenance and strength, give to them from your fulness no stinted measure. Let the dew of your kindness fall on the evil and the good, on the just and on the unjust.

Compass happiness, since happiness alone is victory. On the fragments of your shattered plans and hopes and love, on the heaped-up ruins of your past, rear a stately palace, whose top shall reach unto heaven, whose beauty shall gladden the eyes of all beholders, whose doors shall stand wide open to receive the wayworn and weary. Life is a burden, but it is imposed by God. What you make of it, it will be to you, whether a millstone about your neck, or a diadem upon your brow. Take it up bravely, bear it on joyfully, lay it down triumphantly.

MY BIRDS.

STRICTLY speaking, I have n't any, — only an old cage thrust away up garret under the eaves, — nor, in fact, do I want any. Do not, however, for a moment suppose that I indulge in a sentimental compassion for caged birds, for I don't. I consider such a thing entirely uncalled for, and misplaced. I have no doubt that a canary-bird, with a cup of seed and a glass of water, finds every aspiration of his soul satisfied. A sorrow's crown of sorrow is remembering happier things. He was born and bred in a cage, and, so far from being discontented with a restraint of which he is not conscious, freedom would bewilder him and bring him to grief. But, though I do not take into account the bird's feelings, I do mind my own; and a prisoned bird always gives me a cramped, asthmatic sensation, if I know what cramp and asthma are, which I don't.

My birds, the birds that furnish my right to that possessive pronoun, are the little darlings which this moment brighten the cold, damp, clammy spring earth with their flutter and chirp and song, — little, happy-hearted, hollow-boned braves, who dare untimely frosts, and the whirling snow-wreaths which winter, forced to leave, flings spitefully behind him, — daring the long, cold, dismal rains which chill to the heart this sweet May month, — merry messengers of the storm-king, bearing the olive-leaf of peace; twittering prophecies of summer; tender little bars struck off from the music of the spheres; faint, sweet echoes, in their wooing and winning, their prudence and painstaking, their tender protection and assiduous provision, of the strong, careful, passionate, loving humanity that swells and surges beneath them.

I love birds; I do not mind if it is nothing but a hawk or a crow, or a sooty little chimney-swallow. I even like chickens till they become hens and human. I cannot look with indifference upon turkeys standing out forlorn in the rain, too senseless to think of going in for shelter, and so taking it helplessly, with rounded backs, drooping heads, dripping feathers, and long, bare, red, miserable legs, quite too wretched to be ridiculous. I dote on goslings, — little soft, yellow, downy, awkward things, waddling around with the utmost self-complacency, landing on their backs every third step, and kicking spasmodically till they are set right side up with care, when they resume their waddle and their self-complacency as if nothing in the world had happened. The only fault one can find with them is, that they will grow up; and goslings grown up are nothing but geese, with their *naïveté* degenerated into stupidity, their awkwardness crystallized into vulgarity, and their tempers unspeakably bad. But the little birds that sing to me from the apple-trees, and hop about on the sunny southern slope, are not of these. Purer blood runs through finer veins. Golden robins, a fiery flash of splendor, gleam in the long grass, and put the dandelions to shame. There are magnificent bluebirds, with their pale, unwinking intensity of color; and homely little redbreasts, which we all called robins when we were young, and invested with the sanctity of that sweet, ancestral pity which has given them a name in our memory and a place in our hearts, till somebody must needs flare up, and proclaim that they are nothing but thrushes! As if this world were in a general way such an Elysium that people can afford to make themselves unnecessarily disagreeable. If there is any one thing more than another that is an unmitigated abomination and bore, it is those persons who are always setting you right; who find their delight in pricking your little silk balloons of illusion with their detestable pins of facts; who are always bringing their statistics to bear upon your enthusiasms;

who go around with a yardstick and a quart-measure to give you the cubic contents of your rapture, demonstrating to a logical certainty that you need not have been rapt at all; proving by the forty-seventh proposition of the first book of Euclid that spirits disembodied cannot have any influence upon spirits embodied; setting up that there is n't any Maelstrom and never was, — that the Aurora Borealis is a common cloud reflecting the sunlight, and turning the terrible ocean-waves that ran mountain-high when you were a child into pitiful horse-pond shivers, never mounting above the tens. As for me, I don't believe a word of it. I believe the equatorial line cuts through Africa like a darning-needle, that the Atlantic waves would drown the Himalayas if they could get at them, that eclipses are caused by the beast which Orion is hunting trying to gulp down the moon, and I should not wonder if the earth was supported on the back of a great turtle, which hypothesis has at least the advantage of explaining satisfactorily why it is that we all travel heavenward at such a snail's pace, and founds in a sympathetic and involuntary attraction the aldermanic weakness for turtle-soup. When one has been born and brought up in an innocent belief, one does not like to have it disturbed on slight grounds; and people who have an insane proclivity to propagandism would do well to go to heathendom, where they will find ample room and verge enough in overthrowing mischievous opinions. But no punishment is too severe for him who roots up a thrill, and plants in its place only a fact. Suppose it is a fact, what then? Facts are not necessarily truth. Facts are often local, incidental, deceptive. But a thrill is the quiver of the boundless, fathomless life that underlies humanity, — a sign and a symbol of that infinite from which we sprang, and towards which, perforce, we tend. Come then, my robin redbreast! Never shall my hand rise sacrilegious to wrest from you heraldic honors. Always shall you wear an aureole of that golden light that glimmers down the ages, the one bright spot in a dark and deathful wood. Always shall you sing to me angels' songs, of peace on earth, good-will to men.

So they hop through the May mornings' shade and sun, robins, and bluebirds, and dingy little sparrows as thick as blackberries, at once wild and tame, familiar yet shy, tripping, fluttering, snatching their tiny breakfasts, cocking their saucy heads as if listening to some far-off strain, then, moved by a sudden impulse, hopping along again in a fork-lightning kind of way, and again coming to a capricious full stop and silence, with momentary interludes of short, quick, silvery jerks of head and tail. And, as they sit and sing, — as I watch their ceaseless busyness, their social twittering, their energetic, heart-whole melody, their sudden flights, their graceful sweeps, and agile darts, — I recognize the Pauline title-deeds, and, having nothing, yet possessing all things, I say in deed and in truth, "My birds."

But I came very near having a proprietary right in one small family last summer. I discovered a ground-sparrow's nest just on the overhanging edge of the cornfield. There were three little eggs in it, gray and mottled, and not very pretty. But eggs forerun birds, so I visited it regularly every day to take observations. All the corn-people were sworn not to disturb it. A stick was set up to beacon-mark the plough away in case of momentary forgetfulness ; and, notwithstanding all this care and caution, that selfish, cowardly old mother-bird took a panic, shattered my hopes, and went away leaving her helpless egglets to their fate. Their fate was to have a hole bored through them from stem to stern, their embryotic souls blown remorselessly through it, and then be transported, nest and all, to a what-not in my room, where to this very day they stand looking seaward, a hollow monument of the heartlessness of birds, and of the mournful extent to which children are — shall I say it? — *humbugged* by their judicious parents. When we were young, were we not all exhorted to be very pitiful and of tender mercy to the birds? Was it not represented to be the height of cruelty to plunder their nests? Were not pathetic changes rung on the depth and strength of their domestic affection? And will anybody tell me, then, why this unnatural sparrow deserted her home, that was not even threatened? Domestic affection! I have no doubt the story was originally trumped up to keep us from tearing our clothes by climbing the trees. I have come to the conclusion that, though birds may take on airs of tenderness, it is all a dainty acting. They have no rights which mankind is bound to respect, and I hereby give public notice that I intend for the future to rob every bird's-nest that I can lay my hands on.

I came still nearer to owning birds in the winter. A pair of doves — pigeons, some people call them, with perverted taste, but *pigeon* has no character. It is a generic name, without history or associations. It savors of gunning and game, and nothing else. Dove is the word, bubbling up and boiling over with the sweetness of honeymoons. So it was not pigeons, but a pair of brown doves, that began to make nervous raids upon our back-yard when the frosts began to whiten and blacken. They were old acquaintances of mine. Their summer residence had been under the roof of a barn a few yards off, and I had watched the process of their courtship with great interest. It had not run smooth at all. A little dove-cot had been constructed under the eaves, with a doorway and platform outside for the accommodation of any solitary who might desire to be set in families and I was startled one morning by a succession of strange, angry, guttural sounds proceeding from the barn. I went out. A lively scene was enacting upon the platform under the eaves. There sat a lady-bird in the doorway, and there were her two suitors before her, putting each other into a terrible passion. Number One held possession of the platform, and Number Two was making frantic efforts to carry it by assault. Number One strutted back and forth, ruffling his feathers, dilating his throat, and swearing frightfully in dove dialect. Number Two was calmer, but persistent and determined. He attacked in front and flank and rear. He made desperate dashes from above. Where-ever Number Two planted his adventurous foot, thither Number One betook himself in great force, and ousted him. If Number Two stole a march, and sidled up to my lady, Number One made a sortie and shoved him off. There was no rest for the sole of his foot but the ridge-pole of the neighboring corn-barn, where he occasionally alighted to take breath. Evidently both were very plucky, very much in love, quite conscious that they were fighting under the eye of their mistress, and equally determined never to show the white feather. She, most gracious lady, all this while preserved an imperturbable and thorough-bred indifference. I have no doubt she saw every ebb and flow of the contest, and probably had her own preferences about the victory, but her face said nothing of it. Sometimes she sat immovable, looking far out into the intense inane, as if on sublimer thoughts intent Sometimes she would rise, arch and coquettish, jauntily shake out her plumage, and trip lightly to and fro, displaying her fine face and figure in the most bewilderingly charming attitudes. This was a sure signal for her belligerent lovers to fall to with renewed and indescribable rancor. Sometimes she gave herself up to a fascinating languor. The silken lids would creep slowly and softly over her brilliant eyes, as if weariness at the prolongation of a struggle in which she was so little interested had positively overpowered her. Long time in even scale the battle hung. But possession is nine points of the law of might, as well as of right. Number One fought under the immense advantage of being on the spot, and able to rest directly after one round, and come fresh to the next, while Number Two had to make long journeys between each, with nothing to stand on when he got there. Fighting on a firm footing is nothing, but fighting on nothing is a good deal; and Number Two was at length forced to desist, leaving the fair one and her successful admirer to devote themselves to the pursuits of peace.

Which they did with such assiduity that for many weeks they were scarcely visible to the naked eye; but if Fate led any to the vicinity of the barn scaffold, they became at once conscious of a mysterious stir and bustle and flutter, a certain sign that something was happening. When the fulness of time was come, the something turned out, or rather chipped out, to be two little brown doves, the very image of their respected parents. These respected parents it was who, impelled by the *res angustæ domi*, came foraging in our back-yard. I determined to befriend them, to attach them to me as far as possible. They surely needed friendship and attachment if they were to stand the long, cold Northern winter that was setting in, and I was very sure that I should be extremely glad of some little life to keep the genial current of my own soul from freezing. So I made advances by scattering a few kernels of corn on the porch-roof under my chamber window. They mounted the shed-roof and eyed it longingly. I mounted the window-seat and eyed them. They wished they dared, but they did n't. They were evidently suspicious of masked batteries and infernal machines. Then I hid behind the curtain. They stepped nearer. No appearance of hostility. Nearer still. All quiet along the Potomac. A twitching of wings, a stretching of neck, a settling of body for about five minutes, and down they came to the outmost verge of the porch, balancing themselves on the wire edge just one second, and immediately flying back, alarmed at their own temerity. But though retreating so precipitately, that one onset had given them assurance, and they soon returned, stepping daintily and gingerly along, with many starts and tremors, to where the corn lay. Then they became ridiculous. They would shoot at a kernel, and rush back alarmed at the noise which their beaks made against the tin roofing. The least breath of wind, the buzzing of a fly, startled them. They gobbled up the corn in a perfect hysteric of hurry, darting about twenty times at a single kernel before they could get possession of it. I don't think they were very skilful at best,—I am sure I could hit better than that if I were a dove; but they were in great trepidation of mind, and that is not favorable to accuracy of aim. After a few days they became reassured, and demonstrated their confidence by bringing their young and interesting family along with them. Their family, it must be confessed, were not difficult to bring; they evinced not the slightest backwardness. They entered into the spirit of it at once. They appropriated the corn with the most self-confident alacrity. I fed them regularly twice a day, filching their meals from the garret without remorse. The corn had no business to be there in the first place, tolling all the mice in the neighborhood; and I reasoned that there was no cause why scores of mice should overflow with milk and honey, and a brood of doves die of starvation. So they did not, and so daily we established more amicable and more intimate relations. Regularly every morning, at about eight o'clock, the swoop of their white wings cleft the frosty air, click, click, click, went their horny little toes over the tin plating, and in a moment their little round eyes were peering in through the window as they perched upon the sill outside. (I trust there is no truth in the doctrine of the transmigration of souls!) I believe they formed and cherished for me a real affection, — something quite beyond the loaf-and-fishy attachment of the general animal race,— something, in short, sentimental and super-dovian; for, after they had been abundantly fed, they still sat on the window-sill from morning till late in the afternoon. Through driving sleet and snow, or wrapped in the winter sunshine, they held their post, occasionally hopping down upon the roof to get the kinks out of their legs, but returning soon to take up their old position. When I spoke to them, they would flutter, and wink, and snap their eyes, and look mightily pleased. If I sat by the other window, round they swept to that, nodding and cooing a "Here we are!"

But one morning — woe worth the day! — I heard a noise overhead, a wild, violent, muffled, murderous noise of struggle and assault, and suddenly down past my window floated a tiny cloud of white, fleecy feathers, — dripped three drops of blood. I started up, suspicious at once of crime and the cat. The cat's name is Moses, — a treacherous fellow, striking you when you caress him; a totally depraved cat by nature, choosing evil when the good is not only better, but sweeter, turning away from his allotted food to steal whatever he can lay his paws and claws on ; a quarrelsome fellow, and cowardly withal, attacking where he is sure of success, and yowling frightfully where he is not. But he is a good mouser, and you manage about cats as you do about congressmen, generals, and other public officers. If they will do the work you want done, and do it well, you have to take them, though they may abuse their wives, tell lies, and be otherwise abominable. You execrate their moral character, but you need their special ability, and you use it, not indorsing them thereby. So we tolerated our cat, because he would not tolerate mice, though as a cat and a gentleman he could never be introduced into good society. The garret was his peculiar haunt. There lay the golden corn in forty-thievic profusion. Thither came the mice to levy blackmail for themselves and their little ones, and there I feared my tender dove, lured by the tempting repast, might have flown through the open window and met his fate. I rushed up garret. On the floor by the window lay a clawful of white, fleecy feathers, clotted with blood. Yes, it must be, but where was the murderer? I called to Moses. The echoes alone called back from the rafters. I walked up and down, peering behind the boxes and the barrels. No Moses, no dove. Marvelling at the mystery, I turned to go, and encountered the gleam of two green, phosphorescent eyes, glaring at me through the darkness under an old bed in the corner. I went near, and lifted the corner of the quilt. There lay the mother dove on her back, her beautiful white and brown feathers dabbled with blood, her stiff, pathetic legs stretched upwards and outwards, her bright eyes closed, her fond heart still. Over her stood the fiend Moses, burning his fierce, fiery eyes into my soul; and as I tarried there, bending to behold, with my two hands resting on my two knees, pitying the dove and confounding the cat, a snip of theology came into my mind. Let not envy or bigotry interpose a scornful smile. If the great magician of literature could see tongues in the trees, books in the running brooks, and sermons in stones, may not I, who am indeed no magician, but a humble little page, read theology in a cat's eyes?

I desire to say preliminarily that I am a Calvinist. I say it because the Atlantic Monthly has been in sundry quarters suspected of a certain leaning the other way, and I may be suspected of leaning with it out of an ignoble subserviency. Not that what I am about to say does at all deviate from the right line of Orthodoxy; but "liberal Christians" have a way of exercising their liberality to an astonishing extent on themselves. Whenever I give out anything unusually brilliant in the line of ethics or theology, up jumps a Unitarian, and exclaims, "That is Unitarianism." Whatsoever things are true, whatsoever things are honest, whatsoever things are just, whatsoever things are pure, whatsoever things are lovely, whatsoever things are of good report, if there be any virtue, and if there be any praise, — all the grist goes to their mill. But what right have they, I should like to know, to monopolize just thinking and wise uttering? Is there nothing sensible, philosophic, natural, judicious, catholic, in Orthodoxy? Does every good gift and every perfect gift come from the Gospel according to Channing, and no good thing at all out of Emmons? Do not the "Evangelical" sometimes drop their lines into the great ocean of truth and get a nibble? and is it generous or liberal for the un-Evangelical to snatch at it? Truth belongs to him who recognizes it. There may be certain points not held in common, but they are few when compared to the myriads which are the inheritance of humanity, and which bind men together in golden bands of brotherhood. In this rich, unfenced land, one may make perpetual forays, and draw off laden with spoil, yet trench on no man's rights, appropriate no man's possessions.

I must confess that the Orthodox are only too ready to play into their opponents' hands. When the latter take me up, the former drop me instantly. Instead of tightening their hold, and saying to their antagonists, "No, you don't! Antichrist is not going to pre-empt all the sense and sparkle there is in the world. We have right and title to this, and we mean to defend it against all comers. Go and raise your own prodigies. We want ours for home consumption," — they take the Unitarians' word for it, and give me over as a reprobate mind concerning the faith. They have such a heresy-phobia, that heretics have only to raise the cry, "Mad dog!" and out they tumble with broom-stick and shillalah to hunt me down, never stopping to inquire whether I am only labelled mad, or whether I do indeed foam at the mouth.

What's in a name, Miss Capulet? Everything, my dear.

But for all this, I am not to be lured or fisticuffed away from the faith of my fathers. A Calvinist I was born, and a Calvinist I remain. It does occur to me sometimes that I should like to know what Calvinism is; but that is not essential. Whatever it is, I believe in it. I accept its points, all five of them; and if there were five thousand of them I should accept them just the same. Original sin, total depravity, natural ability, — nothing is too hard for me. I follow wherever Calvin leads. If he could stand it, I can. Servetus does not stagger me. I could swallow a good deal larger camel than he is, and not make faces. I don't believe, in the first place, that Calvin burned Servetus, and if he did, I dare say Servetus richly deserved it. Why could he not keep still? Why must he needs jump from the hot water of Toulouse into the frying-pan of Basle and the fire of Geneva? Why could he not content himself with being a doctor and killing other people, instead of turning theologian and killing himself? It is just these very wilful, pushing, impracticable, one-idea men that make the mischief. If people would only eat their dinners and let things alone, there would be no trouble. But every age and country has its pestilent fellows, who are never easy unless they are poking into somebody's pet belief, or custom, or prejudice, and turning the world upside down. Only the nineteenth century has grown squeamish about cauterizing for disease, and so lets it run till the whole head is sick and the whole heart faint. Our own country furnishes a melancholy example of this. If Hopkins and Phillips and Beecher, and two or three hundred more, could have been summarily Servetized, our friends would not now be up to their necks in Southern mud, and slaveholders would be cracking their whips in peace over our heads and those of their negroes. Moreover, whatever Servetus's opinions deserved, his manners certainly merited the stake; and I wish there could be a law passed to-morrow, that everybody who does not try to make himself agreeable, everybody who is arrogant, or surpercilious, or sneering, or biting, or in any way gratuitously uncomfortable, should be toasted on a gridiron like St. Lawrence, without even the privilege of turning the other side to the fire, until he promises to mend his ways. For my part, I believe I would about as soon be burnt at the stake — I know I would rather be considerably scorched — as come in contact with those tremendous people that one sees occasionally walking up and down the earth, seeking whom they may devour.

If I have now stated my position, and made it sufficiently clear that I do not design to conceal or assume any views out of deference to any institution, I will return to my muttons, as the French say.

It chanced to me once to overhear a company of theologians talking. They were discussing responsibility, penalty, and such things, and, as far as an uninitiated person could gather, the gist of it was whether babies sinned before they began, or not till afterwards. The thing which they all evidently agreed upon was, that beings did not have moral responsibility till they had moral ideas, — that is, till they knew right from wrong. This, I am sure, all must agree to. But as I stood steadfastly gazing at that cat, I went a step beyond, and I remembered a little girl whose education had advanced to the degree that she could make feint of articulating single words, but was in no wise equal to the effort of stringing two words together. This tiny maiden, tempted of the Devil, and aided and abetted thereby, had feloniously abstracted a lump of sugar from the sugar-firkin, and retired behind the closet-door to enjoy her prize. There she was overtaken in her iniquity Her eyes looked up to see her mother's eyes fixed on hers; and whoever saw the shame and guilt and remorse that settled in those eyes, and spread over that three-cent-piece of a face, — whoever, indeed, saw the tiny figure smuggled behind the door, or felt the unwonted silence occasioned by her temporary withdrawal from the world, — could have had no doubt that she knew in the half-inch depths of her frail little heart that she was doing wrong. Yet how far was she morally responsible? If she had died that moment, would she not have gone straight up to the arms of the Christ? I verily believe so. And looking into the eyes of Moses, my belief found confirmation there; for Moses exhibited just as unmistakable signs of moral ideas as did Metty. Both took what they knew they had no right to take. Metty's mamma called to her, and Metty did not reply, though usually both feet and tongue were swift to meet that voice. I called "Moses!" and silence was my only response, though he generally leaped with great strides to the stairs the moment the garret door was opened. Metty took her sugar behind the door to eat it. Moses took his bird under the bed. Metty spoke no word of justification. No more did Moses. The fact I believe to be, that one was just about as morally responsible as the other; only a human soul is grafted on. and will bud and blossom from the little girl's animal instincts, and the poor old cat will grope along forever through his blind brute life.

But he shall not have my dove to sustain him in it, I said. He shall not crown his grievous transgression with festive orgies. He shall at least suffer the torture of seeing the prize snatched from him in the moment of victory. I went to the head of the stairs and gave a general call for assistance. Dr. Sangrado came. Dr. Sangrado said at once that he should pick the dove and have her cooked. I turned away in disgust without opening my lips. Moses's arrangement was but ferocity. Dr. Sangrado's was cannibalism. He did pick her, and brought me the wings, — two spotless, appealing white wings. One is laid away, the other is tied with a pink satin ribbon and hangs under my mantelpiece. If you should mistake it for an ordinary, household wing, and should begin to sweep up the hearth with it, you would experience a sudden difficulty of respiration. This wing is only a memento. Occasionally, I apply it to such æsthetic uses as brushing a silk cushion or a velvet cover, but never to any profaner purposes.

The next morning I was rejoiced to hear that Dr. Sangrado, having prepared his victim for the vile obsequies which he designed, had hung her in the cellar, and Moses, prowling around as usual in search of prey, had got at the bird and fared sumptuosly. As concerning Moses against the dove, I was implacable; but as concerning Dr. Sangrado against Moses, I took sides with the latter. So, though I would have preferred decent interment for my pet, I yet felt that the worst had been spared; the king had come to his own again, and I was content.

For one day the widower dove looked bewildered. Then he disappeared for three days. Then he returned jubilant with the handsomest dark slate-colored mate it is possible to conceive. Her feathers gleamed and glistened in the sun, flashing through green and purple and pink, dazzling and magnificent. Then I saw exemplified the truth of the old adage:

> "A mother 's a mother all the days of her life;
> A father 's a father till he gets him a new wife."

The two young doves immediately began to suffer an unrelenting persecution, not from their step-mother, but from their father, though I dare say she privately egged him on. He determined to drive them away. He chased them all around the edge of the roof. He pecked at them furiously when they came for food as aforetime. He would not suffer them to take a single grain of corn in peace, while the Black Princess settled on her lees and waxed fat. His unnatural treatment at length effected the desired object. His persecuted offspring took leave of him forever, the tawny bride reigned triumphant, and he basked in the sunshine of unclouded prosperity. But his delight was short-lived. Swift justice overtook him. His beautiful brunette assumed a sudden pique and freak, and repulsed him severely. Before he had recovered from the shock of astonishment, she turned his discomfiture into annihilation by introducing a new actor to the scene, — a handsome stranger, snow-white and resplendent. Both set themselves remorselessly to work against the head of the family. The chalice which he had forced upon his innocent offspring was commended to his own lips. He tasted to the full the bitterness of being shoved and pecked and outraged in his own home, till he fled, a broken-hearted bird, from his violated hearth. I should have pitied him if his previous ill-behavior had not alienated from him the sympathy of all virtuous people. As it was, I confess to a grim satisfaction in the cruel chagrin which must have torn his bosom as he sat on the ridge-pole of the barn, contemplating the ruin of his domestic happiness, while his faithless bride and her new companion made love to each other on my window-sill in full view. And it is surprising to see how much love birds can make when they set about it. They actually *kissed!* I should not suppose there could be much pleasure in it. Two ten-penny nails might as well attempt caresses, but they seemed to enjoy it. They ran the sharp points of their hard bills over and around each other's bills, and buried their noses in each other's feathers, and cooed and simpered, as fond and silly as you please. Perhaps it is this demonstrativeness that has made "dove" a term of endearment, but I suspect there may be a good deal more in that application of it than comes to the surface at once. My observations have led me to conclude that doves are of a decidedly quarrelsome disposition, capable of developing into viragoes, termagants, and downright scolds. Also their tenderness, though laid on pretty thick while it lasts, very soon gives out. Has not some close observer, a little cynical, perhaps, given the word its erotic turn as a delicate but sharp satire?

Since the spring has come, my doves have flown. I neglected to feed them one day, and they left me. When I have been from home a week at a time they never seemed to mind it, but frequented me as usual on my return. I suppose my offence lay in being at home and not feeding them; and as the mild weather and the resurrection of insect-life made it practicable for them to gratify their resentment, they concluded to do so.

I am consoled for their absence by the advent of those delicious little beings, those true fairies of the air, those tiny marvels of creative power, — the protest of this new world against the Transatlantic notion that its grandeur is not exalted by a corresponding finish, — humming-birds. A paper of round, black, microscopic seeds, labelled "humming-bird balm," sent me by an honored and valued friend, who, amid the stern duties of life finds time for its small, sweet courtesies, was sown in the fall, ripened through the frosts and snows, and sprang up with the spring into green and flowery strength. Attracted by some mysterious influence, the little birdlets come flying from east and west and north and south. I hear their lively chirp in the warm morning. On they dart with rapid flight, — their forked tails fluttering, their black eyes sparkling, their black bills aiming straight ahead, their brown wings deepening into royal purple, their glossy backs gleaming out a golden-green splendor, their breasts and throats now dazzling me with ruby fire, now throbbing like molten gold, changing from intense black to burning orange and fiery crimson, the brilliant scales instinct with glowing life, — more beautiful than tongue can tell. Now he poises himself, a quivering, shining mist, above the balm. Now he thrusts his slender tongue into the flower-cup, and rifles its hidden honey. And now I see indeed the force of Sidney Smith's advice to women to give a kiss as a humming-bird runs his bill into a honey-suckle, — deep, but delicate.

TOMMY.

SOMETIMES when I am sitting in my room, I hear a prolonged "g-a-a-h!" Then I know that Tommy is out. Tommy has escaped from his keepers, and is pursuing his investigations in the world at large. So I go to the window, and a pink gleam flashes up from the grass, and there, sure enough, is Tommy, climbing up toward the house with slow, tottering, uncertain steps, but with a face indicative of a desperate resolve to get somewhere, and with both arms acting as balancing-poles. Then I call out, "*Hul*-lo! little Tom-*mee!*" and everything changes. The arms drop, the feet stop, the resolution fades out of his face. He looks blankly towards all points of the compass, and when finally his eyes alight on me, what a smile! An ordinary curve of his generous, Irish lips does n't seem at all adequate to his feelings. He smiles latitudinally and longitudinally, — away round towards the back of his head, up to his nose, and down into his chin. Out goes his right arm as far as it can stretch, with the fat forefinger extended towards me, and a more intense "g-a-a-h!" bursts from the little throat. Then, with renewed energy, he resumes his travels. He does very well so long as the ascent is gradual, but when it becomes abrupt, his troubles begin. It is n't the tumbling down, however, that hurts him. Like all the rest of us, he can do that very easily, but it is the getting up again that plays the mischief. He rears himself on his toes and fingers, and there he stands, a round-backed little quadruped, utterly at a loss what to do next; for Tommy does not yet understand the use of his knees. If he thinks I am looking at him, he will stand there and squeal till he becomes convinced that I have gone away and left him to his own resources, which I generally do; when he drops, or rolls, or squirms along, in some illegal and unanatomical way, and at last stands radiant in the porch. Then he steers straightway to the side-lights. Those side-lights are an unfailing source of admiring wonder. If somebody is on the opposite side to play bo-peep, he is ecstatic. If nobody is there, he is calmly blissful.

Tommy is a great nuisance during the "fall cleaning." He is always getting into the soapsuds and hot-water generally. I volunteered once to take charge of him. I was going to tack down a carpet. Tommy looked on in amazement. Then he got down on the floor, and tried to take the tacks in his soft fingers. I rapped the soft fingers with my carpet-hammer. He gave one yell, and drew them back. I kept on with my work. In a minute, the soft fingers were creeping in among the tacks. Another rap, another yell, another creep, — rap! yell! creep, — till I grew tired of rapping, if he did not of being rapped. I suppose I did n't hit quite hard enough, but one does n't like to take liberties with other people's babies. Then I took hold of him by the back of his frock with one hand, carried him, with head and feet hanging, to the farthest side of the room, and deposited him in a corner. I had hardly driven one tack in, before the little rascal was rounding up his back again under my very eyes. I gathered him up once more, and dumped him in the corner as before. Evidently it was fine fun for him. Nothing could exceed the alacrity with which he crawled over to me. In despair, I at length put up the tacks, and proceeded to arrange some curtain-fixtures. Tommy was suspiciously still for several minutes, and when I went to ascertain the cause, I found he had got a bucket of sea-sand that had been left in the room, had emptied it on the carpet, and was flinging it about in royal style. I regretted to stop his enjoyment, for I have a fondness for sand myself, but it did not seem to be appropriate under the circumstances, and I scooped it up as well as I could, and put it beyond his reach. The next time I looked at him, which was in about a quarter of a minute, he was exerting himself to the utmost in pushing a large pitcher off the lower part of the wash-hand-stand. I caught it just as it was toppling over the brink, and before I could get that out of harm's way, he had tumbled a writing-desk out of a chair, scattering pens, ink, and paper in all directions. I saw at once that, if I was going to take care of Tommy, I must "give my mind to it." I took him into the kitchen, as the place best prepared to resist his incursions. He struck a bee-line for the stove, and covered himself with crock. I could n't undertake to wash him, but I mopped him up a little, put on his hat, and took him out to walk. Everything went on blithely till I turned to go home, then he raised the standard of rebellion. Tommy seldom cries, but he has a gamut of most surprising squeals at his command. On the present occasion, he exhibited them in wonderful variety, and with remarkable compass of sound. I might say every step was a squeal. The neighborhood rushed to the windows, not unreasonably fearing a repetition of the "babes in the wood." I covered his eyes, and swung him around rapidly three or four times, to bewilder him so that he should not know which way he was going. But Tommy was too old a bird to be caught by such chaff. He pulled backward, sidewise, every way but the way he ought to have pulled. I sat down on the root of an old elm-tree, and gazed at him in silent despair. He smiled back at me serene as a summer morning but the moment I showed symptoms of starting, he showed symptoms of squealing, till at length I conquered my compunctions, took him up in my arms, crock and all, and carried him home.

Tommy has a little black kitten, and the understanding between them is wonderful to see. Whenever you see Tommy's pink dress, you may be sure the kitty's glossy fur is not far off; and she whisks around him, and tantalizes him in the most provoking manner. Sometimes they both run a steeple-chase after her tail; kitty is too wise, by far, to let anything so valuable as her tail get into the clutch of those undiscriminating fingers; but she frisks and gambols around him delightfully, and Tommy turns, too, as fast as he can, and does n't know that the flashing tail is never to be got hold of by him. It is surprising how slowly children develop compared with other animals. Tommy's kitten is a good deal younger than he, yet she makes nothing of climbing up to the ridge-pole of the barn after the doves, which she never catches, or scudding up the tall cherry-tree and peeping down at Tommy from the upper branches. I believe she does it to excite his envy.

Tommy is intimate only with the kitten, but he makes friends with the chickens, and cultivates the acquaintance of the pig by throwing the clothes-pins over into his pen. An old rooster, nearly as tall as himself, seems to have attracted his especial regard. His efforts to catch him are persistent, though as yet unsuccessful. He evidently has perfect faith in his ultimate success, however, and every time Rooster heaves in sight, Tommy makes a lurch after him with both arms extended. Rooster understands perfectly how matters stand, and preserves a dignified composure till Tommy gets within a foot of him, when he leisurely withdraws. Tommy stops a moment, takes a survey, and goes at it again.

The days, and the weeks, and the months pass on, and Tommy's rich Irish blood ripens in the summer sunshine. His tottering legs grow firmer. His dimpled arms forebode strength. As I sit at my window, I see the apple-trees in the orchard grow white with bloom, and under them my best silk umbrella is marching about, as the courts say, without any visible means of support. While I gaze in astonishment, it suddenly gives a lurch, and reveals Tommy under its capacious dome in a seventh heaven of ecstasy. Or I am startled, while sitting alone in the warm afternoon, by seeing a blue eye, just a naked, human eye, peering in through the lowest chink of a closed blind opening on the porch. It turns out to belong to Tommy, who, by standing on tiptoe in the porch, can just get one eye in range. Now I see him trotting down the lane alone, clad in a gay scarlet frock, *et præterea nihil*, his fat little legs brown with dirt, his white neck, face, and arms mottled with the same, and his curly hair a jungle. From his abstracted and eager manner, I infer that he is bent on some grave errand. "Where going, Tommy?" I call, suspicious of a secret expedition. "O-gah-gi-bah!" shouts Tommy, without slackening his pace. Out comes his mother, with a twig, and gives chase. Tommy becomes cognizant of a fire in the rear, and his eager walk tumbles into a trot, for he feels that he is verily guilty, and knows that he is easily accessible; but fate overtakes him, and he is borne ignominiously back. Then his mother explains that she had just been trying on his new frock, and had remarked that she must get some buttons, and so Tommy had stolen away, and was going "over-shop-get-buttons."

Accidents, we are told, will happen in the best of families, and Tommy awoke one morning and found that his nose was out of joint. A little, lumpy baby sister had sadly deranged the machinery of his life, and he did n't know what to make of it. Formerly, when he stole out-doors unawares, his pretty young mother used to run out after him, and toss him up in her stout, bare arms into the house. Now an old woman in a cap came, and brought her hand down very heavily on his sensitiveness. Then, too, he was ousted out of his cradle by the interloper, and his life was in a fair way of becoming a burden to him. But his good-nature never failed. To be sure, he would throw the plates, and the flat-irons, and the coal into the cradle, but it was probably "all in fun." When I went in to see "the baby," the first time, he pointed to it with great exultation, and as soon as the blanket was rolled down, first poked his finger into her eyes, and then, quick as thought, gave her a rousing slap on the cheek. Baby screamed, as she had a right to do, and Tommy had the slap returned with compound interest, as he richly deserved.

Yet, in senseless, instinctive fashion, in his wild, Irish way, Tommy loved his baby sister. The little life drooped and died while the roses were yet in bloom. Tommy's baby sister was borne to her burial, and Tommy's heart was troubled with a blind fear. What it was he did not know, but something was wrong. He lingered about the cradle where she lay, and when the tiny form was taken up to be placed in the coffin, he plucked wildly at her white robe, crying bitterly, and refused to be comforted.

Darling little Tommy! The very thought of your happy face, white and soft, and fine as a lily-cup, of your merry blue eyes, with their long, curling, black eyelashes, of your bungling little feet, and your meddlesome little fingers, warms my heart. If I could have my way, you should always stay just as you are now, only having your face washed semi-occasionally. But I cannot have my way, and you will by and by run to school barefoot, and wear blue overalls, and smoke bad tobacco in a dingy pipe, and carry a hod, and vote the "dimmocratic ticket."

So I said last year with foolish human prophecy, and now, behold! there is no democratic ticket to vote, and there is no Tommy to vote it. For Tommy is gone. Never any more while I live shall the gleam of his shining hair light up the greensward, or the irregular thumping of his copper-toed shoes bring music to my ears as he stumbles up the yard and clatters across the kitchen-floor. A dreamy October morning, all gold and amethyst with the haze of the Indian summer, took him beyond my sight over the blue waters to the fair island of his fathers, which has been to me ever since a "summer isle of Eden, lying in dark purple spheres of sea"; and it seemed to me for the moment that nothing would be so delightful, nothing looked so winning, as to leave this surging, eager, battling land, and sail over the sea with Tommy, and live quietly in a little brown cottage on the border of Donegal bog, with a well-burnt pipe in the cupboard, plenty of peat on the fire, potatoes smoking in the ashes, a fine fat pig in the corner, and nothing to be careful or troubled about all the days of my life.

While I grieve for Tommy gone, I reflect that he would probably be a little pest if he had stayed. Already his feet were swift to do mischief. His rosy lips could swear you as round an oath as any Flanders soldiers, and he beat the calf, and chased the hens, and worried the sheep, and poked the cow, and pulled the cat's tail, and worked the key out of the door and lost it, and was perpetually carrying off the hoe, and making the gravel fly, and surreptitiously possessing himself of the whip. Fumble, rattle, — Tommy is at the door; creak, creak, — he has got it open; thump, thump, thump, — he is making for the whip; silence, — he is getting it down. "Tommy! Tommy! don't touch the whip, will you?" "No," says Tommy, stoutly, in the very act of marching off with it firmly clasped in both hands, brandishing it right and left, and whisking every living thing, and dead ones too, that came in his way, or that did n't, either, for that matter.

In the warm, moonlight evening, Tommy sits again in a high chair in the porch, and his mother tells me of the home to which she is going in Ireland, and of the schools which Tommy will attend, and the books that he will study, and she promises to send me one to look at, but I greatly fear it will never reach me. As the conversation proceeds, I am driven into a corner, and forced to admit that I do not reckon among my acquisitions an acquaintance with the Irish language. She is silent for a moment, and never fails in the politeness of her race; but I do not think I shall ever quite recover the ground which that revelation cost me. I fear me my reputation is permanently lowered. Tommy, climbing in and out of his high chair, up his mother's neck, and down the porch steps, wiggling everywhere, and clawing everything, takes part in the pleasant chat. "Where are you going, Thomas, by and by?" asks his mother, designing to show his paces. "K-t-ty, k-t-ty," gurgles Tommy, making a dive after the kitten. "Now, Thomas," says she, drawing him back with a strong arm, "tell 'em where you 're going next month, in a ship, you know, over the water." "Cōw," says Tommy, perversely, having a mortal aversion to water, wholesale and retail. But I know a quick way to his tongue. "Tommy, tell me where you are going, and I 'll give you a sugar-plum." "Irle," says he, with a fine brogue, rapidly coming to his senses. "An' tell 'em what 'll your gran'father be sayin' to you, when he sees you." A pink peppermint in my hand becoming visible to the naked eye, he answers promptly, "Ye! ga! Tom! wi! ko! yah! bk!" which, being interpreted, means, "Here comes Tom with the clock on his back," referring to a clock which is to be carried with them, and which he evidently believes will be his own personal luggage. Sometimes his answer turns into "Here 's Tom, coming in at the door!" which seems to me to indicate a decided dramatic power. "Tommy," I say, pathetically, "I am afraid you will forget all about me when you go to Ireland." "Iss," roars Tommy, backing out from under his chair. "But I want you not to forget. Stand still, now, and tell me what my name is." "Yah!" shouts Tommy, jumping up and down. "Yah what?" "Yah *Yah!*" And even when the last morning comes, — when Tommy, gay with scarlet frock and feather, and "bran new" shoes, is borne in his mother's arms up the steps to say his last good-by, — the hard-hearted little pagan is utterly unmoved by her tears, and only jounces up and down, and cries, "Ride! Horse!" and, in virtue of a doughnut in each fist, marches off for fatherland, triumphant.

But Ireland is glorified henceforth. I see no more there want, nor squalor, nor suffering, but verdurous meadow-depths, and a little child crowned with myrtle and arbutus, flinging around him the crushed wealth of daisy and primroses and gold cups, while his upturned face, shining against the morning sun, is as it were the face of an angel.

God bless the Irish! I cannot choose but love them. They do unearthly things, I know, and are a grief of heart to the sorely-tried housewives. One whole winter did Bridget sweep my room, and invariably set the table with the drawer toward the wall. Never by any mistake did it happen to come right side out. Patsy had a way of swooping up all the contents of all the wash-hand-stands, in her regular round with broom and duster, and distributing them again without respect of persons. Accordingly, your own stand would be garnished with the tooth-brush of your neighbor on the right, the nail-brush of your neighbor on the left, the hair-brush of your neighbor above, and the hat-brush of your neighbor below. But Patsy is a diamond in the rough. I wrote a love-letter for her once. She came to me beaming with ruddy shyness, and, after backing and filling for fifteen minutes, gave me to understand that her lover was by "the far wash of Australasian seas," and would I write him a letter for her. He was a fond swain, but she had been coy and coquettish, and, now that he was so far away, her heart relented. Did I write to him? Of course I did, conjecturing, to the best of my ability, what manner of document a love-letter should be, and determining that at least it should not lack the quality which gives it a name. So, after exhausting my own vocabulary, I had recourse to the poets, and quoted Tennyson. It smote me in the heart to look up when I had read it to her, and see her beautiful almond eyes filled with tears; for though one's own love-letters may be a serious enough matter, one can hardly voice another's tenderness with entire good faith. "Oh!" said Patsy, with a sigh from the very bottom of her warm Irish heart, "them is *jes'* my feelin's," and even put her head back through the door after going out, to add, "An' sure, ye must have had them feelin's yourself, or ye niver could have done it." "Ah, Patsy!" I said, — but never mind what I said.

God bless the Irish! They supply an element that is wanting to our Anglo-Saxon blood, the easy, eloquent, picturesque race. Their rest is such a cushion to our restlessness. As they mount the ladder, their individualities lose outline, but an Irish poor family is world-wide from an American poor family. The Americans will be so sharp and angular, and clearly defined. They will have such an air of having seen better days, and not giving up seeing them again. Their poverty is self-conscious, and draws comparisons. A painful scrubbiness is in the air. Everything is neat, whitewashed, and made the most of. Evidently they are struggling against fate. They contest every inch of ground. If you offer them assistance, you must double and turn, and ten to one give mortal offence after all. I know these are the very things that the books applaud, and I suppose they are one of the bases of greatness; but for solid comfort, give me an Irish shanty, where all are dirty and happy and contented. For the spare, stooping American mother, with thin hair, pointed elbows, and never fewer than forty years, you have the Irish matron, always young, — red, round arms, luxuriantly full figure, great white teeth, head set back, and peerless hair. You are received with nonchalant courtesy, and your "remainder biscuit" with graceful gratitude. No care furrows any forehead. If the baby creeps into the ashes, one blacksmithy arm whips him out again as good as new. In winter the air is warm with the mingled odor of soapsuds, boiling cabbage, and fragrant tobacco. In the summer they set their wash-tubs at the back door, and, in a sensible scantiness of costume, rub to the robin's song, and never seem to look forward to a possible presidency. They float across the tide acquiescent. Thus poverty is robbed of its sting.

If one must be poor, it is so much easier to be comfortable about it. And if one is thoroughly comfortable, what matter whether one lives in one room or twenty?

God bless the Irish! Their strong arms are lifted, their warm hearts are beating, side by side with ours, for the honor and life of their adopted country. Does famine impend over their island home? We have enough and to spare. From our bursting granaries, from our larders over-full, let their tables be spread with plenty. Surely the bread, the few crumbs which we cast upon the waters, many days ago, are already returned to us in Irish truth and loyalty. And when their civilization and Christianity are brought abreast of their inborn poetry, Ireland shall come forth fair as the sun, clear as the moon, and terrible as an army with banners.

Tommy, Tommy, I am loath to leave you. I do not see how you can possibly grow up good; but your angel, always beholding the face of our Father which is in heaven, may read there plans of love which my dim eyes cannot discern. To God I commend you. Wherever you go, the Lord give his angels charge concerning you, to keep you in all your ways, and even though you worship him blindly, with bell and incense and crucifix and rosary, may he none the less keep your eyes from tears, your feet from falling, and your soul from death.

Boston and Home Again.

ONE thing there is in the world which I admire. It is *blasé* people, — people, as Curtis expresses it, who have pumped life dry, and the pump only wheezes, — people who are not interested in anything, — people who have gone through the whole round of sensations, and have the satisfactory consciousness of having nothing more to feel, — people who are always self-possessed, never thrown off their balance. Attacked from any quarter, they are ready. There is the English Quarterly Reviewer. He has all things under his feet. He is calmly superior to the world, the flesh, and so forth. He holds in his hands the reins of the universe. He embraces the whole circle of knowledge. Nothing ever happens to which he cannot assign its true cause and prophesy its remotest future. He knows more of poetry than the poet, more of art than the artist, more of history than the historian. He can get more out of anything than ever was in it. The scanty grains of information which you have been able to gather by hard digging into dictionaries and grammars, and which you reserve for grand occasions, dwindle to nothing before the huge boulders of learning which he scoops up and tosses about with his finger-tips on the slightest provocation. But the seal of his royalty is the air of quiet superiority, of having been born to it, with which he handles his resources, and, awed by which, you abdicate at once, feeling it an honor to be tyrannized over by such a one. But this is a remarkable world in many respects, and in none more so than in a certain organic disjointedness. Causes do not seem to produce effects. Sequences are arbitrary. There is general law, but a great deal of special lawlessness. You lay all your plans to accomplish an object, and miss of it; while the good that you never dream of obtaining comes to you unsought. Machines that work well in theory will not work at all in iron. There seems to be no reason why the stove should smoke, but it does. I knew a man who, at twenty, was given up by his physicians. His lungs were gone, his stomach was going, his heart was capricious, — in short, all his internal apparatus seemed to be destroyed or deranged; it is plain that, under such circumstances, he ought to have died. If this were a logical world, he would have died. On the contrary, he most unreasonably persisted in living, and is now, at forty, roaming over Europe, climbing the

Alps, braving the Pontine Marshes, tampering with Rhein wine, sauer-kraut, and all manner of foreign edibles, and threatens to live out his threescore years and ten, unless death comes to him from without. Certainly, there is a hitch in the world somewhere. So, though I would give any reasonable sum to be *blasé* and *au fait* myself, I am in fact very far from it. I often become bewildered in cities. I lose my purse, and I lose my way, and I almost lose my senses. I admire, and am astonished. I like to look in at shop windows, to see a monkey capering to a hand-organ, to buy fruit of old women crouching at the corners of streets. When I get into an omnibus, I never can remember to get out again, and once I rode from Boston to Cambridge three times before I remembered to pull the strap at the place where I wanted to be left. I like to be in a crowd, if I am not in a hurry (in a carriage, — I should n't like to be on foot, and have all sorts of people knocking against me), and see the feathers and silks trying to get on, and can't, and men elbowing through by the skin of their teeth, and truckmen shouting, and wheels interlocking, and horses pawing, and timid people looking scared. That sounds rather malignant, but it is n't. I would not scare them myself for the sake of the fun; but as they are scared independently of any effort of mine, I enjoy it simply as a part of the pantomime. Besides, I don't see any use in being frightened in such a case. I don't expect a coachman to have any especial regard for my individual bones, but I do expect him to have a regard for his own reputation as a coachman, and for his pocket, both of which demand that he should not upset his coach and injure his passenger, unless circumstances absolutely require it. I take it for granted, also, that he understands his business a great deal better than I do; and as he does n't fret about my writing, I won't fret about his driving me through a crowd. I also like, in passing through streets, to count the windows, and see how many stories the shops have. I like to talk with newsboys, and rag-pickers, and the little beggar-girls, and with all sorts of out-of-the-way people. It seems to take you into another world. I am always awed in the presence of milliners and dressmakers. If I have an opinion before I go in, it presents itself to them in the form of the meekest and timidest suggestion, and melts away and evaporates before their slightest objection. There is something in their art perfectly incomprehensible to me. I can understand how a locomotive engine or a sewing-machine can be made. I think I could make one myself, if I were educated to it, and had the proper tools; for a ponderous machine cuts out your work by rule, and you put it together, one engine just like another. But a milliner must have creative power. She must conceive an idea of every bonnet separately, and then, from a wilderness of silk and straw and lace and flowers, she must evoke the perfect bonnet, every one separately, and every one adapted to the figure, complexion, and character of every separate wearer, — and this for months and years continuously.

But of course all this is incompatible with that air of *savoir faire* which is at once my admiration and my despair. You cannot be tranquilly indifferent and keenly interested at the same time. And how can one go up from the country, where the quiet is a perpetual Sabbath, into the city, where life whirls in ten thousand different forms, and not be interested, — and not show it? I have had opportunities to observe my sex in the transition state, and I am forced to say that I do not think the female traveller is always a pleasant object of contemplation. She is never quite free from anxiety or bundles, and is generally pretty highly charged with both. She asks the conductor the same question twice, as if she believed he might undergo a moral reformation between the first and second asking, and tell the truth at last, though he told a lie at first. Sweetly patient at home, sublimely patient in great pain or peril, she is ludicrously impatient on her travels. She cannot wait the march of events, but outstrips the present, anticipates the future, and asks the conductor "if we change cars at B." Trustful to a fault in the domestic circle, she becomes a very sceptic in the cars, and never believes him unless he says "Yes."

When he announces at B., "Passengers change cars for the East," she steps out with alacrity upon the platform, and immediately asks him, "Do we change cars here?" Acute of vision, and rapid in perception at home, abroad a glamour seems to fall upon her. The time-table invariably hangs upon the station-walls, but, as if incapable of calculation, she invariably asks the ticket-master at what hour the train is due; and if it is five minutes late, she goes to him again, and asks him how long before it will arrive. Of course, observing the inconsequence of these and similar vagaries, I am especially careful to avoid them. You will presently see how I succeed.

I will, however, say this in extenuation, that no city has any moral right to be as crooked as Boston. It is a crookedness without excuse, and without palliation. It is crooked in cold blood, and with malice aforethought. It goes askew when it might just as easily go straight. It is illogical, inconsequent, and incoherent. Nowhere leads to anywhere in particular. You start from any given point, and you are just as likely to come out at one place as another. Of course, all this can but have an effect on the inhabitants. Straightforwardness becomes impossible where you are continually pitching up against sharp points. People born and bred in angles, and blind alleys, and cross-ways, cannot fail to have a knack at tergiversation and intrigue. Diplomatists should be chosen from Boston, or should at least take a preparatory course of five years there, as soldiers do at West Point.

The number of the streets is amazing. The Bostonians seem to have a perfect frenzy for them. If they can squeeze in a six-foot passage between two houses, they are happy. Half a dozen stairs and a brick platform is an avenue and an elysium. They build their houses in the shape of a letter V, with the point sticking out in front, apparently for no other reason than the exquisite satisfaction of having a street pass up each side; and they make their streets crooked to look at, and then make alleys to get there. Washington Street, the principal thoroughfare,

"Like a wounded snake drags its slow length along."

I have heard that it was originated by cows, meandering down to drink. This hypothesis may answer in the one case, but it won't apply to the smaller streets, for a cow could not make so acute angles if she tried. Owing to this vaccine inability, Washington street rolls on with considerable dignity for awhile, but it goes off into a delirium tremens down by Cornhill and Dock Square. Everything is as shifting as a kaleidoscope. When you set out from the Revere House, you observed the landmarks. There was "Oliver H. Brooks, Eating-House," set in the middle of the road, and peaked of course. That is easy to remember. But when you get back into the maze, the thing is there, to be sure, wedging itself into space, but it is no longer Oliver H. Brooks's Eating-House; it is B. F. Paine's Fruit of all kinds Chamois. You go to the very spot where the Revere House stood in the morning. It has died and left no sign, and a block of brick houses reigns in its stead. When you went up Cornhill, "V. B. Palmer" stood at the head of it in gold letters, but when you come back V. B. has trotted off, and the various religious and publishing societies which congregate there have, in the incredibly short space of two hours, given way to Mr. Blake's Furnishing Rooms, or the Quincy House. As for Faneuil Hall, it is perpetually dancing a jig with Dock Square. Places that you are in a hurry to come at, are never "at home." Places that you don't want, are continually turning up. You may wander about in that benighted region for hours, and every corner you turn, there will be Faneuil Hall prancing before your eyes as pert and coquettish as if each time were the first. It is always within a stone's throw, but you never get close to it. I don't believe anybody ever did get close to it. And you never see it standing square. You never have a front view, nor a side view, but always a corner view. It must have secret springs, for if you make a flank movement, with the sole object of getting it in a straight line, it will manage to cut a pirouette, and present angles. Jefferson Davis threatened to go into winter quarters in Faneuil

Hall. I wish he had. A sure way to stop the rebellion without bloodshed would be to bring him and his whole army to Faneuil Hall and suburbs. They never would find their way out again. I would not blindfold them. I would give them every clew that they chose. After they were once in, Boston could just shake herself, the clews would be good for nothing, and Massachusetts nurseries for a thousand years would shiver at twilight over stories of wandering ghosts, with phantom barred flags and shadowy Golden Circles, wandering, weeping, wailing, in the alleys of Dock Square, and moaning ever and anon, like Sterne's starling, "I can't get out." I mention only Dock Square, but there are, as the Yankees say, "lots of 'em." That one has made the deepest impression on me, for whenever I am lost, I drift into that, and it seems like the nightmare. I suppose it is called "Square," on the same principle that the only man in the House of Representatives who cannot make a speech is called Mr. Speaker. Certainly there never was such a misnomer as Dock *Square*. Dock Dodecagon would be nearer the truth, but that would only approximate it, for a dodecagon has regular sides, and there is not a regular side to anything, from one end of Boston to the other, let alone Dock Square, which has no sides at all, but consists solely of corners.

That the crookedness of Boston is not external

only, but strikes in, there is abundant proof. You go into a shop, — Kinmonth's, for instance. You founder at once in a raging sea of agitated silks and laces and feathers. Appalled, you turn to Turnbull's, next door. Another sea, but something must be done. You want sixpence worth of galloon. At home, in your one little "cheap cash store," you could get it, and be gone, in two minutes; but the female population of the rural districts has a mortal aversion to buying anything at home that can be bought in Boston. The grandeur of the metropolis seems to cling around whatever radiates from it into the country, even though it be only a paper of pins. So, feeling very tall, and awkward, and conspicuous, you timidly ask the first clerk to whom you gain access for galloon. "Back part of the store," says he, briskly, and turns to the next comer. You color away up to your hair, and down under your collar, feeling guilty and ashamed, and very rustic, — as if you ought to have known, by instinct or education, that galloon is never to be found in the front ranks. You flounder through the press into the back part of the store, and repeat your request with as much *au fait* as you can assume. "Back part of the store," jerks clerk No. 2, and is off in a twinkling, and there you are, stranded high and dry. It turns out that what you thought was the back part of the store is only the beginning of another room at right angles with the first, — and so you go on, and the rooms go on. You are shot up by some pop-gun of a clerk from counter to counter, from room to room, fondly thinking every one to be the last, but finding in the backest part a backer part, — (*vide* Milton,) — till, after making half a dozen angles of incidence and reflection, you get your galloon, and — there is the door close by you! Is Turnbull's, then, built circularly? Have you circumnavigated it till, as the old geographies used to say, you have arrived at the point from which you started, in an opposite direction? In your bewilderment, this is not difficult to believe, and you depart, but everything without is changed. The din seems hushed, or far off. The tide of drays and omnibuses has ebbed. You remember that Kinmonth's was next door, — yes, there is Kinmonth's, but no longer next door; it has stepped across the street and stands opposite, and the big sign has dwindled into a little one. Terror-struck, you strike out at random, fearful lest the Merlin, or Math, or Michael Scott, who roams in Boston, stretch forth his wand again; sign, shop, and city disappear before your eyes, and you find yourself wandering among the forests and wigwams of Shawmut.

Boston, moreover, has a way of contracting and expanding herself that is marvellous in country eyes. You shall, for instance, be in search of Number Thirty-three. Passing up the street, reading eagerly every sign, you count "twenty-seven, twenty-eight, twenty-nine," — and then there is a sudden leap over to thirty-eight! What now? You look again, fancying you must have made a mistake. No, this door is certainly twenty-nine, and the next is certainly thirty-eight, if you can read Arabic characters. Eight houses, therefore, must be squeezed into one brick partition-wall. You think of microscopes. You wonder if the houses are to be pulled out one after another, as Mr. Hermann *prestidigitates* twenty apples and fifty tin cups out of one empty old hat. Presently, you summon courage to go into a neighboring shop, and request to be enlightened. They inform you that the missing numbers are attached to the doors of rooms inside. A most extraordinary circumstance! It is generally supposed that a house means a house. In Boston, however, it appears to mean only a room. Number Ten does not necessarily indicate the tenth house on the street. You must fumble through the dark passages and over the strange staircases within before you can be sure that it does not point out the tenth room. If we should go and do likewise in the country, numbering and labelling every barn, corn-barn, cider-press, pig-sty, dog-kennel, hen-coop, and dove-cot, we should have quite a little settlement at every homestead.

The result of it all is, that you never know

how much ground you have been over, nor where you ought to stop. You make your way to the dry-goods desk in a shop, and ask for poplins, overhaul them all, find nothing to suit, and go on till you come to another shop, and by a similar process are passed up to a similar desk, and repeat your meek inquiry. "You looked at all our poplins a few moments ago," says the clerk, politely. You lift your eyes quickly to his face. Yes, it is the same man and the same place that you went to before, — and then do you not feel amiable? Yet you have been a Sabbath-day's journey since then. How in the world, then, came you back again? Because these wary merchants open doors and send out feelers in all directions, and there is nothing for a poor, silly little fly like you to do but walk into their parlors whichever way you turn.

But Boston, though crooked and inexplicable, is not without her charms. "God made the country and man made the town," as a general fact. But there is a good deal in Boston that man never made and never will make.

Come, behold the works of the Lord. You need not turn yourself into a polar bear with furs, live on raw frozen walrus beef, tallow candles, and blubber, be drawn by dogs, and sleep in a hut with a naked Esquimaux baby for a pillow, — nor need you brave the snakes and scorpions and hurricanes of the tropics, or plunge full many a fathom deep in the ghost-enpeopled sea, — to gaze upon the wonderful works of God; for behold they are nigh you, even at your doors.

Right in the thick of Boston is a glass tank, big enough to sail a small fleet, and in that tank a huge white whale bulges his billowy bulk in a never-ending round of treadmill travel. I call him huge, but it is relatively. He is, in fact, rather diminutive for a whale, but he is prodigious for a fish. You have studied in Parley's Geography about a whale as big as the steeple of the meeting-house, — an indefinite, but sublime comparison. You have read thrilling narratives of whale captures, — long and perilous voyages, boats stove, races run, men submerged, shipwreck and suffering and death in far-off, mysterious seas. Think then what a triumph of mind over matter is implied in the fact, that for twenty-five cents you can go and sit in your best clothes, and look at a whale. But you must look closely, or you will not see him; he but just heaves above the surface to breathe, and then sinks down till he is only a white mist in the green water. What a fortitude the poor fellow needs to sustain his change of fortune. Surely, if any one ever had right to complain of "reduced circumstances," it is he, wrested from the halls of his fathers, from the forests of the vivid-tressed mermaidens, from the crystalline corridors "of his dim water-world," to a glass tank, — admission twenty-five cents; children under ten years of age fifteen cents. And what a lonely life it is! There are sturgeons and lobsters and a dolphin, to be sure, but they are not like "own folks." A whale cannot be expected to be hand and glove with a lobster. A sturgeon cannot enter into the feelings of a whale. So, as was said of Napoleon, "grand, gloomy, and peculiar, he sits upon his throne, a sceptred hermit, wrapped in the solitude of his own originality."

The little dolphin is alone too, but he does not seem to mind it. I call him little, but that is also relative. Little beside the whale, he is a giant among the dolphins, and he sports around the whale, a dusky satellite, as gay as a lark, doubling, bobbing, and seeming to take life in a very free and easy manner.

"This is a weary world, little Dolphin," one can fancy the melancholy whale saying, in sepulchral tones, and with that dignity of bearing which the great are wont to employ towards the small.

"Not a bit of it, Whaley," retorts the dolphin, cheerily, with the smart familiarity of ignorance.

"I am haunted evermore, O Dolphin, by the dull brilliancy of golden memories. Did I ever sweep around the illimitable shores of an icy continent? Were my pearly whiteness and the splendor of my opal tints caught from the glow of an unsetting sun? Whence come the diamond mountains, ruby-crested, that rise forever in my dreams? Do you not remember, O Dolphin, a brighter sky, a broader sea, and other shores than these?"

"None to speak of, Whaley. Nothing that could hold a candle to this. Cold as Greenland, that 's all I remember, and no nice people to look at you. Tip-top world:

'Here we go up, up, up,
Here we go down, down, downy,
Here we go backwards and forwards,
Here we go round, round, roundy.'"

And, with a double-and-twisted frisk of his tail, off he darts, leaving his gigantic companion to roll on his monotonous way "in slow and solemn brightness."

It is amusing to see how the other little fellows in the tank keep out of the whale's and the dolphin's orbit. They have caught the fashion, and revolve, but they hug the shore. I am sure they need not be afraid, for, if there is any truth in physiognomy, that whale is a humane and benevolent individual, and Dolphin is too good-natured, with all his giddiness, to harm a fly. But, from whatever cause, the "small fry" never come in collision with their Anak brethren. It is a very easy matter for them to avoid it. Men have to move on the same plane, but when haddock meets haddock, he can dive, or soar, or pass on one side, as he chooses, and this certainly is one of the compensations for being a fish. You encounter Mr. Smith, and, because you are a reasoning animal, you must keep to the right as the law directs, though you wet your feet and get a lung-fever in consequence; but if you were only a bass or a cod-fish, you could dart down and go under him, or you could strike up and go over him, which would save invaluable time, temper, and health. Here comes Mrs. Jones under full sail, her silken expansiveness resplendent in the morning sun. She needs, and should receive, the whole sidewalk, and a coal-cart presses against the curbstone. What now? A smile, a bow, a graceful undulation, one bird's-eye view of Mrs. Jones, and you have alighted on the sidewalk behind her, resuming your stroll with unspotted boots and unruffled placidity. *Eheu! non omnia possumus omnes;* which means, dear unlearned readers, who have never pushed your researches to the last page of Webster's Spelling-book, that, though it is possible to be a fish, and possible to be a man, it is not possible to be both at one and the same moment.

Around the central tank are small tanks full of unimagined beauty. The exquisite, elaborate forms, and the intense green of sea-plants; the multiplied hues, shifting, flashing, dazzling, — green, and purple, and pink, and gold, — of the millions of little lives; the feathery waving of the sea-anemone, the burnished scales of the humblest trout, the sluggish torpor of the slow, and the electric agility of the quick, — inspire you with delighted wonder. Little marvellous outbursts of life! For what service were they formed and fashioned? We see but one, and the ocean teems with myriads which no human eye hath seen, or shall see; but does not the great Creator, whose name is Love, enjoy the happiness of his lowliest creations? May not his eye dwell delighted on the work of his hands? What presumption for us to marvel at the production of beauty which *we* cannot see! As if in the broad universe there were no eyes but ours!

Here is a den of tortoises, excessively ugly, and inconceivably heavy of movement. What is remarkable about a turtle is, that he is not only sluggish, but he does not seem to try to be otherwise. He takes pains to be lazy. If he wants to go from the upper to the lower story of his cage, instead of climbing or jumping down, he lolls to the edge, and then drops off. I have lost my early faith in the fable of the hare and the tortoise. I believe a hare could get anywhere sooner than a tortoise, if he slept all the time.

Up and down, up and down, tramp the lions, and the leopards, and the bears, tramp, tramp, tramp, — their fierce hearts beating against their prison-bars like restless souls chained in the cage of circumstance, hungering, thirsting, maddened, for their native jungles, and the freedom of their uncramped, strong limbs. No philosophy, no religion, gives them resignation. They cannot "find, for outward Eden lost, a paradise within." No self-control ennobles them. Their savage souls know no restraint but the iron bars against which they press in vain. No reason for their stolen liberty mitigates the severity of its loss. It is nothing to them that they are daily waiting on the pleasure and the wisdom of a higher race. So, perhaps, our sufferings, — the blow that shocks us out of all conventionalities, and the inward, silent, hidden torture, — all the ache and agony, — "the dull, deep pain, and constant anguish of patience," — shall work out for other lives, if not for ours, a far more exceeding and eternal weight of glory.

Time would fail me to speak of the deers, and the snakes, and the squirrels, the porcupines, the woodchucks, and the guinea-pigs, the rats, and the cats, and the kangaroos. There will always be a crowd watching the frisky little monkeys, whose bodies are so rollicking, whose faces are so dismal, and whose gymnastics are so almost incredible. And if you are not too fastidious to join the crowd, you will see some display of human, as well as of *simic* nature. A little boy near me had long been silently devouring the monkeys with his eyes; presently his father came along, and, anxious that his son should — as *his* old copy-books doubtless enjoined upon him — devote every moment of his time to the acquirement of useful knowledge, began, in the regular Harry and Lucy style, to advise him to "watch their motions, observe the variety," &c.

Why, you dear, good man, as I know you must be, what in the world did you suppose your boy was doing with those great wide eyes of his? Set any boy down before a cage of monkeys, and see if you can make him do anything else than watch their motions!

Do not forget the seal, the sea-dog, round, fat, and sleek, with full, pathetic eyes. What nameless tragedy, far back in the history of the race, has left those mute, appealing eyes? — a monument more durable than brass. Fortunately, the tragedy has not affected his appetite, as the alacrity with which he gulps down a piece of fish as big as your arm, and then looks up at you as tragic and trusting as if he had not swallowed a morsel, and you never suspected he had, abundantly testifies. Our seal has accomplishments, too. He jerks a waddling kind of a duck at you, and thinks it is a bow. He flops up and turns a crank, calling it a hand-organ. As his education is still going on, there is no telling what attractions he may not finally attain.

So the tropics and the frozen North-land meet. Sea and shore give up the wonders which are in them; and in the midst of man's work and man's devices, we say, with reverent hearts, "The earth is full of the riches of the Lord."

And Boston is not only valuable as a depository of curiosities and dry-goods, but she has her beautiful aspects. I will tell you how to arrive at one of them. Sleep soundly through a winter night in one of those rural cities in her suburbs that lie toward the sunset. Rise early on the fine, frosty morning. The snow lies six inches deep on the ground, and is covered with ice. Every tree is heavy fruited with gems, pale and pearly now, but the up-coming sun shall kindle them to prismatic fire. Take possession of some good friend who owns a ——, I have forgotten the name, but it is a square box on runners, and is either a pun, or a pung, or a bun, or a bung, and coax him to harness his horse and drive you into Boston. Then you shall see her glorified. The keen air clarifies your vision, thrills your blood, and tingles through your soul. At first, Boston wraps herself in mist, and is a city of the clouds, invisible to earth-born. But the sun, coming up from the Under-Land, sends his heralds before, and the vapor glows into amethyst. Still the heralds come, — the sky grows rosy, the swelling dome that crowns the three-hilled city mounts up from the vapor sea, the church spires shoot golden arrows into the ruddy heavens, — all is soft, and sparkling, and beautiful.

Boston, you are more beautiful than this. When, after long absence and wandering, I come over the marshes to meet you, you are lovely as the day. I wait for you as they that watch for the morning, and when your stately dome curves its clear contour against the blue sky, "my heart swells and my eyes are dim." Beloved Queen of my beloved State, the archers have sorely grieved you, and shot at you, and hated you, but your bow abides in strength. When envious rivals traduce you, I make no defence. "She needs none. There she is. Behold her, and judge for yourselves." When I am asked, "What is thy beloved more than another beloved?" I only say, "My beloved is *mine*," but I think of all the grandeur garnered there, of all your inheritance, all your possession, and all the promise of your future.

Yet, O Boston, I have somewhat even against you. There are stains upon your escutcheon. There is blood upon your garments. I have heard that you once, in blind fury, placed a rope around the neck of an innocent man, and dragged him through your streets. What tears shall wash out the footprints you made that day? I have heard that iron chains once clanked around your noble court-house, that white-haired judges passed under the yoke, and that you let a man be dragged back into the Valley of the Shadow of Death. Do you say that it was not your fault? Did your loyalty to law clash with your loyalty to God? But how was it when, not two years ago, you stood up with deliberate intent to crush free speech? Where then was your loyalty to law? Where was your manhood? Where was your honor? Where was your chivalry? Where your high birth and breeding? With malice prepense you assembled your "merchant princes," and lewd fellows of the basest sort, and placed a knife at the throat of liberty You stabbed the breast that cherished your infancy You shamed the mother that bore you. The guilt, if not the stain, of blood is at your door.

O Boston, Boston! be as crooked as you like, waltz as bewilderingly as you will, but keep yourself pure. Sully not your fair fame. Play not false to humanity. Shame not the memory of your fathers. Make atonement to-day for the sins of the past, if so be the Lord will yet have mercy upon you. Now is the accepted time. Gird thy sword upon thy thigh, and in thy majesty ride prosperously, because of truth and meekness and righteousness. Let thine arrows be sharp in the hearts of the king's enemies. Love righteousness and hate wickedness. So shall the king greatly desire thy beauty, and make thy name to be remembered in all generations.

But shopping and sight-seeing, like all things earthly, must come to an end, and having accomplished a few of my thousand and one errands, I — for whether I have in this narrative said "you" or "I," it all means myself — turned my face homeward. I did not wish to go by the direct route, but through Salem, stopping over one train at Melrose. Geography, I regret to say, has always been my weak point, and I was quite ignorant of the situation of Melrose, and consequently did not know what railroad ran through it. To my country eyes there are railroads and depots enough in Boston to give a separate one to every village in the vicinity. I inquired at a shop on Cornhill from what depot I should leave for Melrose. They advised me to take the horse cars. I did not know horse cars went there. They believed they did; at any rate I could inquire at the car-office just above. I started for the car-office. "Just above" not seeming to develop such an institution, I went into another shop, and asked a clerk if he could tell me where the car-office was. He asked me what car-office. I was vexed with myself for asking such a question, as if, like the man who inquired the way to Boston meeting-house, I supposed there was but one in the city. I answered, with as much intellectuality and cosmopolitanism as I could call up, "The Melrose office." "Why," said he, "there it is, right there." There, sure enough, it was before my face and eyes, in staring capitals, "Malden and Melrose Railroad." I launched another thunderbolt against myself for my blindness, and went in, determined to be on my guard and ask no more foolish questions. A woman was transacting business with the clerk, and, while waiting, I reflected that the question I set out with, viz. if the cars went to Melrose, would be a foolish one, after seeing the sign, and I would therefore simply ask at what hour they left. Having made this resolution I had leisure to observe the woman who was talking with the clerk. She seemed to be rather excited. She had, it seemed, paid her fare in the car, the conductor had not given the right change back, and she wanted the clerk to make it right. *I* could see that it was none of his business, but she could not, and was highly indignant at his refusal. He directed her to the Superintendent of the road as the proper person. She remarked, with the air of a Nemesis, that she should not come to the office again about it. He seemed resigned. She went away, woman-like, declaring with her last breath, "You owe me twenty-three cents." He had been as polite as could be expected, but it was not in human nature not to retort, "I don't owe you a cent," and then, turning to a gentleman near by, he added, "There 's a woman says I owe her twenty-three cents, and I never had any dealings with her in my life." All my womanhood blushed at this woman's unreasonableness; I determined to try to obliterate the impression from his mind by the utmost consideration and politeness; and blandly asked, putting a good deal of sympathy for his embarrassing position into my manner, "Will you be so good as to tell me at what hour the cars leave for Melrose?"

"They don't leave at all. They don't go there."

I could have borne the disappointment of fruitless search with fortitude; but to be baffled in my magnanimity was too much. I am afraid I lost my temper for a moment, and that the clerk found it in my impetuous question, "What under the sun do you have that sign there for then?" He muttered something about a charter, which was probably satisfactory to himself, but of little avail to my wounded feelings, and, in the chaotic state of my mind, I could hardly be blamed for asking the first question that came up, "What time do the steam-cars go to Melrose?" He did n't know, and I perceived that I had fallen into a trap again. Of course he did n't; he had nothing to do with steam-cars. I went back to the original shop. They were very polite, and looked up evidence, and decided that the Boston and Maine Railroad was the one. They directed me to the depot, but they killed me with kindness, for one told me to take this street, and another said that street was nearer, and a third said the first street was just as near, and they all seemed to talk together, though I don't suppose they did, and I was conscious of nothing but a din of "Union Street," and "Brattle Street," and "Haymarket Square," which quite bewildered me, though I endeavored to look as if I comprehended everything clearly, and said yes all round, anxious only to get out doors and into the next shop, to inquire the way to the Boston and Maine Railroad depot. Only one thing I understood, — that, instead of going out at the front door, I was to go "right out this way," but "out this way" I could see nothing but windows, though, all the while they were talking, I cast stolen glances to catch any sign of a door. I was determined, however, not to ask another foolish question, and merely remarked that I saw no mode of egress that way except through the windows. Then they showed me a basement door, through which I made good my escape, grateful for their kindness, but not much the wiser.

By assiduous inquiry, I found my way to the depot, and gathered my various packages together. Observation and experience both combine to make me a firm foe to packages. I lose half my self-respect and all my independence unless my hands are free. At this time, by circumstances entirely beyond my control, I was the proprietor of five different articles, — a package of books and paper, cumbrous and heavy, a travelling-basket bursting full, as I particularly dislike to see travelling-baskets, a roll of cloth, a parasol, and a bottle of yeast. One of the pleasantest feelings in the world is that of being master of one's position; but when one is weighed down with bundles, one is its victim, and I got into the cars under a deep sense of degradation, though innocent of any palpable sin. The cars were full. I walked slowly through till a gentleman arose and gave me his seat. Men make so much ado about the ingratitude and impoliteness of travelling women, that I make a point of acknowledging the smallest courtesy; but just as I was putting on my most grateful expression to thank him in, it suddenly occurred to me that this seat, being next to the stove, might prove fatal to my yeast-bottle. I had been particularly warned not even to let it come in contact with my person more than was necessary, lest the warmth should make it ferment, — and to sit in front of a red-hot air-tight stove! I could have borne to lose the yeast, though it was a new kind, said to be of a superior quality, which I was taking home for trial; nor should I have been inconsolable for the loss of my dress, though it was my best silk; but I did not feel that I could endure *the scene.* In my consternation, I forgot to thank the gentleman, to whom I now make this public apology and explanation. I at length managed to lift the window about an inch and a quarter, and held the bottle in the draft, and my peace as well as I could.

I thought Melrose was the first station from Boston, but it was not. The second one did not sound like Melrose, and I kept my seat. Then I began to fear that I had missed it, so I compromised with my principles, and asked my seat-mate if he knew which station from Boston Melrose was. He said he did not, but should know it when he saw it. By and by he said this was it. I do not like to see people, particularly women, hurry out before cars stop, or in before passengers are out, but I had many encumbrances and could not move rapidly, so I thought I would for once take time by the forelock and just move down the aisle to be near the door when the cars stopped. I accordingly did so, and the conductor opened the door and shouted, "Wy-o-ming!" and, partly to punish myself, and partly because of the difficulty of returning to my seat, I stood up in the aisle, covered with shame, till we reached Melrose.

My errand there being performed, I returned to the station in ample time, — indeed, long before the ticket-office was opened. There was a glass window looking into the ladies' room, and a corresponding one into the gentleman's room. Presently a large boy walked in and established communication between the office and the men's room, but left ours alone. There were several women in the room, who all seemed to take it very coolly, and I was not going to be anxious. Still, as the time passed and the window was not opened, I did think it rather strange. By and by the whistle began to whistle, and the cars rushed in. I supposed they must be some branch, or extra train; but to make certain, I said, carelessly, to an official, "This is not the Salem train." "Yes," was the prompt reply. Surprised into it, I ejaculated, "Not the Salem train?" "Yes," with equal promptness, "last car." I marched along in a most unwilling hurry. I think there must have been at least seven cars, and under the pressure it seemed to me that I never should get to the last one; so I thought I would steal into the nearest, and at the next stopping-place change to the right one. I turned aside, but the fellow called out, "Not that, — the last car. Be spry!" If I had obeyed the impulse of the natural heart, I should have hurled my yeast-bottle at him, telling *me* to be "spry," — me who am famous for my fleetness of foot, — telling *me* to be spry as if I were a barefoot pond-lily boy! My dignity and capacity were both insulted. I was vexed with myself for having disregarded his direction, and vexed with him for having caught me in it. If I had been sure that the cars would wait for me, I should have loitered, simply to show a proper spirit; but as it was, there was no time for indignation, and I put my foot on the step just as the cars started. But when I went to open the door, there was no door there. I fumbled and stared and rubbed my eyes, but no open sesame will unlock a door that does not exist. The conductor came to the rescue, and directed me through a hide-and-go-seek chink passage, such as I never saw or heard of before, away round on one side of the car. In my perturbation I could n't find it for a while, and then I could n't tell whether the door was at the end or one side, and he kept saying, "There, there!" as if I knew where "there" was. I meekly remarked that I did n't like to get in while cars were going, — a moral reflection which I might just as well have spared him. He said I could n't fall off if I tried. I knew I could, for the railing had only one rail, and that was at the top; but I was so utterly humiliated by such a series of disasters, that I let him have everything his own way, and was glad to drop into a seat at last.

We rustics have a phrase "starched up." When we say a man is starched up, we do not at all refer to his linen, but to his character. We also, in continuance of the same figure, talk of taking the starch out of him. That was the way I felt. The starch was completely taken out of me. I did not become reglutinated till I impinged upon Halicarnassus. With him, whatever my feelings may be, I find it necessary always to maintain an aspect of superiority and self-satisfaction. If I should once suffer him to see me discomfited by any opposing force whatever, I should at once lose all power over him. The sole basis of my authority is his implicit belief in my thorough invulnerability. Therefore, nothing and nobody as I felt myself, I sloughed it all off when I stepped from the train and stood before him, an invincible armada. My foot was on my native heath, and my name was McGregor.

Brown-Bread Cakes.

TASTES differ.

That is not an original remark, but it is a true one. The Frenchman rolls as a sweet morsel under his tongue the hind legs of a frog. To the patriotic Chinese, no savor is so savory as that which arises from roasted mouse or broiled puppy. The Esquimaux, plunged into the pots and kettles of civilization, moans for the delicious blubber and whale-oil which once gladdened his heart. Connecticut delights in the frying-pan. Meat, bread, rice, turnovers, apples, potatoes, hasty-puddings, "whatever goods the gods provide her," — and every dweller in her valleys will attest they are neither few nor small, — she casts incontinently into the sputtering fat, till Connecticut joints, from constant lubrication, acquire a suppleness which neither age, nor time, nor travel, nor the burden of her traditionary nutmegs, clocks, and hams, can overcome.

But thou, O Massachusetts! land of my birth, and thrice and four times land of my love! queen mother of men, reverent children, who turn to thee from every shore, and bind on thy brow the laurels they learned from thee to win, — will any wanderer from thy sturdy soil ever

> " Forget the sky that bent above
> His childhood, like a dream of love?
> The stream beneath the green hill flowing,
> The broad-armed trees about it growing,"

the smoke from thousand fires ascending, with fragrant odors sweetly blending, of thousand pans, bright, glazed, and red, a thousand pans of hot brown-bread?

Nor is thy fame confined to thy children alone. From the lumbering and fishing East to the miasmatic and ague-atic West, an unfortunate race, whose veins have never throbbed with Bay State blood, who have not sufficient ingenuity to step out of the even tenor of their wheat-bread way, but whose stomachs have been endowed with a sensibility denied to their brains, weekly distend their pliant throats with " Boston brown bread."

Can such a generation be supposed, in the highest flights of its imagination, ever to have soared to brown-bread *cakes?* Is not the attempt to rouse, in these sluggish minds, an enthusiasm for the ambrosial food, Quixotic to the last degree? Nay, is it possible to introduce into their stolid souls any conception of the ethereal flavor which penetrates my inmost frame when I sit down to a repast of brown-bread cakes? Yet, in the great multitude gathered from every nation under heaven, the mighty throng that are making the wilderness of this New World to bud and blossom as the rose, there must needs be a few who have an eye for the curve that swells the luxuriant sides of a sweet potato, a nose to discern the fumes that rise, incense-like, from a fair, young beefsteak, floating in its own savory juices, a soul to mount upwards on the wings of smoking Mocha; and since

Bonnet	: Head	
Shoe	: Foot	
Bay	: Soul	
Canvas	: Faces	: : Brown-bread : Brown-Bread Cakes.
Cup	: Wine	
Dew	: Rose	
Noon	: Evening	
Earth	: Heaven	

or, less mathematically, as a beautiful bonnet to the beautiful head that bears it, or a delicate satin shoe to the delicate foot that wears it, as the green of the deathless bay to the lofty brow that won it, as the canvas is to the faces that startlingly glow upon it, as the grace of the golden cup to the mantling wine that fills it, as the quivering globe of dew to the regal rose that distils it, as the glare of the midsummer noon to the scented breath of Eden, as the homely and kindly earth to the grand and star-lit heaven, — so is the "home-felt bliss" which a loaf of brown bread makes, to the exquisite thrill of delight arising from brown-bread cakes. Because of all this, I will make the attempt.

Let me give the *modus operandi*. Of fine

maize flour, yellow as the locks of the lovely Lenore, take — well, take enough — I cannot tell exactly how much; it depends upon circumstances. Of fresh new milk, white as the brow of the charming Arabella, take — I don't know exactly how much of that, either; it depends upon circumstances, particularly on the quantity of meal. If you have not new milk, take blue milk, provided it be sweet; or if you have none that is sweet, sour milk will answer; or if "your folks don't keep a cow," take water, clear and sparkling as the eyes of the peerless Amanda; but whether it be milk or water, let it be scalding as the tears of the outraged Isabel. Of molasses, sweet as the tones of the tuneful Lisette, take — a great deal, if it is summer, in the winter not quite so much (for the reasons therefor, see Newton's *Treatise on the Expansive Power of Fluids*, Vol. I. p. 175). Of various other substances, animal, vegetable, and mineral, which it becomes not me to mention, — first, because I have forgotten what they are; secondly, because I never knew; and, thirdly, because, as the immortal Toots remarks, "it is of no consequence," — take whatever seems good in your sight, and cast them together into the kneading-trough, and knead with all your might and main. Provide yourself, then, with a tin plate, not bright and new, for so will your cakes be heavy, your crust cracked, and your soul sorrowful, but one blackened by fire, and venerable with time, and rough with service. With your own roseate fingers scoop out a portion of the pulpy mass. Fear not to touch it; it is soft, yielding, and plastic, as the heart of the affectionate Clara. Turn it lovingly over in your hands; round it; mould it; caress it; soften down its asperities; smooth off its angularities; repress its bold protuberances; encourage its timid shrinkings; and when it is smooth as the velvet cheek of Ida, and oval as the classic face of Helen, give one "last, long, lingering look," and lay it tenderly in the swart arms of its tutelar plate. Repeat the process, until your cakes shall equal the sands on the sea-shore or the stars in the sky for multitude, or as long as your meal holds out, or till you are tired. I am prescribing for one only. "Ab uno disce omnes."

To the Stygian cave that yawns dismally from the kitchen-stove, consign it without a murmur. Item: said stove must have a prodigious crack up and down the front. A philosophical reason for this I am unable to give. I refer the curious in cause and effect to Galen's deservedly celebrated *Disquisition on the Relations of Fire and Metals*, *passim;* also *Debrauche on Dough*, p. 35, Appendix. I only know that the only stove whence I ever saw brown-bread cakes issue had an immense crack up and down the front.

[Since writing the above, a new stove has been

substituted for the old one, and still brown-bread cakes are duly marshalled every morning. Con sequently, you need not be particular about the crack. Still, I would advise all amateurs to consult the authorities I have mentioned. It will be a good exercise.]

When your cake has for a sufficient length of time undergone the ordeal of fire, bring it again to the blessed light of day. If the edge be black and blistered, like a giant tree blasted by the lightning's stroke, or if the crust be rent and torn as by internal convulsions, cast it away. It is worthless. Trample it under foot. Item: put on your stoutest boots, and provide yourself with cork soles; otherwise, the trampling may prove to be anything but an agreeable pastime. But if the surface be a beautiful auburn brown, crisp, brittle, and unbroken, —

> "Joy, joy, forever! your task is done!
> The gates are past, and breakfast is won"; —

or, as the clown said of the apple-dumplings, "Them 's the jockeys for me."

If you are an outside barbarian, ignorant of the refinements of civilized life, you will at once proceed to cut open with your knife the steaming cake, as you would an oyster, and thereby render it heavy as the heart of the weeping Niobe; but if you are a gentleman and a scholar, you will gently sunder its clinging sides without "armed interference," and so preserve its spongy, porous texture. To the uninitiated, one part is as good as another; but let me confidentially whisper in your ear, if it should be your duty to pass the plate, present to your neighbor that side which bears the under-crust, as that is liable to be burnt and unpalatable, and reserve to yourself the smoothly-rounded upper crust, which is deliciously toothsome. Lay your portion on your plate, crust downward. With your own polished knife (the reason of this you will presently perceive) carve from the ball of golden butter a lump of magnificent dimensions. Be not niggardly in this respect. Exercise toward yourself a large-hearted generosity; for butter sinks into itself, and in itself is lost with wonderful rapidity, when it rests on a pedestal of hot bread. Press your butter, still adhering to your knife, down into the warm, soft bread, in various places, forming little wells, whose walls are unctuous with the melted luxury, and then — O THEN! but I cannot sustain the picture which my fancy has drawn.

> "My eyes are dim with childish tears,
> My heart is idly stirred;
> For the same sound is in my ears
> That in those days I heard.
>
> "Thus fares it still in our decay,
> Yet mourns the wiser mind
> Less for the crusts time takes away,
> Than those he leaves behind."
>
> "The bridegroom may forget the bride
> Was made his wedded wife yestreen;
> The monarch may forget the crown
> That on his head an hour hath been."

but never, O brown-bread cakes! never may your taste pass away from my lips, your odor from my nostrils, or your memory from my heart, till "my eyes shall be turned to behold, for the last time, the sun in the heavens."

"Et dulces moriens reminiscitur Argos."

A Complaint of Friends.

IF things would not run into each other so, it would be a thousand times easier and a million times pleasanter to get on in the world. Let the sheepiness be set on one side and the goatiness on the other, and immediately you know where you are. It is not necessary to ask that there be any increase of the one or any diminution of the other, but only that each shall pre-empt its own territory and stay there. Milk is good, and water is good, but don't set the milk-pail under the pump. Pleasure softens pain, but pain imbitters pleasure; and who would not rather have his happiness concentrated into one memorable day, that shall gleam and glow through a lifetime, than have it spread out over a dozen comfortable, commonplace, humdrum forenoons and afternoons, each one as like the others as two peas in a pod? Since the law of compensation obtains, I suppose it is the best law for us; but if it had been left with me, I should have made the clever people rich and handsome, and left poverty and ugliness to the stupid people; because — don't you see? — the stupid people won't know they are ugly, and won't care if they are poor, but the clever people will be hampered and tortured. I would have given the good wives to the good husbands, and made drunken men marry drunken women. Then there would have been one family exquisitely happy, instead of two struggling against misery. I would have made the rose-stem downy, and put all the thorns on the thistles. I would have gouged out the jewel from the toad's head, and given the peacock the nightingale's voice, and not set everything so at half and half.

But that is the way it is. We find the world made to our hand. The wise men marry the foolish virgins, and the splendid virgins marry dolts, and matters in general are so mixed up, that the choice lies between nice things about spoiled, and vile things that are not so bad after all, and it is hard to tell sometimes which you like best, or which you loathe least.

I expect to lose every friend I have in the world by the publication of this paper — except the dunces who are impaled in it. They will never read it, and if they do, will never suspect I mean them; while the sensible and true friends, who do me good and not evil all the days of their lives, will think I am driving at their noble hearts, and will at once haul off and leave me inconsolable. Still I am going to write it. You must open the safety-valve once in a while, even if the steam does whiz and shriek, or there will be an explosion, which is fatal, while the whizzing and shrieking are only disagreeable.

Doubtless friendship has its advantages and its pleasures; doubtless hostility has its isolations and its revenges: still, if called upon to choose once for all between friends and foes, I think, on the whole, I should cast my vote for the foes. Twenty enemies will not do you the mischief of one friend. Enemies you always know where to find. They are in fair and square perpetual hostility, and you keep your armor on and your sentinels posted; but with friends you are inveigled into a false security, and, before you know it, your honor, your modesty, your delicacy are scudding before the gales. Moreover, with your friend you can never make reprisals. If your enemy attacks you, you can always strike back and hit hard. You are expected to defend yourself against him to the top of your bent. He is your legal opponent in honorable warfare. You can pour hot-shot into him with murderous vigor; and the more he writhes, the better you feel. In fact, it is rather refreshing to measure swords once in a while with such a one. You like to exert your power and keep yourself in practice. You do not rejoice so much in overcoming your enemy as in overcoming. If a marble statue could show fight, you would just as soon fight it; but as it cannot, you take something that can, and something, besides, that has had the temerity to attack you, and so has made a lawful target of itself. But against your friend your hands are tied. He has injured you. He has disgusted you. He has infuriated you. But it was most Christianly done. You cannot hurl a thunderbolt, or pull a trigger, or lisp a syllable, against those amiable monsters who with tenderest fingers are sticking pins all over you. So you shut fast the doors of your lips, and inwardly sigh for a good, stout, brawny, malignant foe, who, under any and every circumstance, will design you harm, and on whom you can lavish your lusty blows with a hearty will and a clear conscience.

Your enemy keeps clear of you. He neither grants nor claims favors. He awards you your rights, — no more, no less, — and demands the same from you. Consequently there is no friction. Your friend, on the contrary, is continually getting himself tangled up with you "because he is your friend." I have heard that Shelley was never better pleased than when his associates made free with his coats, boots, and hats for their own use, and that he appropriated their property in the same way. Shelley was a poet, and perhaps idealized his friends. He saw them, probably, in a state of pure intellect. I am not a poet; I look at people in the concrete. The most obvious thing about my friends is their avoirdupois; and I prefer that they should wear their own cloaks and suffer me to wear mine. There is no neck in the world that I want my collar to span except my own. It is very exasperating to me to go to my bookcase and miss a book of which I am in immediate and pressing need, because an intimate friend has carried it off without asking leave, on the score of his intimacy. I have not, and do not wish to have, any alliance that shall abrogate the eighth commandment. A great mistake is lying round loose hereabouts, — a mistake fatal to many friendships that did run well. The common fallacy is, that intimacy dispenses with the necessity of politeness. The truth is just the opposite of this. The more points of contact there are, the more danger of friction there is, and the more carefully should people guard against it. If you see a man only once a month, it is not of so vital importance that you do not trench on his rights, tastes, or whims. He can bear to be crossed or annoyed occasionally. If he does not have a very high regard for you, it is comparatively unimportant, because your paths are generally so diverse. But you and the man with whom you dine every day have it in your power to make each other exceedingly uncomfortable. A very little dropping will wear away rock, if it only keep at it. The thing that you would not think of, if it occurred only twice a year, becomes an intolerable burden when it happens twice a day. This is where husbands and wives run aground. They take too much for granted. If they would but see that they have something to gain, something to save, as well as something to enjoy, it would be better for them; but they proceed on the assumption that their love is an inexhaustible tank, and not a fountain depending for its supply on the stream that trickles into it. So, for every little annoying habit, or weakness, or fault, they draw on the tank, without being careful to keep the supply open, till they awake one morning to find the pump dry, and, instead of love, at best, nothing but a cold habit of complacence. On the contrary, the more intimate friends become, whether married or unmarried, the more scrupulously should they strive to repress in themselves everything annoying, and to cherish both in themselves and each other everything pleasing. While each should draw on his love to neutralize the faults of his friend, it is suicidal to draw on his friend's love to neutralize his own faults. Love should be cumulative, since it cannot be stationary. If it does not increase, it decreases. Love, like confidence, is a plant of slow growth, and of most exotic fragility. It must be constantly and tenderly cherished. Every noxious and foreign element must be carefully removed from it. All sunshine, and sweet airs, and morning dews, and evening showers, must breathe upon it perpetual fragrance, or it dies into a hideous and repulsive deformity, fit only to be cast out and trodden under foot of men, while, properly cultivated, it is a Tree of Life.

Your enemy keeps clear of you, not only in business, but in society. If circumstances thrust him into contact with you, he is curt and centrifugal. But your friend breaks in upon your "saintly solitude" with perfect equanimity. He never for a moment harbors a suspicion that he can intrude, "because he is your friend." So he drops in on his way to the office to chat half an hour over the latest news. The half-hour is n't much in itself. If it were after dinner, you would n't mind it; but after breakfast every moment "runs itself in golden sands," and the break in your time crashes a worse break in your temper. "Are you busy?" asks the considerate wretch, adding insult to injury. What can you do? Say yes, and wound his self-love forever? But he has a wife and family. You respect their feelings, smile and smile, and are villain enough to be civil with your lips, and hide the poison of asps under your tongue, till you have a chance to relieve your o'ercharged heart by shaking your fist in impotent wrath at his retreating form. You will receive the reward of your hypocrisy, as you richly deserve, for ten to one he will drop in again when he comes back from his office, and arrest you wandering in Dreamland in the beautiful twilight. Delighted to find that you are neither reading nor writing, — the absurd dolt! as if a man were n't at work unless he be wielding a sledge-hammer! — he will preach out, and prose out, and twaddle out another hour of your golden eventide, "because he is your friend." You don't care whether he is judge or jury, — whether he talks sense or nonsense; you don't want him to talk at all. You don't want him there any way. You want to be alone. If you don't, why are you sitting there in the deepening twilight? If you wanted him, could n't you send for him? Why don't you go out into the drawing-room, where are music, and lights, and gay people? What right have I to suppose, that, because you are not using your eyes, you are not using your brain? What right have I to set myself up as judge of the value of your time, and so rob you of perhaps the most delicious hour in all your day, on pretence that it is of no use to you? — take a pound of flesh clean out of your heart, and trip on my smiling way as if I had not earned the gallows?

And what in Heaven's name is the good of all this ceaseless talk? To what purpose are you wearied, exhausted, dragged out and out to the very extreme of tenuity? A sprightly badinage, — a running fire of nonsense for half an hour, — a tramp over unfamiliar ground with a familiar guide, — a discussion of something with somebody who knows all about it, or who, not knowing, wants to learn from you, — a pleasant interchange of commonplaces with a circle of friends around the fire, at such hours as you give to society: all this is not only tolerable, but agreeable, — often positively delightful; but to have an indifferent person, on no score but that of friendship, break into your sacred presence, and suck your blood through indefinite cycles of time, is an abomination. If he clatters on an indifferent subject, you can do well enough for fifteen minutes, buoyed up by the hope that he will presently have a fit, or be sent for, or come to some kind of an end. But when you gradually open to the conviction that *vis inertiæ* rules the hour, and the thing which has been is that which shall be, you wax listless; your chariot-wheels drive heavily; your end of the pole drags in the mud, and you speedily wallow in unmitigated disgust. If he broaches a subject on which you have a real and deep living interest, you shrink from unbosoming yourself to him. You feel that it would be sacrilege. He feels nothing of the sort. He treads over your heart-strings in his cow-hide brogans, and does not see that they are not whip-cords. He pokes his gold-headed cane in among your treasures, blind to the fact that you are clutching both arms around them, that no gleam of flashing gold may reveal their whereabouts to him. You draw yourself up in your shell, projecting a monosyllabic claw occasionally as a sign of continued vitality; but the pachyderm does not withdraw, and you gradually lower into an indignation, — smothered, fierce, intense.

Why, *why*, WHY will people inundate their unfortunate victims with such "weak, washy, everlasting floods"? Why will they haul everything out into the open day? Why will they make the Holy of Holies common and unclean? Why will they be so ineffably stupid as not to see that there is that which speech profanes? Why will they lower their drag-nets into the unfathomable waters, in the vain attempt to bring up your pearls and gems, whose lustre would pale to ashes in the garish light, whose only sparkle is in the deep sea-soundings? *Procul, O procul este, profani!*

O, the matchless power of silence! There are words that concentrate in themselves the glory of a lifetime; but there is a silence that is more precious than they. Speech ripples over the surface of life, but silence sinks into its depths. Airy pleasantnesses bubble up in airy, pleasant words. Weak sorrows quaver out their shallow being, and are not. When the heart is cleft to its core, there is no speech nor language.

Do not now, Messrs. Bores, think to retrieve your characters by coming into my house and sitting mute for two hours. Heaven forbid that your blood should be found on my skirts! but I believe I shall kill you, if you do. The only reason why I have not laid violent hands on you heretofore is that your vapid talk has operated as a wire to conduct my electricity to the receptive and kindly earth; but if you intrude upon my magnetisms without any such life-preserver, your future in this world is not worth a crossed sixpence. Your silence would break the reed that your talk but bruised. The only people with whom it is a joy to sit silent are the people with whom it is a joy to talk. Clear out!

Friendship plays the mischief in the false ideas of constancy which are generated and cherished in its name, if not by its agency. Your enemies are intense, but temporary. Time wears off the edge of hostility. It is the alembic in which offences are dissolved into thin air, and a calm indifference reigns in their stead. But your friends are expected to be a permanent arrangement. They are not only a sore evil, but of long continuance. Adhesiveness seems to be the head and front, the bones and blood, of their creed. It is not the direction of the quality, but the quality itself, which they swear by. Only stick, it is no matter what you stick to. Fall out with a man, and you can kiss and be friends as soon as you like; the recording angel will set it down on the credit side of his books. Fall in, and you are expected to stay in, *ad infinitum, ad nauseam.* No matter what combination of laws got you there, there you are, and there you must stay, for better, for worse, till merciful Death you do part, — or you are — "fickle." You find a man entertaining for an hour, a week, a concert, a journey, and *presto!* you are saddled with him forever. What preposterous absurdity! Do but look at it calmly. You are thrown into contact with a person, and, as in duty bound, you proceed to fathom him: for every man is a possible revelation. In the deeps of his soul there may lie unknown worlds for you. Consequently you proceed at once to experiment on him. It takes a little while to get your tackle in order. Then the line begins to run off rapidly, and your eager soul cries out, "Ah! what depth! What perpetual calmness must be down below! What rest is here for all my tumult! What a grand, vast nature is this!" Surely, surely, you are on the high seas. Surely, you will now float serenely down the eternities! But by and by there is a kink. You find, that, though the line runs off so fast, it does not go down, — it only floats out. A current has caught it and bears it on horizontally. It does not sink plumb. You have been deceived. Your grand Pacific Ocean is nothing but a shallow little brook, that you can ford all the year round, if it does not utterly dry up in the summer heats, when you want it most; or, at best, it is a fussy little tormenting river, that won't and can't sail a sloop. What are you going to do about it? You are going to wind up your lead and line, shoulder your birch canoe, as the old sea-kings used, and thrid the deep forests, and scale the purple hills, till you come to water again, when you will unroll your lead and line for another essay. Is that fickleness? What else can you do? Must you launch your bark on the unquiet stream, against whose pebbly bottom the keel continually grates and rasps your nerves — simply that your reputation suffer no detriment? Fickleness? There was no fickleness about it. You were trying an experiment which you had every right to try. As soon as you were satisfied, you stopped. If you had stopped sooner, you would have been unsatisfied. If you had stopped later, you would have been dissatisfied. It is a criminal contempt of the magnificent possibilities of life not to lay hold of "God's occasions floating by." It is an equally criminal perversion of them to cling tenaciously to what was only the *simulacrum* of an occasion. A man will toil many days and nights among the mountains to find an ingot of gold, which, found, he bears home with infinite pains and just rejoicing; but he would be a fool who should lade his mules with iron-pyrites to justify his labors, however severe.

Fickleness! what is it, that we make such an ado about it? And what is constancy, that it commands such usurious interest? The one is a foible only in its relations. The other is only thus a virtue. "Fickle as the winds" is our death-seal upon a man; but should we like our winds unfickle? Would a perpetual North-easter lay us open to perpetual gratitude? or is a soft South gale to be orisoned and vespered forevermore?

I am tired of this eternal prating of devotion and constancy. It is senseless in itself and harmful in its tendencies. The dictate of reason is to treat men and women as we do oranges. Suck all the juice out and then let them go. Where is the good of keeping the peel and pulp-cells till they get old, dry, and mouldy? Let them go, and they will help feed the earth-worms and bugs and beetles who can hardly find existence a continued banquet, and fertilize the earth which will have you give before you receive. Thus they will ultimately spring up in new and beautiful shapes. Clung to with constancy, they stain your knife and napkin, impart a bad odor to your dining-room, and degenerate into something that is neither pleasant to the eye nor good for food. I believe in a rotation of crops, morally and socially, as well as agriculturally. When you have taken the measure of a man, when you have sounded him and know that you cannot wade in him more than ankle-deep, when you have got out of him all that he has to yield for your soul's sustenance and strength, what is the next thing to be done? Obviously, pass him on; and turn you "to fresh woods and pastures new." Do you work him an injury? By no means. Friends that are simply glued on, and don't grow out of, are little worth. He has nothing more for you, nor you for him;

but he may be rich in juices wherewithal to nourish the heart of another man, and their two lives, set together, may have an endosmose and exosmose whose result shall be richness of soil, grandeur of growth, beauty of foliage, and perfectness of fruit; while you and he would only have languished into aridity and a stunted crab-tree.

For my part, I desire to sweep off my old friends with the old year, and begin the new with a clean record. It is a measure absolutely necessary. The snake does not put on his new skin over the old one. He sloughs off the first, before he dons the second. He would be a very clumsy serpent, if he did not. One cannot have successive layers of friendships any more than the snake has successive layers of skins. One must adopt some system to guard against a congestion of the heart from plethora of loves. I go in for the much-abused fair-weather, skin-deep, April-shower friends, — the friends who will drop off, if let alone, — who must be kept awake to be kept at all, — who will talk and laugh with you as long as it suits your respective humors and you are prosperous and happy, — the blessed butterfly-race who flutter about your June mornings, and when the clouds lower, and the drops patter, and the rains descend, and the winds blow, will spread their gay wings and float gracefully away to sunny Southern lands, where the skies are yet blue and the breezes violet-scented. They are not only agreeable, but deeply wise. So long as a man keeps his streamer flying, his sails set, and his hull above water, it is pleasant to paddle alongside; but when the sails split, the yards crack, and the keel goes staggering down, by all means paddle off. Why should you be submerged in his whirlpool? Will he drown any more easily because you are drowning with him? Lung is lung. He dies from want of air, not from want of sympathy. When a poor fellow sits down among the ashes, the best thing his friends can do is to stand afar off. Job bore the loss of property, children, health, with equanimity. Satan himself found his match there; and for all his buffetings, Job sinned not, nor charged God foolishly. But Job's three friends must needs make an appointment together to come and mourn with him and to comfort him, and after this Job opened his mouth, and cursed his day,—and no wonder.

Your friends have an intimate knowledge of you that is astonishing to contemplate. It is not that they know your affairs, which he who runs may read, but they know you. From a bit of bone, Cuvier could predicate a whole animal, even to the hide and hair. Such moral naturalists are your dear five hundred friends. It seems to yourself that you are immeasurably reticent. You know, of a certainty, that you project only the smallest possible fragment of yourself. You yield your universality to the bond of common brotherhood; but your individualism — what it is that makes you you — withdraws itself naturally, involuntarily, inevitably, into the background, — the dim distance which their eyes cannot penetrate. But, from the fraction which you do project, they construct another you, call it by your name, and pass it around for the real, the actual you. You bristle with jest and laughter and wild whims, to keep them at a distance; and they fancy this to be your every-day equipment. They think your life holds constant carnival. It is astonishing what ideas spring up in the heads of sensible people. There are those who assume that a person can never have had any grief, unless somebody has died, or he has been disappointed in love, — not knowing that every avenue of joy lies open to the tramp of pain. They see the flashing coronet on the queen's brow, and they infer a diamond woman, not recking of the human heart that throbs wildly out of sight. They see the foam-crest on the wave, and picture an Atlantic Ocean of froth, and not the solemn sea that stands below in eternal equipoise. You turn to them the luminous crescent of your life, and they call it the whole round globe; and so they love you with a love that is agate, not pearl, because what they love in you is something infinitely below the highest. They love you level: they have never scaled your heights nor fathomed your depths. And when they talk of you as familiarly as if they had taken out your auricles and ventricles, and turned them inside out, and wrung them, and shaken them, — when they prate of your transparency and openness, the abandonment with which you draw aside the curtain and reveal the inmost thoughts of your heart, — you, who are to yourself a miracle and a mystery, you smile inwardly, and are content. They are on the wrong scent, and you may pursue your plans in peace. They are indiscriminate and satisfied. They do not know the relation of what appears to what is. If they chance to skirt along the coasts of your Purple Island, it will be only chance, and they will not know it. You may close your portholes, lower your drawbridge, and make merry, for they will never come within gunshot of the "Round Tower of your heart."

There is no such thing as knowing a man intimately. Every soul is, for the greater part of its mortal life, isolated from every other. Whether it dwell in the Garden of Eden or the Desert of Sahara, it dwells alone. Not only do we jostle against the street-crowd unknowing and unknown, but we go out and come in, we lie down and rise up, with strangers. Jupiter and Neptune sweep the heavens not more unfamiliar to us than the worlds that circle our own hearth-stone. Day after day, and year after year, a person moves by your side; he sits at the same table; he reads the same books; he kneels in the same church. You know every hair of his head, every trick of his lips, every tone of his voice; you can tell him far off by his gait. Without seeing him, you recognize his step, his knock, his laugh. "Know him? Yes, I have known him these twenty years." No, you don't know him. You know his gait, and hair, and voice. You know what preacher he hears, what ticket he voted, and what were his last year's expenses; but you don't know him. He sits quietly in his chair, but he is in the temple. You speak to him; his soul comes out into the vestibule to answer you, and returns, — and the gates are shut; therein you cannot enter. You were discussing the state of the country; but when you ceased, he opened a postern-gate, went down a bank, and launched on a sea over whose waters you have no boat to sail, no star to guide. You have loved and reverenced him. He has been your concrete of truth and nobleness. Unwittingly you touch a secret spring, and a Blue-Beard Chamber stands revealed. You give no sign; you meet and part as usual; but a Dead Sea rolls between you two forevermore.

It must be so. Not even to the nearest and dearest can one unveil the secret place where his soul abideth, so that there shall be no more any winding ways or hidden chambers; but to your indifferent neighbor, what blind alleys, and deep caverns, and inaccessible mountains! To him who "touches the electric chain wherewith you 're darkly bound," your soul sends back an answering thrill. One little window is opened, and there is short parley. Your ships speak each other now and then in welcome, though imperfect communication; but immediately you strike out again into the great, shoreless sea, over which you must sail forever alone. You may shrink from the far-reaching solitudes of your heart, but no other foot than yours can tread them, save those

"That, eighteen hundred years ago, were nailed,
For our advantage, to the bitter cross."

Be thankful that it is so, — that only His eye sees whose hand formed. If we could look in, we should be appalled at the vision. The worlds that glide around us are mysteries too high for us. We cannot attain to them. The naked soul is a sight too awful for man to look at and live. There are individuals whose topography we would like to know a little better, and there is danger that we crash against each other while roaming around in the dark; but, for all that, would we not have the Constitution broken up. Somebody says, "In heaven there will be no secrets," which, it seems to me, would be intolerable. (If that were a revelation from the King of Heaven, of course I would not speak flippantly of it; but though towards Heaven we look with reverence and humble hope, I do not know that Tom,

Dick, and Harry's notions of it have any special claim to our respect.) Such publicity would destroy all individuality, and undermine the foun dations of society. Clairvoyance — if there be any such thing — always seemed to me a stupid impertinence. When people pay visits to me, I wish them to come to the front-door, and ring the bell, and send up their names. I don't wish them to climb in at the window, or creep through the pantry, or, worst of all, float through the keyhole, and catch me in undress. So I believe that in all worlds thoughts will be the subjects of volition, — more accurately expressed when expression is desired, but just as entirely suppressed when we will suppression.

After all, perhaps the chief trouble arises from a prevalent confusion of ideas as to what constitutes a man your friend. Friendship may stand for that peaceful complacence which you feel towards all well-behaved people who wear clean collars and use tolerable grammar. This is a very good meaning, if everybody will subscribe to it. But sundry of these well-behaved people will mistake your civility and complacence for a recognition of special affinity, and proceed at once to frame an alliance offensive and defensive while the sun and the moon shall endure. O, the barnacles that cling to your keel in such waters! The inevitable result is, that they win your intense rancor. You would feel a genial kindliness towards them, if they would be satisfied with that; but they lay out to be your specialty. They infer your innocent little inch to be the standard-bearer of twenty ells, and goad you to frenzy. I mean you, you desperate little horror, who nearly dethroned my reason six years ago! I always meant to have my revenge, and here I impale you before the public. For three months, you fastened yourself upon me, and I could not shake you off. What availed it me, that you were an honest and excellent man? Did I not, twenty times a day, wish you had been a villain, who had insulted me, and I a Kentucky giant, that I might have the unspeakable satisfaction of knocking you down? But you added to your crimes virtue. Villany had no part or lot in you. You were a member of a church, in good and regular standing; you had graduated with all the honors worth mentioning; you had not a sin, a vice, or a fault that I knew of; and you were so thoroughly good and repulsive that you were a great grief to me. Do you think, you dear, disinterested wretch, that I have forgotten how you were continually putting yourself to horrible inconveniences on my account? Do you think I am not now filled with remorse for the aversion that rooted itself ineradicably in my soul, and which now gloats over you, as you stand in the pillory where my own hands have fastened you? But can Nature be crushed forever? Did I not ruin my nerves, and seriously injure my temper, by the overpowering pressure I laid upon them to keep them quiet when you were by? Could I not, by the sense of coming ill through all my quivering frame, presage your advent as exactly as the barometer heralds the approaching storm? Those three months of agony are little atoned for by this late vengeance; but go in peace!

Mysterious are the ways of friendship. It is not a matter of reason or of choice, but of magnetisms. You cannot always give the premises nor the argument, but the conclusion is a palpable and stubborn fact. Abana and Pharpar may be broad, and deep, and blue, and grand; but only in Jordan shall your soul wash and be clean. A thousand brooks are born of the sunshine and the mountains: very, very few are they whose flow can mingle with yours, and not disturb, but only deepen and broaden the current.

Your friend! Who shall describe him, or worthily paint what he is to you? No merchant, nor lawyer, nor farmer, nor statesman, claims your suffrage, but a kingly soul. He comes to you from God, — a prophet, a seer, a revealer. He has a clear vision. His love is reverence. He goes into the *penetralia* of your life, — not presumptuously, but with uncovered head, unsandalled feet, and pours libations at the innermost shrine. His incense is grateful. For him the sunlight brightens, the skies grow rosy, and all the days are Junes. Wrapped in his love, you float in a delicious rest, rocked in the bosom of purple, scented waves. Nameless melodies sing themselves through your heart. A golden glow suffuses your atmosphere. A vague, fine ecstasy thrills to the sources of life, and earth lays hold on heaven. Such friendship is worship. It elevates the most trifling services into rites. The humblest offices are sanctified. All things are baptized into a new name. Duty is lost in joy. Care veils itself in caresses. Drudgery becomes delight. There is no longer anything menial, small, or servile. All is transformed

"Into something rich and strange."

The homely household-ways lead through beds of spices and orchards of pomegranates. The daily toil among your parsnips and carrots is plucking May violets with the dew upon them to meet the eyes you love upon their first awaking. In the burden and heat of the day you hear the rustling of summer showers and the whispering of summer winds. Everything is lifted up from the plane of labor to the plane of love, and a glory spans your life. With your friend, speech and silence are one; for a communion mysterious and intangible reaches across from heart to heart. The many dig and delve in your nature with fruitless toil to find the spring of living water: he only raises his wand, and, obedient to the hidden power, it bends at once to your secret. Your friendship, though independent of language, gives to it life and light. The mystic spirit stirs even in commonplaces, and the merest question is an endearment. You are quiet because your heart is over-full. You talk because it is pleasant, not because you have anything to say. You weary of terms that are already love-laden, and you go out into the highways and hedges, and gather up the rough, wild, wilful words, heavy with the hatreds of men, and fill them to the brim with honey-dew. All things great and small, grand or humble, you press into your service, force them to do soldier's duty, and your banner over them is love.

With such a friendship, presence alone is happiness ; nor is absence wholly void, — for memories, and hopes, and pleasing fancies, sparkle through the hours, and you know the sunshine will come back.

For such friendship one is grateful. No matter that it comes unsought, and comes not for the seeking. You do not discuss the reasonableness of your gratitude. You only know that your whole being bows with humility and utter thankfulness to him who thus crowns you monarch of all realms.

And the kingdom is everlasting. A weak love dies weakly with the occasion that gave it birth; but such friendship is born of the gods, and immortal. Clouds and darkness may sweep around it, but within the cloud the glory lives undimmed. Death has no power over it. Time cannot diminish, nor even dishonor annul it. Its direction may have been earthly, but itself is divine. You go back into your solitudes: all is silent as aforetime, but you cannot forget that a Voice once resounded there. A Presence filled the valleys and gilded the mountain-tops,—breathed upon the plains, and they sprang up in lilies and roses, — flashed upon the waters, and they flowed to spheral melody, — swept through the forests, and they, too, trembled into song. And though now the warmth has faded out, though the ruddy tints and amber clearness have paled to ashen hues, though the murmuring melodies are dead, and forest, vale, and hill look hard and angular in the sharp air, you know that it is not death. The fire is unquenched beneath. You go your way not disconsolate. There needs but the Victorious Voice. At the touch of the Prince's lips, life shall rise again and be perfected forevermore.

Dog-Days.

DOUBTLESS they have their uses, but they are not agreeable. That must be conceded. There is no out-doors. You wake in the morning with a mild sense of strangulation, though all your windows are open at top and bottom. You thrust your head out into the morning air, but there is n't any. It has all run to fog. Fog lies heavy and gray on the grass. Trees and hills and fences are smothered in fog. It creeps into your house, tarnishes all your gilt, swells your drawers and doors so that you can't open them, and when you have opened them you can't shut them. It breathes upon your muslin curtains, and they turn into limpsy strings. It steals into your closet, and little blue specks and white feathery spots appear on your pies. A pungent taste develops itself in your pound-cake. The stray cup-custard filched from the general larder for private circulation is a keen and acid disappointment. Milk refuses to curdle into cheese, and cream will tumble about in your churn for hours, and come out mitigated buttermilk at last.

Flies are rampant. If the cover is left off the sugar-bowl, a colony of flies take immediate possession. If your bare arm happens to be carrying a vase of flowers with special care, a fly lights on your elbow, and proceeds by short and easy stages (to him) to your wrist. If you are writing, a horde of flies institute an investigation of your head and hands, with a special commission for your nose. You brush them off, and they only rub their fore legs together, bob their heads, brush down their wings, and go at it again. Your kitchen ceiling looks like huckleberries and milk. All the while it is very warm, but not so warm as it is sticky, only the stickiness is all on the outside. Within, you feel a constant tendency to fall to pieces, because there is n't *brace* enough in the air to hold you together. If we were English, we should say it was nasty weather. Being Americans, we only sigh, "Dog-days!"

But they must have their uses. Everything is good for something. Let us see. First, they are excellent for the complexion, — a matter in which, whatever we say, we are all more or less interested. Bile-y, jaundice-y, sallow faces clear up into healthy tints. Freckles "try out." Pale cheeks tone up into delicate rose, and dry, parched, burning flushes tone down into a cool liquescence. All the pores are opened, and the whole system languishes in a pleasant helplessness, — pleasant, if one has been so industrious all the year, that he can afford to be idle during the dog-days.

Dog-days are good as tests. Their effect on curl-paper curls is melancholy, but natural curls laugh them to scorn, and riot in twistings. Just so the temper. Placidity at Christmas often dissolves in an August fog. What you thought was amiability, may have been only oxygen. If you wish to see whether your temper can really bear the strains of wind and weather, just remember how you went to the middle drawer in your bureau for gloves, fearing you should be too late for the cars, — how the drawer would only come out by hitches, first one side, then the other, and then not at all, — how you thrust in your hand up to the wrist, and could just not reach the gloves with the end of your longest finger, while your wrist was tortured by the sharp edge of the drawer on one side, and the sharp edge of the bureau on the other. Did you possess your soul in patience? When a shower came suddenly pelting down through the fog, and you tried to close the window, and got yourself wet through for your pains, and could n't move it an inch for all your shaking and pounding, — when you put your cake into the oven to "scald," and forgot it, till a sense of something burning travelled up-stairs to stir your passivity, and you rushed down to snatch too late a burnt and blackened loaf, — did you remember the first three words of Psalm xxxvii. 1?

In the calm complacency of a balmy spring morning, we look down with a serene smile on the follies of the world. We assume a calm and quiet superiority, give it a pat on the shoulder, and say condescendingly: "Yes, you will do very well; a little rickety in the joints; a slight softening of the brain; but very passable for your age." Nothing can exceed our amiability when we are pleased and comfortable; but, floundering up to the neck in July, keeping the breath of life in us only by becoming amphibious and web-footed, bound to the earth by no stronger tie than ice-cream and sherbet, wooing to our side every passing breeze, as if it were the king's daughter, — then, a beflowered, bespangled, bedizened abomination, coming betwixt the wind and our nobility, is the spear of Ithuriel to our smiling good-nature, and we feel disposed to pluck its eyes out with a demoniac delight.

Dog-days can teach us trust. You have heard of the woman who, when her horse ran away, trusted to Providence till the breeching broke. A good deal of our trust is like this. We call it Providence, but it is really breeching. Not that breeching is not a very good thing to trust to as far as it goes, — only it is not Providence. So, when our doors can be bolted and locked, we lie down in peace and sleep; but when they won't go to, and we have to make a precarious arrangement of sticks and strings, we feel more keenly that we awake because the Lord sustained us.

Dog-days are friendly to greenness. Our lawns smile with velvet verdure. The fog goes into the soil and wraps it around the tender strawberry-vines that we have just transplanted, and in soft swaddling-clothes the young fruit will slumber till next summer's sun shall bid it leap to luxuriant life, and a creamy and glorious death. Down into the heart of the sweet-pea, deep into the cup of the morning-glory, steals the kindly mist, and a pink and purple splendor crowns the rising day. The cucumber swells its prickly sides and snuffs the coming vinegar. The squash-vine creeps along the ground, sorrowing that it has all turned to pumpkin, but catching from the moist air a deeper shade for the generous gold of its blossom. Ah! in the laboratories of nature the fog has a great work to do.

But the best of dog-days is their departing. Grateful for the returning sun, and the sweet west wind, we see a deeper blue in the sky, and a denser green in the fields. The tall corn waves with statelier grace. The trees are fretted with fresh-springing life. The earth is a billowy and dimpled emerald, tender and smiling; but the sky — the ever-shifting sky — is an absorbing and perpetual joy. Sometimes its sweep of stainless blue is glorious afar. Then the dying sun leaves its legacy in the west, of saffron, and amber, and pale green. Now the clouds sail out white and warm into the central blue, or rush exultant, whirling up masses of lavender rimmed with gold, or shoot from the glowing west spires of rosy pink, or mount to the zenith in delicate shells of pearl, or lie above the horizon, passionate, breathless, and ruddy, floating in seas of fire. Anon they group themselves in all fantastic shapes. A turreted castle sends down shafts of light from its pearly gates. The mailed warrior places his lance in rest, and a couchant lion

> "Scatters across the *sunset* air
> The golden radiance of his hair."

"Cloud-land! Gorgeous land!" All grace of outline, all wealth of color, are gathered there. Tropical splendor and heavenly purity kiss each other, and the angels of God can almost be seen ascending and descending.

So gazing with thankful and reverent hearts, we remember that great city, the holy Jerusalem, descending out of heaven from God, whose light is like unto a stone most precious, for the glory of God doth lighten it, and the Lamb is the light thereof.

So, when the west winds come laden with fragrance from the prairies, and the cold winds blow down from the north, bearing us healing and strength, we will gird up our loins anew to the work of the Lord of light, contented to rest and stand in our lot at the end of the days.

SUMMER GONE.

HOPE, a throb, a memory, — that is summer in these high latitudes. The sorrow of her going follows close upon the jubilee of her welcome. The lips that part to ring out her joyous "Salve!" close, white and tremulous, upon her thrice-wailed "Vale!" The same breath wafts her Hail! and Farewell!

But be not cast down, O my soul, nor disquieted within me. The beauty that budded with the opening spring is not yet gone, though autumn winds wail, and chilly nights prophesy dismantled woods. That beauty will be a joy forever. No time, no tyranny, can rob me of the riches which the summer brought. Wherever I go, my walls will be always spread with pictures that no artist can rival. I have but to close my eyes, and the hill-sides whiten with Innocence once more. I see again that strange, hardy, frail-looking thing, with the soft, delicate, liquescent "feel" of a month-old baby, yet popping up its audacious little head close upon the heels of the departing snow. Defiant of frost, and storm, and wind, — tremulous, mellow, luscious, — yet pure, and sweet, and saintly, it meets me everywhere. On the very top of the hill, where the moss is only a brown crisp in the sun, a little clump of white richness sways in the scented air. I put aside the dark, dense grass under the apple-trees, down in the moist meadow-land, and it laughs up at me with joyful recognition. Sometimes it takes on a deep, creamy white; sometimes it is tinted with pearl, or lavender, or pale violet deepening at the border into a purple rim, but always spreading purest white around the centre, where, in a silver palace, the baby-prince lies sleeping, crowned with a golden crown.

Here in my quiet room, with the curtains drawn and the red fire-light setting the room aglow, I gather them once more into a swelling wave of white loveliness, circled with deep green moss or the velvet purple of pansies. I do not mingle them with other flowers, because I think it destroys their individuality. They look crowded, and uncomfortable, and overlooked, but by themselves they are the sweetest, happiest little company in the world. Their talk is of the floating of angel-garments, the fathomless depths of mothers' hearts, and the souls of little children that went to God unstained. They are like fluttering memories of some sweet, strange sphere long ago, and they murmur rare melodies if you but lean your heart close and listen.

Side by side with the Innocence, the purple violet rears its slender stalk and bends its swan-like neck with a queenly condescension. This is an age of iconoclasm. Dr. Livingstone has demolished the traditional valor of the lion, and Alphonse Karr makes count that the violet is one of the most ambitious and aspiring of flowers. I marvel, however, that it needed Alphonse Karr to show us that the violet is not modest. I do not mean that it is *im*-modest, — far from it; but only that in looking at it, modesty, humility, do not seem to be its prevailing or most striking characteristic. I should rather say it was stateliness. Innocence, which has never been accused of modesty, to my knowledge, conveys to me a far stronger impression of it. It springs up with a light, unconscious air, as if it were not thinking about itself at all, — peeping and peering into the great mystery of sun and sky with an investigating, curious, wide-awake, humble look, as if quite aware that it was an ignorant little good-for-nothing of a flower, but would thankfully receive information from any quarter on any subject. Not so the violet. It does not shoot up like the Innocence with any definite object in view, but rather glides deliberately, having decided that, on the whole, it may as well dispose of its elegant leisure in that as in any way, and once up, it seems to take a comprehensive survey of the universe, concludes that nothing therein is especially worthy of its august notice, and then — does n't *droop* its head as many people persist in asserting, though, if you will but notice its two winged petals expanding laterally from a certain inward prompting, and the two upper ones flung spiritedly back and curling over, you will see that there is no more droop to it than there is to a — I don't think of anything to finish my comparison with, so it must hang as it is — and then, as I was saying, it bows its stately head as a queen might to a chimney-sweeper who raises his tattered cap as she rides past.

It is true that the violet does seem to delight in obscure, out-of-the-way places, "half hidden from the eye"; for though it does sometimes appear in the open fields, it is shorn of its glory, — a pale, spiritless thing, afraid of its own shadow, and clinging so timorously to its mother Earth that you can hardly find it in your heart to stoop and pluck it thence; while, if you chance to leap over an old, tumbling-down stone wall, you will see hosts of them rising on the other side, with tall, juicy stems, and deep, rich petals, fearless and free. In my stroll one morning, I came unexpectedly upon a bed of — I beg everybody's pardon, but I never heard it called anything but "skunk-cabbage." It was in a low, swampy ravine, and I was turning vigorously away, when the sudden twinkling of flowers beckoned me forward. Treading very insecurely among the mushy hassocks, and thrusting aside the uncouth leaves, lo! a great army of violets rollicking under their odorous shade, in all the intensest passionate purple of tropical luxuriance. Strange! They love the sunshine. It nourishes their strength and beauty. Grace of form and wealth of color come to them from its beneficence. They would fade and die without it, yet they hide from it. They pale in it. They keep their richest bloom for dark shady dells, where sunshine only drips through lazily. It is no coquettish teasing, but a real shyness, — not the petty tyranny of a weak vanity, but the shrinking of a true heart, a-tremble in the grasp of its own passion, hiding involuntarily, in silence and solitude, from the love that has evoked it, and that glows, and flames, and dazzles in lambent embrace around it, yet in voiceless solitude feeding on nothing else than the fullness of that very love, drinking in its sweetness, softening down the brilliancy to its own white lustre, and filling up the springs of life with an inward and unspeakable joy.

Still the place does not make, though it often does reveal, the man. Let many a one who passed in his cottage for a quiet, sensible, well-bred person be raised suddenly to a palace; or, since, notwithstanding the newspapers, we don't have palaces in this country, say a five-story, brown-stone front, with income to match, and his innate vulgarity crops out. Or *vice versa*, the large-hearted, hospitable master of the aforesaid palace, falsely so called, coming suddenly to grief and a pittance per annum, is transformed into a fretful, jealous, petty, and pitiful soul. The springs of his generosity lay in his pocket, not in his heart. His bank-book, not himself, made him a gentleman. A little, fat, good-natured woman is not majestic because she dons a diadem; nor was Godiva ever more a queen than when she swept down the turret stairs, clad only in her loveliness. Circumstances may veil or obscure for a time, but cannot prematurely hide, —

> "May cloud the soul with shadows, but may not
> Its glory blot."

Pomp disguises meanness, and poverty shackles grandeur; but sooner or later the heaven-lit flame plays around the brow of the true prince, and reveals his royal birth, — whether it be Havelok in the fisherman's hut, or Iulus in burning Troy.

So, little violets, wax pallid on the hill-tops if you will, and shun the garish day. Nestle under the shadows of gray old rocks, and verdurous, large-leaved plantain. I know you. In your self-sought solitude your royal blood reveals itself. By your amethystine locks, by your incense-breathing vestments, by your princely port and mien, I read your noble lineage. Your kinghood stands confessed.

Still with closed eyes I see thousands of dandelions gleaming sun-ward. All the highways and by-ways are mottled with their generous gold. Dust cannot choke them, — can scarcely dim their shining. On the warmest summer noon, place one against your cheek, and it has the same cool, soft, fresh feeling. Little curling tendrils nestle lovingly among the petals. Young eyes untrained to minute uses are attracted by their unblinking gaze, and dimpled hands pluck at them with ill-aimed eagerness, and hold them in unsteady grasp. Obedient to "waxen touches," their satin-smooth stems curl in involute circles, adorning child-brows with fantastic grace, or link themselves in tremulous chains about little white throats. When their yellow disks round into nebulous globes of pale, feathery softness, merry hands clutch them afresh, and puckered red lips and puffed cheeks send out as strong a blast as juvenile lungs can furnish; because, you know, if you can blow away the down with one breath, it is a sure sign that "your mother wants you"! Happy little lion-toothed flower, with nothing of the lion but the tooth, and with neither the power nor the wish to use that, — woven in with the unconscious sunshine of childhood, with the memories of continual spring-time, and innocence, and blissful ignorance, — the blessing of all baby-life be upon you! Never cease to fringe the dusty road with sunlit smiles, — a boon and a benediction alike to the infant and to him that is an hundred years old.

All the knolls are studded with star-flower, but you must go down on your knees to see it, and gather with painful care, one by one, if you gather at all. I should let them be. They look pretty where they are, sprinkling the somewhat bare slope with a crystalline delicacy, and their leaves have an elaborate, clear-cut beauty; but they do not make much figure in a — must I say bouquet? O that the old English nosegay might be reinstated in its ancient dignity, and the stiff, foreign, unmeaning, wrong-meaning, cut-and-dried bouquet ousted from the throne where its presence is a perpetual usurpation! It never will be naturalized, and never is natural. We don't know how to pronounce it; we don't know how to spell it; and if any of us do happen to know, the printer does n't, and he goes straightway and spells it wrong. Let us have the nosegay, brimful of rich old meanings, replete with associations; and reserve the foreign word for the only thing which it fits, — namely, the round, stiff, hard, close-clipped, tightly-squeezed horror that comes from the hand of professional hot-house men, — solid enough to knock you down, if thrown with sufficient force, and so ugly that you are divided between pity for the poor little things forced into such unnatural contiguity, — divested of the green which relieved their brilliancy from the charge of gaudiness, and laced into a hideous regularity, — and wrath against the man who has so misused his eyes and hands as not to be able to construct any better imitation of the viny, sprayey, feathery, airy, slender, pendulous lightness, winsomeness, and grace of nature than that artificial knob. Call that a bouquet, and with merciful hands rend off its swaddling-clothes, tone down its rainbow hues with all tints of green, from the pale tenderness that springs up on the sunny, sheltered side of the wood, to the deep luxuriance that lurks in its unsunned and unstirred heart, and make of it twenty nosegays, whose colors shall delight, and whose odors shall intoxicate; in which nosegays, as I have said, my little star-flowers would make but a poor figure. Their stems are so short, that it is difficult to group them with any effect. Their tiny faces become quite hidden behind their sturdier kinsmen. But in their own haunts they lead a quiet, noiseless life, which well repays an observer.

If you went away to foreign lands when you were young, and your knowledge of buttercups is only a childish memory hanging on an obscure peg in some inner chamber of your brain, you will very likely — as I did — look upon the first star-flowers that you see as juvenile buttercups, — just as children invariably suppose mice to be young rats, and rats adult mice; and though you have a vague, half-unconscious feeling that those wee things do not quite satisfy your sense of buttercups, you will attribute it to the difference between the eyes of childhood and of maturity. "Years dwarf so many of our grandeurs, and dim so many of our lustres!" you will begin to sigh. Don't. It 's no such thing. Wait awhile, just a few days, and — whence comes that shining? Is it the twinkling of a star-flower? Not a bit. It is the gleam of knightly armor. It is the glitter of burnished gold. There stands the real buttercup. Does it pale before your young memories? Your memories were, on the contrary, but a faint herald of its splendor. Yon little star-flowers might grow for an age of summers, and never attain such form and comeliness. Their timid, delicate, soft sweetness is to the defiant, glittering, manly beauty of buttercups

"As moonlight unto sunlight, or as water unto wine."

Think of the merry scorn with which, hiding in the grass, they must have heard your mournful musing on their short-comings; and the sturdy self-confidence with which they bided their time. No wonder they toss their heads a little saucily as you pass by, and nod and wink at each other in ill-concealed jubilee over your undisguised admiration. One idea concerning them, however, I have discarded, — my belief in the traditional test-ship. In fact, now that I am grown up and out of harm's way, I will say that I never did believe it. I think if you hold a buttercup under *anybody's* chin, near enough, his chin will turn yellow, and it is no sign at all that he is inordinately fond of butter. But when I was little, I was not as bold as an eagle, and often waived, or at least suppressed, my convictions, for the sake of being let alone. Moreover, I was conscious of a weakness in the direction indicated by the buttercups; so I suffered them to be brought in confirmation strong, and only smiled in outward acquiescence, but with inward protest. I am older now, and have learned that Paul's order of sequence is best, — first pure, *then* peaceable; that peace is not so precious a treasure as to be bought at any price; that, in fact, it is a curse

> "Till the Might with the Right and the Truth shall be."

> "Better war, loud war by land and by sea,
> War with a thousand battles and shaking a hundred thrones."

Nay, so fearful, so deceitful, so dangerous, is the calm of a stagnant peace, — a peace that scums the pool in whose foul depths lurk dishonesty and oppression and cowardice, lust and rapine and murder, — that I rather feel

> "'T is better to have fought and lost,
> Than never to have fought at all."

The anemones have passed into my heart forever. Their reign was short, but they bloomed in beautiful profusion. Almost before I thought of looking for them, I found a bed two feet in diameter on the edge of a swamp where I least expected to find any. I don't suppose a soul had seen them but myself,—a soul in a mortal body, I mean,— for I dare say many of the shining ones had looked upon them, and lent perhaps some ray of whiteness to their pure garments ; but there in their sheltered nook, unseen, unknown, they revelled in sunny, exuberant life, every petal springing back with joyous eagerness. It seemed as if they gladdened at sight of me, — as if they wanted mortal eyes to be refreshed with a glimpse of their overflowing happiness ; and the breath of the soft morning — a June morning dropped into the stormy lap of March — that gently swayed their pliant stems, seemed to intone a song of peace on earth, good-will toward men. I think they are very human. Perhaps it is because we associate them with those

"Who in their youthful beauty died."

Gazing upon their exquisite tracery, we see once more the tender grace that grew so deep into our hearts, but vanished from our aching eyes long ago, — the first little baby-daughter, who learned only in heaven how dear she was on earth ; the sister who fell asleep while the dew of life was yet fresh on her brow ; the young wife who glided out of the arms, strong but utterly powerless, that would have held her forever ; the young mother who could have found her angel-garments scarcely whiter than the robes of her sacred motherhood ; — so, with tear-dimmed eyes, we press the anemones to our white lips, and bless the memories, sad, yet passing sweet, which they awaken. There is a pain which is better and higher and holier than pleasure. Since that morning I have seen many anemones springing up from their warm bed of dry leaves which the fall frosts scattered and the fall winds spread, and where, safe as in the hollow of His hand who metes out heaven with a span, they slept to a glad resurrection; but none came so near me, none so took hold of my strength, as the stray little cluster that awoke first in the embrace of the sun on the edge of that Dismal Swamp.

Faerily, daintily, bewilderingly, they troop around me now, — the sun-born, gala-robed sprites. Advancing, receding, bending their lithe forms in airy dances to the music of vocal brooks, rocking dreamily back and forth in the lap of soft south gales, surging into my soul, but mocking my yearning arms, now pensive with dewy tears, now laughing softly to little, cooling showers, now drunken with the fierce wine of the northwest wind, they circle me in elfin ring. The wild columbine flings out his scarlet banner, but gives me no Open Sesame to the vaults where his nectared honey is stored. The gay geranium leaps from his lurking-place beneath the maple-trees, but I have no charm to bid him stay. The tawny wood-lily glares sylvan rage, and will not be soothed by my caresses, but his white-bosomed sister in the valley pours crisp coolness from her crystal cups, and whispers of rippling waters, and golden sunshine glinting down the greenwood. The spiræas rise before me still and stately; the vervain shoots at me his slender arrows, purple-tipped; the honeysuckle vies with the sweet-brier to flood me with heavenly odors; and the garden of God is my perpetual heritage.

"We all do fade as a leaf." The sad voice whispers through my soul, and a shiver creeps over from the churchyard. "How does a leaf fade?" It is a deeper, richer, stronger voice, with a ring and an echo in it, and the shiver levels into peace. I go out upon the October hills and question the Genii of the woods. "How does a leaf fade?" Grandly, magnificently, imperially, so that the glory of its coming is eclipsed by the glory of its departing; — thus the forests make answer to-day. The tender bud of April opens its bosom to the wooing sun. From the soft airs of May and the clear sky of June it gathers greenness and strength. Through all the summer its manifold lips are opened to every passing breeze, and great draughts of health course through its delicate veins, and meander down to the sturdy bark, the busy sap, the tiny flower, and the maturing fruit, bearing life to the present, and treasuring up promise for the future.

Then its work is done, and it goes to its burial, — not mournfully, not reluctantly, but joyously, as to a festival. Its grave-clothes wear no funereal look. It robes itself in splendor. Solomon in all his glory was not arrayed like one of these First there is a flash of crimson in the low lands, then a glimmer of yellow on the hill-side, then, rushing on, exultant, reckless, rioting in color, grove vies with grove, till the woods are all aflame. Here the sunlight streams through the pale gold tresses of the maple, serene and spiritual, like the aureole of a saint; there it lingers in bold dalliance with the dusky orange of the walnut. The fierce heart of the tropics beats in the blood-red branches that surge against deep solemn walls of cypress and juniper. Yonder, a sober, but not sombre, russet tones down the flaunting vermilion. The intense glow of scarlet struggles for supremacy with the quiet sedateness of brown, and the numberless tints of year-long green come in everywhere to enliven, and soothe, and subdue, and harmonize. So the leaf fades, — brilliant, gorgeous, gay, rejoicing, — as a bride adorned for her husband, as a king goes to his coronation.

But the frosts come whiter and whiter. The nights grow longer and longer. Ice glitters in the morning light, and the clouds shiver with snow. The forests lose their flush. The hectic dies into sere. The little leaf can no longer breathe the strength-giving air, nor feel juicy life stirring in its veins. Fainter and fainter grows its hold upon the protecting tree. A strong wind comes and loosens its last clasp, and bears it tenderly to earth. A whirl, an eddy, a rustle, and all is over, — no, not all, its work is not yet done. It sinks upon the protecting earth, and, Antæus-like, gathers strength from the touch, and begins a new life. It joins hands with myriads of its mates, and takes up again its work of benevolence. No longer sensitive itself to frosts and snows, it wraps in its warm bosom the frail little anemones, and the delicate spring beauties, that can scarcely bide the rigors of our pitiless winters, and, nestling close in that fond embrace, they sleep securely till the spring sun wakens them to the smile of blue skies, and the song of dancing brooks. Deeper into the earth go the happy leaves, mingling with the moist soil, drinking the gentle dews, cradling a thousand tender lives in theirs, and springing again in new forms, — an eternal cycle of life and death "forever spent, renewed forever."

We all do fade as a leaf. Change, thank God, is the essence of life. "Passing away" is written on all things; and passing away is passing on from strength to strength, from glory to glory. Spring has its growth, summer its fruitage, and autumn its festive in-gathering. The spring of eager preparation waxes into the summer of noble work; mellowing, in its turn, into the serene autumn, the golden-brown haze of October, when the soul may robe itself in jubilant drapery, awaiting the welcome command, "Come up higher," where mortality shall be swallowed up in life.

Why, then, should autumn tinge our thoughts with sadness? We fade as the leaf, and the leaf fades only to revivify. Though it fall, it shall rise again. Does the bud fear to become a blossom, or the blossom shudder as it swells into fruit, and shall the redeemed weep that they must become glorified? Strange inconsistency. We faint with the burden and heat of the day. We bow down under the crosses that are laid upon our shoulders. We are bruised and torn by the snares and pitfalls which beset our way, and into which our unwary feet often fall. We are famished, and foot-sore, and travel-stained from our long journey, and yet we are saddened by tokens that we shall pass away from all these. Away from sin and sorrow, from temptation and fall, from disappointment and weary waiting, and a fearful looking for of evil, to purity and holiness, and the full fruition of every hope, — bliss which eye hath not seen, nor ear heard, nor heart conceived, — to a world whence all that made this dreary is forever banished, and where all that made this delightful is forever renewed and increased, — a world where the activities and energies of the soul shall have full scope, and love and recognition wait upon its steps forever.

Let him alone fear who does not fade as the leaf, — him whose sources are not in God, and who does not draw his life thence, — him whose spring is gathering no strength, whose summer is maturing no fruit, and whose autumn shall have no vintage. Is not this the real sorrow of us all? not a dread of change, but a secret consciousness of wasted power, — of disloyalty to God as the supreme object of our love and service? Yet even here the fading leaf brings hope. Our future is always before us. The past is fixed. No tears can wash away its facts. Let us waste no vain regrets upon it, but, from the wisdom which its very mistakes and sins have bequeathed us, start afresh on the race. Though yesterday we were weak, and selfish, and indolent, let us to-day, at this moment, begin to be strong, and brave, and helpful, and just, and generous, and considerate, and tender, and truthful, and pure, and patient, and forgiving. "Now" is a glorious word. "Henceforth" is always within our grasp.

> "O, my soul, look not behind thee. Thou hast work to do at last:
> Let the brave toil of the Present overarch the crumbling Past.
> Build thy great acts high and higher, build them in the conquered sod,
> Where thy weakness first fell bleeding, where thy first prayer rose to God."

WINTER.

SOME people have a way, you probably, my dear friend, among the rest, of going into the country. When the sun beats down hot and hard, when the earth gets parched and arid, when the fields have gone gray for lack of rain, and all the little leaves have curled themselves to dry death, and the heavens are dull, shimmering brass, and the roads are ankle-deep in fine, powdery dust, and the thirsty oxen stand panting in muddy bogs that were once pools of water, and the grasshopper has become a burden, and your desire for everything but ice-water has failed, — then you wrap the chairs in brown holland, turn the pictures to the wall, carry the silver down to the bank, pack a dry-goods store into your trunk, leave your cool, blinded, shaded city house with its large rooms, its ample baths, and its attentive well-trained servants, join a great dusty caravan, in a little dusty, cindery, clamorous railroad-car, whirl off to a great hotel, pitch about among hackmen and porters till you have ensconced yourself somewhere in a seven by nine room, with the clatter of a legion of feet continually above, around, beneath, and the prolonged torture of a gong forever summoning you to the two-hundredth part of a table, when you unpack your dry goods, and put on your flounces and laces and diamonds, and sit up straight, graceful, and lady-like, and dine off the same meats, and hop with the same hoppers, and talk with the same talkers, and see the same faces, and do the same things you did yesterday at home; and this you call "going into the country."

Or, being a notch lower in the social scale, and not able to contribute your part to the splendors of a great establishment, you go to a little village, eight miles away, and engage a southwest chamber in a house set on a hill, without blinds, with a tank of rain-water directly under the window, a feather bed, wooden chairs, and red-flowered carpet, where you slumber out your mornings, simmer out your middays, and fight out your nights with mosquitos,—to all of which I have not the slightest objection—if you like it. It is change, and that, after all, is what you need; and even if you have jumped out of the frying-pan into the fire, it will serve to make the frying-pan more tolerable when you go back to it. But if, having done this, you consider that you have been in the country, that you have exhausted nature, and that there is nothing new under the sun for you to see, why, I must take the liberty of respectfully informing you that you don't know what you are talking about.

Nature is very exacting. You may make her a flying visit in August, and she will indeed unfold to you the beauties of dew-drop, and thunder-shower, and evening sky; but to know her in her wholeness, to drink in full measure the "life that hides in marsh and wold," to conceive all her magnificent possibilities, you must woo her from New Year to New Year, and every New Year shall bring you a fairer picture, a richer blessing, than the last.

You shall look out upon a gray, frozen earth, and a gray, chilling sky. The trees stretch forth naked branches imploringly. The air pinches and pierces you, a homesick desolation clasps around your shivering, shrinking heart, and then God works a miracle. The windows of heaven are opened, and there comes forth a blessing. The gray sky unlocks her treasures, and softness and whiteness and warmth and beauty float gently down upon the evil and the good. Through all the long night, while you sleep, the work goes noiselessly on. Earth puts off her earthliness, and when the morning comes she stands before you in the white robes of a saint. The sun hallows her with baptismal touch, and she is glorified. There is no longer on her pure brow anything common or unclean. The Lord God hath wrapped her about with light as with a garment. His Divine charity hath covered the multitude of her sins, and there is no scar or stain, no "mark of her shame," no "seal of her sorrow." The far-off hills swell their white purity against the pure blue of the heaven. The sheeted splendor of the fields sparkles back a thousand suns for one. The trees lose their nakedness and misery and desolation, and every slenderest twig is clothed upon with glory. All the roofs are blanketed with snow; all the fences are bordered. Every gate-post is statuesque; every wood-pile is a marble quarry. Harshest outlines are softened. Instead of angles, and ruggedness, and squalor, there are billowy, fleecy undulations. Nothing so rough, so common, so ugly, but it has been transfigured into newness of life. Everywhere the earth has received beauty for ashes, the oil of joy for mourning, the garment of praise for the spirit of heaviness. Without sound of hammer or axe, without the grating of saw or the click of chisel, prose has been sculptured into poetry. The actual has put on the silver veil of the ideal.

Will you look more closely? A part is, if possible, more beautiful than the whole. On the Brobdignagian texture of your coat-sleeve, one wandering snow-flake has alighted. Gaze at it or ever it vanishes from your sight. What a world of symmetry it discloses to you! What an airy, fairy, crystalline splendor! What delicate spires of feathery light shoot out from the centre with tiny fringes, and rosy, radiating bars. In all your life you have never seen anything more beautiful, more perfect, and you may stand "breast-high" in just such marvellous radiance. Talk of robbers' caves and magic lamps! No Eastern imagination, rioting in "barbaric pearl and gold," can eclipse the magnificence in which you live and move and have your being.

And there is a deeper beauty than this. It is not only that the snow makes fair what was good before, but it is a messenger of love from heaven, bearing glad tidings of great joy. Hope for the future comes down to the earth in every tiny snow-flake. Underneath, as they span the hill-side, and lie lightly piled in the valleys, the earth-spirits and fairies are ceaselessly working out their multifold plans. The grasses hold high carnival safe under their crystal roof. The roses and lilies keep holiday. The snow-drops and hyacinths, and the pink-lipped May-flower, wait as they that watch for the morning. The life that stirs beneath thrills to the life that stirs above. The spring sun will mount higher and higher in the heavens; the sweet snow will sink down into the arms of the violets, and, at the word of the Lord, the earth shall come up once more as a bride adorned for her husband.

And "as the rain cometh down, and the snow from heaven, and returneth not thither, but watereth the earth, and maketh it bring forth and bud, that it may give seed to the sower, and bread to the eater: so shall my word be that goeth forth out of my mouth: it shall not return unto me void, but it shall accomplish that which I please, and it shall prosper in the thing whereto I sent it."

Native land! Fatherland! Is not the word spoken to you?

O beautiful, sorrowful country! for whom the watch-fires of freedom have been lighted on the hills, for whom the flames of sin lurk ghastly and baleful in the valleys; baptized in the blood of heroes; consecrated with the prayers of saints; precious for your priceless past, unspeakably precious for the hope of your mighty future; for all your faults never more dear than now; rocked with the throes of a mortal agony; shuddering through all your frame in the slimy coil of a monster; your young strength once prostrated, but now alive, your young life poisoned, but renewed again; — shall not "Nature bring you solace"? Already the winter is past, the flowers appear on the earth; the time of the singing of birds is come, and the voice of the turtle is heard in our land. Shall we not therein read a sweet prophecy? The winter of your discontent shall be made glorious summer. You too shall go out with joy, and be led forth with peace; the mountains and the hills shall break forth before you into singing, and all the trees of the field shall clap their hands. Instead of the thorn shall come up the fir-tree; and instead of the brier shall come up the myrtle-tree; and it shall be to the Lord for a name, for an everlasting sign that shall not be cut off.

There is nothing like winter in the country to develop one's resources and mature one's graces. Blocked up by the snow, driven in by the cold, forced to subside on yourself, it stands you in hand to be agreeable and inventive. If your chimney smokes, if your door-knobs loosen and come off, if the rain soaks through the walls, if the roof is leaky, if holes yawn in your shoes, if your skate-straps are too short, or your sled-runner is broken, or your note-paper gives out, you cannot jump upon the train and go to the next market-town to be set up again. You must either wait for the spring or a January thaw, or you must contrive some remedy yourself.

If your Decembers have been genially warmed into Junes without any intervention of your own, and you find yourself suddenly in a remote village, under the necessity of attending to your fire or going without it, you will often be in that state of mind which will demand for solace a constant repetition of the old saw, "It takes a fool to make a fire." If, worse than this, you suffer yourself to be lured by siren songs of warmth, convenience, and economy from the good old groves of hickory and oak and maple, to try, like the old man in the spelling-book, what virtue there is in stones, you will have an admirable opportunity to cultivate the virtue of patience; and patience is a divine virtue. When we look at God, holy, just, and kind, and at his creatures, rebelling against him, cruel to each other, polluting themselves with sin, and violating his wise laws, — and yet see how he ever makes his sun to rise upon evil and good, and sends his rain upon just and unjust, continuing to all alike the blessings of seed-time and harvest, — we are ready to say, that patience is of all virtues the most divine.

But it is not only divine, it is pre-eminently a human virtue. It works into daily life a sweetness, a balm, a peacemaker, a consoler. It makes home happy. It shames vice. It disarms ill-temper. It goes far to make society tolerable. So important is this virtue esteemed in the Divine economy, that a large part of our experience is framed so as to strengthen and improve it. We deviate into no path in which we cannot find some circumstance fitted to exercise and perfect it. It is, however, a solemn thought, that opportunities wasted are burdens upon our shoulders. If we grow wicked by a means which was intended and adapted to make us grow good, we grow a great deal more wicked than we should if such means had never been tried. A blessing turned into a curse is doubly accursed. Sorrows that do not soften, harden. Life is full of little occasions which may help us to grow in grace, and may show us whether we have already done so; but neglected or perverted, they deteriorate us.

But these reflections will not occur to you in the early stages of your experience with coal fires. On the contrary, you will begin your work full of hope. Careful to follow to the letter every direction, you are confident of success. With half-contemptuous commiseration, you think of some cousin, or aunt, or friend, who has been appalled by the lions in the way, and turned back. You consider it a weakness of character, rather to be pitied than severely censured. You are charitable to all the world as you lay in your kindlings with mathematical regularity, — paper, shavings, splinters, sticks. You apply the match. A furious roar springs up. You start back, half delighted, half scared. What if the chimney should catch fire. You hustle on the coal to smother the exceeding fierceness. The roar crackles, sputters, stifles, and dies the death. There is a pause. You open the door, and peep in furtively. A faint suggestion of flame and half a dozen sparks. A second peep, — the flames have disappeared, the sparks are diminished. A third peep, — black as Acheron. The kindlings burned charmingly, but they mistook means and ends, and kindled nothing. You put in your hand and pry under the surface to see if anything is happening. Whew! Who could imagine that anything so cold-looking could be so hot, or anything so hard-looking could be so smutty. But your black fingers will be atoned for to-morrow by three little white blisters at this moment developing under the blackness. Then you turn a crank and let the coal down, that you may take it out and try again. Down it comes crashing into the drawer. You proceed to pull it out. Something sticks. You pull and twist, and jerk it in vain. You are forced to thrust your arm into the stove, and take the coal out by handfuls. Then you begin anew, and after consuming wood enough to heat your room all day, and time enough for as much more wood to grow, you succeed in getting a fire. But you do not mind the time spent, for you say to yourself, "It is once for all." You flatter yourself that, once kindled, it will stay kindled. You are doomed to disappointment. You open the stove door in the morning, and it is "upper, nether, and surrounding darkness," abysmal and dismal. You have to go through the whole process again, with the added misery of ashes, which come, puff! into your face, a suffocating cloud, on the slightest provocation. You plod on for a few days. Every separate member of your family has a separate opinion, and proffers different advice,—all entirely conjectural and at random. You have recourse to the experienced. One advises you to shake down the old coal before you put on new, which you do vigorously, and shake all the life out of it. Then you are told that you must keep it quiet, and you tread gingerly, laying in the fresh coal carefully with your own shuddering fingers, — as if you were planning a surprise, and designed to get it on fire before it should know what was going on; but the enemy is on the alert, and baffles you with a "masterly inactivity." Meanwhile there comes a cold snap, and the thermometer plumps down to zero. Everything about the house freezes solid, and breaks. Friends who call are pressed to have a shawl, and stop to dinner. Bores are blandly invited, in rural formula, to "take off their coats and make themselves at home." Then somebody tells you that the grate must be poked to keep it clear. Submissive, you procure a sharp stick in lieu of a poker, which, if it exists at all, is not visible to the naked eye, and, like any Parsee, prone on the floor you fall before your swart divinity, and ram the stick up under the grate. Down come the ashes in a gray shower over your sleeve and hand, covering every thread of the one, and filling every pore of the other; but desperately you poke on, till light shines through. Sometimes your exertions will be rewarded with success, and sometimes not; and this is your great perplexity. Everything is inconsequent. Similar causes produce dissimilar effects. You do, with slavish imitation, everything you are told to do, till it is shown to be useless, when you give rein to genius and branch off on your own account, in brilliant and startling combinations. You shake down, and refrain from shaking. You poke, and you cease poking. You set the wood on fire before you put the coal on, and you put the coal on before you set the wood on fire. You open everything openable, and shut everything shutable, and you never have any inkling of what will happen next. There is no satisfaction when the fire does burn, for it does not burn logically. It is an isolated fact. It does not establish anything, nor indicate anything. No palpable reason exists why it should burn this time, that did not apply with equal force to the four previous occasions when it declined burning. It ought to have gone out last night as well as the night before. It is like the proverbial woman, —

"If she will, she will, you may depend on 't,
If she won't, she won't, and there 's an end on 't."

It is like an over sensitive man, — one of those disagreeable unfortunates who are known as "touchy." If you don't treat it "just so," it is all over with you. Its dignity is as ticklish as that of our self-made aristocrats. You can scarcely look askance at it without disturbing its equilibrium. You begin to believe that some "imp of the perverse" has taken up his abode there, — that some unhoused gnome is wreaking vengeance on you for his violated home, — and you fall gradually into a pugnacious mood. You get a way of looking at the coal as a malicious and skilful foe, and it is a drawn battle between you. You grow, as the country-people say, "short-waisted." The harder it is for the coal to kindle, the easier it becomes for you. Your conversation turns growly and snappish. You wax dangerous. Every inquiry as to your progress, you get to look on as an insult. You suffer under a sense of injury. You feel as if the world and the elements were in league against you. You are sensitive of the slightest allusion to fire. You have a kind of pyrophobia.

No, my dear friend, this will never do. This is all wrong. This is the abuse, not the use, of coal. You are wasting anthracitic opportunities for the development of the noble virtue of patience. Be not deceived. Martyrdom comes to but few. Few are called to resist unto blood, striving against sin, but many are called to resist unto inconvenience, restraint, and self-denial; and an incessant pin-pricking is perhaps harder to bear than the swift-descending axe, or the cranch of a lion's jaws; and if you come off conqueror from the one, you shall in no wise lose your reward, any more than he who calmly faced the horrors of the other. If the trials to which you are subjected seem all the more severe from being so petty, remember that Rome was not built in a day, and it is the constant, hourly chipping at the quarried marble that is to rear in the end — the temple of God. Remember, too, that however out of joint the matter may be, fretting will never mend it. It is bad to feel your hands growing rough, but it is worse to let your temper keep them company. It ruffles you to hear of stoves that run like a clock from November to May, but it won't smooth you to go into a rage about it. It is aggravating to have the fire burn up and warm the room delightfully, just as the stove-man, for whom you have sent to see what the trouble is, arrives, and then to have it go out as soon as he does; but what are you going to do about it? If you are wise, you will remember that you are only sharing the common lot. You will think of the great multitudes who have passed through the same tribulations, and the summer atmosphere of a thousand happy homes will beckon you on to victory. You will think, with admiring gratitude, of the man who first discovered the combustibility and practicability of coal. You will see the fatherliness of your Creator in making this wonderful provision for you, — how the giant trees leaped heavenward at his bidding, and at his bidding died, to become in death your ministers. What wisdom and benevolence wrought this marvellous work in the great laboratories of the earth, — scooped out those vast basins, piled therein these inexhaustible treasures, more precious than gold, and so took care for your comfort ages and ages before you were born! And will you be petulant because you carry your end of the pole a little awkwardly at first? Shall your orisons and vespers be the prayer of the daughters of the horse-leech? Will you not be content that the Lord has given you the coal, but will you require him to work a miracle to kindle it? For you fail only because you are fighting against the nature of things, and here is another lesson which you may learn, — the inexorableness of law. Not a spark of fire, not the smallest black coal-speck on your finger, but follows the law of its being, fixed, relentless. Your intentions are good. You mean to do right. But you are transgressing some chemical or mechanical law, and the dumb coal, which has never deviated from rectitude, is a swift witness against you. With nature, ignorance is no excuse for transgression. The penalty follows surely on the heels of sin. Is the law of matter more fixed than the law of mind? If you cannot sin against lifeless stones with impunity, can you sin against a living soul, and go scot free? If a right purpose will not kindle a fire without wise means, will it fashion a son's mind? Do you not see how the blind may mislead the blind, with utmost tenderness, to destruction?

Above all things, do not "give up." Rise to the height of the emergency. Be master of yourself. Get the victory over impatience; so from the stubborn coal shall you express the oil of joy, and find beauty for ashes. Every lambent tongue of flame shall be to you a messenger from heaven, and every day a pentecost. With a heart open to all pure influences, you shall feel the full force of those sweet words, "Lo! I am with you always," and with eyes which the Lord hath opened, you shall see "sermons in stones, and good in everything."

My Flower-Bed.

 AM oppressed with a feeling that, whatever welcome my literary venture may meet, I have not, so far as appears in this volume, made a brilliant figure at gardening. I think, therefore, that I ought, in justice to myself, to relate the distinguished success which attended my second attempt. An ordinary person would have been deterred, by so unparalleled a series of disasters as befell me, from ever making another endeavor; but, for my part, I like always to retire with the honors of war. Therefore, when February crept away to the north, and March came breezing up from the south, I went to a seed-shop and laid in an entire new supply of garden ammunition.

I began on a smaller scale than before. My ambition had not forgotten the severe lesson of the past spring. I relinquished the idea of supplying our table with vegetables, and concluded to devote myself solely to the department of the beautiful. Instead of taking the whole estate for a centre, and radiating over the land in all directions, I pre-empted from the waste of corn and potato-field a corner, ill-suited, indeed, to my desires and my dreams, but better suited, I was forced to admit, to my inexperience.

A square piece of ground, of moderate size, was the basis of my flower-bed. The circle described by the drapery of a fashionably-dressed woman, standing in the centre, would be scarcely more than contained in it. But does not "Rare Ben" say,

> "In small proportions we just beauties see,
> And in small measure life may perfect be"?

It is amazing to note the interest one has in the weather when one becomes a landed proprietor. It is equally amazing to note the coquetry of the weather when it becomes aware of that fact. With the poets, who have hitherto kept me in Almanacs, April is a sunny, showery month; May melts into music and warmth; and June is redolent of roses. But, O Messrs. Poets, you have dealt treacherously with me, or else you have studied nature from Chaucer, not from herself. What did April do for me this year? Blocked me up with a snow-storm. What did May do? Took advantage of her name, entrapped my coal-stove into the garret, then benumbed my fingers, and turned me into a Nova-Scotian. Nay, Winter, lingering, was not content to chill the lap of May, but even set young June a-shivering. The fact is, Spring as a figure of speech, and the prolific mother of figures of speech, is a good thing; but Spring as an institution ought to be abolished. It has outlived its usefulness. It exists only in tradition; and that tradition is productive of much mischief. Our idea of it, derived chiefly from Old English ballads, bloom with violets, and soft airs, and gay, green woods, and frisking lambs, and golden-throated birds. In pursuance of which idea we get up May parties on May-day, and lay aside our flannels, and make ourselves miserable, let alone the rheumatisms and neuralgias and consumptions whose highway we make straight. The blue skies, the *greening* fields, and the poets aforesaid, conspire to draw us into the trap of raw east wind and chill vapor, from which we return with a stiff neck, a sore throat, and settled melancholy. All this would be obviated if there could only be a general understanding that Winter in this latitude lasts till the Fourth of July, and comes out in spots all summer. We should then know what to depend upon, and the "fair, mild days" would be so many extra blessings thrown in. That is, the rule would be comfortable, and the exceptions delicious; whereas now, the rule is indifferent, and the exceptions intolerable.

Understand, I am not finding fault with the weather, but with our nomenclature. A north-east snow-storm is a splendid thing in its way; only don't let us pretend it is a shower of apple-blossoms, and act accordingly.

But snowy April days and murky May mornings may cultivate the divine virtue of patience, if nothing else, I said to myself, as I stood, flower-seeds in hand, awaiting the Spring. It came at last, or something which a vivid imagination, combined with the Almanac, could call Spring, and I levelled and spaded and raked and squared my flower-bed that was to be. On the north and south I bounded it with a line of currant-bushes; on the east and west with rose-bushes. At least, that is what they were given to me for. In my heart I believed they were mere dry sticks, but I stuck them into the ground, nothing wavering. Between the rose-sticks I set out pansy-roots, and between the currant-sticks dahlias, and whatever is the plural of gladiolus. Next came the question of internal arrangement. You may let a forest grow wild. Nature will group her trees, and drape herself with all manner of creeping mosses, and trailing berries, and sprightly undergrowth, and you shall find nothing amiss. But snip off a little bit of nature, and the case is altered. A garden that you can put in your pocket is nothing if it is not regular. You must have a design, a diagram. I thought of a star. But a star is a great deal easier to think of than it is to make. If you don't believe me, I should just like to have you try it. I have a vague impression that, if I could have got hold of a treatise on geometry, I could have constructed one on scientific principles, and without much trouble; but I don't suppose there was such a treatise within twenty miles; so I had to bungle with sticks and strings. However, the result was an obvious star. To be sure, the rays were rather "peakéd," and not exactly equidistant at the tips, and somewhat skewy at the centre; but it was a very good star for all that. At least, it was more like a star than like anything else. *Aut aster aut nullus!* When I had completed that, I put outside, between the five rays, two gladiolus roots, a pansy, a circle of candy-tuft, and one of lily of the valley. Then there was nothing to do but wait. That is the beauty of being a farmer. A little provision, a few days of hard work, and the sweet sunshine, the soft rain, the silent dews, finish the business. You do not have to hammer away day after day at your lapstone or your sermon. Nature herself puts a shoulder to your wheel, and rolls you on to fortune.

Or would, if it were not for the weeds and chickens and bugs and worms, that choke and peck and gnaw her gifts. A few innocent flower-seeds will make a remarkable number of enemies; and it is surprising to see how much faster weeds grow than flowers. I wonder what the result would be if one should set out Roman wormwood, and tend it carefully. Would it forget it was a weed, fancy itself a flower, and become shy and sensitive? As it is, I have found it one of the most enterprising of individuals. Before I thought of looking for one of my roots or seeds, up came this Italian bitterness, speedily followed by the pig-plant, close on whose heels tramped the smart-weed; and in a twinkling appeared witch-grass, and sorrel, and a mob of little villanous vines, sprawling things, which had never been planted, and never came to anything, and had no business there, and only gave the trouble of pulling them up.

But one warm night something happened. The evening had given no sign; but under the silent moon a host of tiny warriors, clad in Lincoln-green, unsheathed their sharp swords, cleft the brown earth, and when the day dawned there they were marshalled in knightly array, along the white lines of my star.

I know few sensations more exquisitely satisfactory than the springing up of something which your own hands have planted. You have, perhaps, — if you are a neophyte, — had a lurking fear lest you might not detect the difference between the gold and the gilt, have suffered weeds to flourish, lest, in exterminating them, you might ignorantly exterminate something that was not a weed; but when the gold comes, you recognize its gleam. A flower is no more like a weed than if it had never grown. It is pale, and soft, and juicy, and tender. The first lifting of its little face above ground is a mute appeal to your sympathy and protection. It would seem as if a harsh look might crush out its little life. But the weed is a saucy, reckless, pushing, defiant, strong-nerved Yankee fellow. "Here I am," he says, tossing his plumes six inches in the air before you knew he was "anywhere round." "Here I am. You did n't invite me, but I came, and brought all my brothers, and we are going to have a rollicking time of it. You can give me the cut direct. O yes. But I am not sensitive. I am not overladen with modesty. It is a very nice place, this world, with its sun and dew and rain, and I don't intend to be driven out of it in a hurry."

I suppose every school-girl and school-boy in New England has compared weeds and flowers to the vices and virtues of the human heart; but you don't take in the full force of the illustration till you have a flower-bed of your own, and actually see the thing going on with your own eyes. Then you make the illustration yourself, and it seems just as fresh to you as if nobody had ever made it before. This living A. M. 5865, or thereabouts, is very damaging to originality, — when it comes to writing. Adam and Seth and Noah had the advantage of us there. Yet as a matter of living, sun and sky, the broad-bosomed earth and the "many-sounding sea," are newly created for every baby born.

When the world was young, the seed spake

vaguely of the soul. But Paul, standing in the newly-risen light, saw what his fathers could not see, and in unfolding leaf-buds "learned the language of another world." Ever since, the spring's resurrection is a revelation. You lay in the brown soil the ugly, shrivelled, insensate seed, but under that unseemly garb the soul of the plant keeps watch and ward. Life is there, hidden in death. When the fulness of time is come, life shall burst its cerements, and mount upward to its fate, which is sunshine and greenness, and glowing beauty, and matchless grace.

So this mortal puts on immortality.

I suppose a professional gardener might laugh at my flowers. In fact, people do laugh at them who are not professional gardeners, — for that matter, who are no gardeners at all, any more than I am. They think I don't see them, but I do. They think that I think a nasturtion is something very smart, and grand, and *recherché*. I don't think anything of the sort. I know as well as they that it is a very common, kitchen-gardeny kind of a flower. So are poppies. So are mallows. So are lady's-delights, and bachelor's-buttons, and pinks, and candy-tuft, and asters, and coreopsis, and roses; but what of that? Is a thing less beautiful because it is common? The blue sky bends over the evil and the good. The earth unfolds her loveliness to the just and to the unjust. No title-deeds can convey possession of the splendor or the beauty of the universe. No landed proprietor can fence in from lowliest eyes the swell of the hills, or the scoop of the valleys. No gas agent can turn off the bland breezes from those who cannot pay monthly bills therefor. No "merchant prince" can adorn his garden with the grandeur and the glory of the sea; while the clod-hopper may snatch strength from its sturdy waves, be rocked on its heaving bosom, and sink to rest with its surging lullaby. God makes his most beautiful things most common, and shall we baffle his benevolence, spurning his blessings? A nasturtion "common," — with the heart of a thousand sunsets shrined in its kingly cup, or the shadow of royal robes empurpling its "wine-dark depths"! Common! shall I see less beauty in its golden gleam because that gleam has flashed brightness into myriads of hearts? Shall it not rather have an added value? The hard hand of labor, the wasted hand of disease, the restless hand of poverty, have found peace, and hope, and joy, in training these happy flowers to grasp the sunshine, and the glad gifts of the dew. I see on the folds of their scarlet banners the message of good-will to weary souls. Peering into those glowing caverns, the radiant eyes of little children laugh up to meet my own, and the touch of their tender stems is like the touch of groping baby-fingers. Shine on, O fairest messengers of

Heaven, and show to all waiting, toiling, disheartened, sorrowful lives

> "A strange and mystic story, —
> How moistened earthly dust can wear celestial glory."

My horticultural cook-book affirms that nasturtions make a toothsome salad. I dare say. I should like to see the individual, however, who should venture to go browsing among *my* nasturtions. I am strongly opposed to Judge Lynch's code of laws, but I think I should give that person something harder to swallow than the worst salad he ever saw.

A poppy is not like a nasturtion, but it has a fringed, downy beauty all its own. A mystical, crimson languor suffuses the encircling air. Vivid blood-red plashes stain its white bloom. Sometimes, in riotous revelling, it hurls back the arrows of the sun, till my dazzled eyes can hardly endure the brightness. But pale or purple, it is enchanted ground. Under that fretted greenery, the poets lie asleep. Hence, far hence, all ye profaner ones! It is not for you to tread the courts of the poppy-crowned god.

> "Amid the bowels of the earth full steepe,
> And low, where dawning day doth never peepe,
> His dwelling is; there Tethys his wet bed
> Doth ever wash, and Cynthia still doth steepe
> In silver deaw his ever-drouping hed,
> And, more, to lulle him in his slumber soft,
> A trickling stream from high rock tumbling downe,
> And ever-drizzling raine upon the loft,
> Mixt with a murmuring winde, much like the sowne
> Of swarming bees, did cast him in a swoone.

> ..... Carelesse Quiet lyes
> Wrapt in eternal silence farre from enimyes."

So dream the poets. But common people must keep wide awake.

When my nasturtions came, they came with a leap. They hardly seemed to have grown. They lifted their broad, shield-shaped leaves, one morning, and looked as if they had always been there. But poppies tread delicately. There is just a faint line of green, shading the brown soil. For several days it hardly increases. While you are looking at it, you persuade yourself that nothing will come of it, — there is nothing there. But when you are away, you have a very strong impression that something *was* there, and will " turn up." While you are waiting further developments, the " heated term " comes, — dry, dusty, suffocating, blinding, baking, brazen days, — when the sun unmasks his batteries, and opens upon you a steady fire. If you want to know how your flowers feel about it, go out doors barefoot, and the grass that was so tender, and cool, and dewy in the morning, is curled and crisp, and burns your feet. (Nevertheless, it is an excellent thing to go barefoot. Civilization is shocked at the mention of such a thing, but Hygiene rejoices. Physicians tell us that one of the reasons why our Irish population are so healthy, notwithstanding their untidy, irregular habits, is that they go barefoot so much. Certainly the stout frames and brawny arms of Irishwomen are an argument very difficult to overcome; while, in point of comfort, nothing can surpass untrammelled, unhampered feet. It stands to reason. Shoes are bad heat-conductors. They confine and accumulate it; but without shoes and stockings it passes off as fast as it is generated, and not only the feet, but the whole body preserves a pleasant equilibrium. People have only to lay aside their prejudices, and their shoes and stockings will follow, till the summer custom and costume will be as fashionable as Nahant.)

Presently the parched look of your flower-bed excites your compassion. You water it, but the water runs off the hardened surface. You loosen the soil around, and it is a little better. In the height of the drought the spout of the water-pot generally comes off, and then your strong plants are drenched with torrents, and for your weak ones you take a colander, which is not "handy." So you blunder on, day after day, wishing and watching for a thunder-shower or a tin-pedler. By and by a cloud in the west appears, rises, spreads, and descends in beautiful and doubly welcome abundance. The dear, benevolent rain! the kindly, saving rain! It is better than a thousand watering-pots with the spouts all on. It does the business so easily and so thoroughly. You hardly wonder that

"Danae in a golden tower,
Where no love was, loved a shower."

You are in love with it yourself, and as you stand silent, with smiling eyes, a silver voice begins to well murmurously around you; but just here the rumbling of wheels breaks in upon the murmurous voice, and a tin-pedler's cart heaves in sight, blossoming with watering-pots. Of course you don't buy any, but it is "trying" to see them just then. After this, however, you are in no doubt about the poppies. They leap up into rounded vigor and obviousness, and the whole garden is quickened.

I made a mistake in my planting. I put the seeds in too close, and the centre of my star is a perfect tangle. The nasturtions had the advantage at the start, and they keep it; but they are smothered in their own sweetness, and the gilias and geraniums fairly gasp for breath. A sly little portulacca hides under an overgrown marigold, and cheated me for a long while. I thought several mornings that he had buds on the brink of opening, and sometimes I surely thought I saw buds that had opened and closed again, but that was all, so I set a watch, and one day, just at noon, (when I never visited him, and he thought himself safe from intrusion,) I spied a flash of Solferino, rushed upon him, and caught him in the very act. Since then he has hung out his colors quite openly. My rose sticks have prospered beyond measure. I counted fourteen buds on one of them. My gladiolus is the delight of my eyes,

> "A daughter of the gods, divinely tall,
> And most divinely fair."

My dahlias came up headlong, four or five in a group. Somebody said I must break off all but one. I rejected the Vandalism with horror. I am a Republican and a Christian, and I would have no Turks about that could "bear no brother near the throne." It shows the weakness of moral principle, that three weeks after, when I saw a bed of dahlias twice as tall as mine, I came home and broke mine off with a bleeding heart. Then they shot up, and a high wind came and twisted and prostrated them remorselessly. Then I hunted up stakes and poles, worn-out broom-sticks and dislocated hoe-handles, and tied up my dahlias, till my flower-bed might have been taken for a returned regiment from a thirty years' war. Presently one of them "made an effort," and put out a flower, which looked like an agitated turnip. I never saw such a dismal, washed-out rag in my life. I do not think much of dahlias. They are coarse and unsightly in leaf, and forlorn in flower, and ten to one don't flower at all. I call them nothing more than an aristocratic potato. Several of my most beautiful and promising plants I pulled up, because Halicarnassus said they were weeds. I did not believe it then, and the more I think of it, the more I do not believe it still. It was envy on his part, not weeds on mine. Still I pulled them up. So I lost the cream of my garden; but the skim-milk that is left is ravishingly toothsome.

Dear old Earth, "tickle her with a hoe, and she laughs with a harvest." I scarcely so much as tickled her. I did but lay the tip of an unskilful finger in one of her dimples, and she broke forth before me into singing. Dear old mother of us all, what you were before Adam I cannot conceive, for with the burden of his curse upon you, you are more lovely than tongue can tell, or pencil portray, and in your bosom lie hidden treasures of strength, and honor, and glory, and blessing for him who is wise to woo. The earth is full of the riches of the Lord.

Lights among the Shadows of our Civil War.

CIVIL war is a very terrible thing. Because it is terrible, however, it is not necessarily unmitigated. Even civil war may have its sunny side. In the lessons which it teaches, in the sophistry which it demolishes, in the manhood which it develops, we may find wherewithal to stay our souls, when they are ready to faint with the burden and heat of this our bloody day.

And first, what has become of the people who were always talking about the bravery, and virtue, and hardihood, and patriotism of our forèfathers, in sad contrast with the pusillanimity, effeminacy, and selfishness of us their descendants? You have doubtless heard persons, in and out of the newspapers, linger regretfully over the olden devotion to country, sacrifice for a righteous cause, perseverance under difficulties, undaunted bravery in battle, and unshaken fortitude in defeat. They would speak with reproachful admiration of the mothers who beat their pewter spoons into bullets, and sent their sons to battle; and then would come a sigh over these degenerate days, when men think of nothing but to buy and sell, and get gain. I must say that I, for one, never did believe one word of it. I think we are just as good as our fathers, and always have been; but you cannot expect martial virtues in a time of peace, any more than you can expect the triumphs of peace in time of war. I always believed that, if we ever had an opportunity, we should show ourselves just as brave, just as loyal, just as self-sacrificing, as our fathers. Did they fight in a holier cause than we? Did they exercise a greater forbearance than we, so long as forbearance seemed of any avail; and when forbearance would have been weakness, did they spring to arms with greater alacrity? Were they more prodigal of men and money? Have we not brought forward our precious things, laying upon the altar even our prejudices, and preferences, and opinions? Did our fathers fight for liberty? So do we. Was their struggle less for themselves than for the future? So is ours. *We* should have got along very comfortably, letting things go on as they have been going on. That we might leave to the future a righteous legacy, that we might maintain in its integrity a righteous cause, we have sacrificed, not only without a murmur, but with a spontaneous and irresistible enthusiasm, our lives, our fortunes, and our sacred honor, — lives just as dear, honor just as sensitive, and fortunes ten times as large as those of our fathers. The "Spirit of '76" was noble; but its nobleness is rivalled and its power excelled by the Spirit of '61. The blood of our fathers does not run thin, and pale, and sordid in our veins. The canker of peace has not taken out our life. Let us have done forever with this exaltation of the past by the depreciation of the present. The world is richer now in all the elements of greatness than it ever was before, and this is the Golden Age.

Another compensation is the love of country springing up in every Northern heart. It is to many of us a new revelation. Love is always creative. When a man begins to love a woman, a new world unfolds itself to him in this. With every baby born, the mother is herself new-born. When the soul awakens first to the love of Christ, old things pass away and all things become new. We have been living quietly under our vines and fig-trees. We have, as the mood took us, boasted of our government, or rebuked its administrators; but, excepting those who have been abroad, we never had much feeling about it one way or the other. We have been protected by it. We have known it only by its constant benefactions, to which we were born, among which we were nurtured, and of which we were scarcely more conscious than of the air we breathed. It is not that we were especially ungrateful. We did not love, because there was nothing in particular to love. The President is too short-lived to create a strong attachment. Yesterday he was nobody, and to-morrow he will relapse into nobody. The Senate and House are not peculiarly adapted to call forth emotions of tenderness, nor can one in ordinary times wax wildly enthusiastic over a piece of bunting. We have no royal family to define, concentrate, and vivify our loyalty, so it had to go wandering for an object, or lie sleeping in the bottom of our hearts; but the besom of war has swept away all difficulties. We want no princely blood now. A new love is born, strong, vigorous, full grown in a day. I don't know that we could tell precisely what it is that we love now, but it is something! The love is there. It swells and surges in our hearts, it overflows our eyes. It quivers on every lip. It melts down all barriers of sect, and race, and religion, and politics. It throbs wherever a banner floats. It thrills out in brave, tender words, in manly deeds, in public generosities and private heroisms. Selfishness and worldliness shrivel and scorch in its white heat, and the hearts of the nation are welded together as the heart of one man. We are, as we never were before, a united North. Sectional animosities, local hatreds, petty rivalries, are swallowed up in the deep sea of universal brotherhood, whose boundless extent is only made more imposing by the few traitors who are scudding under bare poles over its heaving bosom.

There is another benefit which we would not inaugurate civil war to procure, but in which, since civil war has, unsought, reared his horrid front among us, we will rejoice and be glad. We shall, for a little while at least, be spared our Fourth of July literature and oratory. A certain map of the United States, probably in possession of a good many of my readers, is adorned along its borders with various pictures, one of which is labelled, "An American showing to the Sovereigns of Europe the Progress of his Country." The American stands, with one foot on a bale of goods, pointing to the steamers, and railroads, and schoolhouses, and churches which mark the landscape. Louis Philippe, Victoria, Nicholas, and a mob of kings and queens, with their crowns on, crowd around him, mouths agape, eyes staring, in the most intense and unroyal astonishment and admiration. In England the picture might be relished as a clever caricature, but it comes too near the simple truth for home consumption. It is evidently sketched in perfect good faith, and is the expression of a widely prevalent, not to say universal feeling. We have thought, and have not always exercised the modesty which good taste would have suggested in saying, that

"We are the greatest nation
In all creation."

No more of this for the present. We will, indeed, congratulate each other in a quiet way, among "own folks," (as I have just been doing,) on our many virtues and large capabilities, but we will let our spread eagle go into winter quarters. We will cease for a while to ring changes on our "unexampled prosperity," our "commerce whitening every sea with its sails," our ingenuity filling the world with its products, our cities springing up in the wilderness, our great and glorious Republic, laying hold of the Atlantic with one hand and the Pacific with the other, crowning her head with the snows of the Northern mountains and dipping her feet in the waters of the Southern seas. We have had a sudden check in our career. A strong man armed is at the door. He of our own blood which did eat of our bread has lifted up his heel against us. A brother has struck at his brother, — nay, worse than this, a man has done treason to his mother. The children whom she has nourished and brought up tenderly have rebelled against her, and striven to cut down her strength. Shame and confusion of face belongs to us all, — that our soil should have nourished, our skies spanned, and our airs sustained a treachery so base. We are in a death-grapple with our own, and a most glorious victory, as surely as the most disastrous defeat, bears in its bosom the seeds of a profound sorrow.

Again, the cost of war is undoubtedly very

great. It takes a good deal of money to begin with, and a good deal more to carry it on, and not a little to repair damages after it is over. We must contract an immense debt, but our children must look to it. It will be their business as well as ours. The vices, the virtues, and the debts of the fathers are visited upon the children. The head of Louis the Sixteenth paid for the vices and extravagances and ambitions of the Grand Monarch. This seems an ungracious consolation, but it is not. Our children have the best of the bargain at that. We take the laboring oar. The price is the price of liberty, not of slavery. If we dance for them the dance of death, they may consider themselves well off if they only have to pay the piper. But what is this debt? Where does our government get the money which it borrows? It is loaned by our moneyed institutions, our banks, our citizens. And who are the government? Citizens likewise. The people are the sovereigns. Through their servants, chosen from and by themselves, they borrow of themselves twenty or a hundred millions of dollars, and there is a great debt; but the money is owned as well as owed by themselves. In their capacity as government, they owe money to themselves as people, — which is, to say the least, a rather Pickwickian kind of debt.

Moreover, a debt may be the measure of credit. If a man owes a thousand dollars, it shows that his property is valued at that sum. The fabulous millions of the national debt of England is the lowest sum at which her pecuniary value to the people of England can be rated. This strong, pecuniary, direct interest which the people of England have in the perpetuity of their government, is one of the bulwarks of her Constitution. It helps to keep her throne steady when the Continental thrones are tottering. Her debt is her life insurance. The moment her government is destroyed, the debt is wiped out, and the people, her creditors, are bankrupt. So Louis Napoleon, wise in his generation, issues his coupons, and, by making the people the creditors of his dynasty, makes them at the same time its firmest supporters.

And what becomes of the money borrowed by the government? It levies and maintains and transports armies, and provides the munitions of war. That is, it goes to the farmers, and butchers, and bakers, and grocers, and tailors, and shipbuilders, and gun-makers, — straight into the pockets of the people, just where it came from. It is not sunk in the ocean or burned in the fire, as a general thing. It is still in circulation, which is the only thing money is good for.

And how is this debt to be paid, or upheld? By taxation.

Our people have generally been opposed to direct taxation, both politically and socially. If we want a Sunday-school library, instead of tak ing the money and buying it out and out, we get up a fair. That is, we put ourselves to a world of trouble to make a wilderness of knick-knacks, that we don't want, and nobody else wants, and then we pay twenty-five or fifty cents for the supreme satisfaction of going to look at them, and three or four dollars more for the pleasure of littering our houses with them, and *then* we are ready to buy our library, — at five times the cost, and five thousand times the trouble, that it would have been had each one quietly handed in his share of money in the first place. But each one won't quietly hand in his share, — he won't hand it in at all, and so you must have a fair, or go without. You may demonstrate twenty times over that one course of action is better than another to accomplish a certain end, but so long as people will not adopt the one, and will adopt the other, what are you going to do?

In respect of taxation, the case is somewhat similar. We pay duties on silk, and tea, and wine, and so, ordinarily, make shift to support the government without finding it out. But now the times are becoming extraordinary, the newspapers are discussing taxation, the bankers shut up their vaults demanding taxation, financiers announce the imperative necessity of taxation; now, therefore, let us have done with this child's play. So long as a question of finance is but a question of here or there, we may *prestidigitate* it harmlessly enough, making the burden disappear under any pleasant name we choose, or even turning it into a profit as featly as Mr. Hermann disposes of his pocket-handkerchiefs, or makes a gold dollar out of a walnut; but when it is a question of here or nowhere, it is time to demand new measures and new men. Is it supposed that this people is an infant, to be frightened by a bugbear? Are we a nation of pagans, to fall down before a molten image? Do we shrine our gold and silver in the Holy of holies, with a "These be thy gods, O Israel"? True, a forced taxation, a taxation levied by alien publicans and sinners, an arbitrary, unjust, and unrighteous taxation, we refused to submit to eighty years ago, and we have never repented of it since; but a tax self-imposed, imposed to insure the triumph of a cause in which all our religion, all our loyalty, all our honor, everything that is dear and sacred in life, nay, even life itself, is concerned, should be hailed, and shall be hailed, with acclamation.

It is true there are not wanting those who will bemoan their heavy taxes, who seem already to see their golden eagles putting forth the wings which they are to take to themselves, in order to fly away; but surely they are in a frightful minority, and if they are not, they ought to be. What in the world is money good for, if not for just such a crisis as this? It brings comfort and luxury, and, to a certain extent, position and power; but what are all these to a man whose only child, the heir of his house and heart, lies mangled and dying on his own door-stone? Ah that he prizes his money for, then, is the prompt and efficient aid it may bring to the suffering boy. Does he clench his hands and knit his brow, and mourn over the expense which the surgeon's visit will bring, and lament that the best mattress in the house will be thoroughly spoiled, and wonder if molasses and water won't do instead of French brandy? Yet this is what we should do to groan over taxes. Taxes! Every dollar that goes to put down the rebellion is stamped with the image and superscription of the Lord. Surely, surely, never was money so honored, so glorified, — so sanctified! A handful of gold-dust, a scrap of rag-paper, moistened with our tears, hallowed by our prayers, may help to usher in the millennial year! Shall we grumble? Shall we not rather lay our hand on our mouth, and our mouth in the dust, and cry, "Will God in very deed condescend to accept so poor a gift?" Behold heaven and the heaven of heavens cannot contain Him. All the beasts of the forests are his, and the cattle upon a thousand hills, — nay, the earth and they that dwell therein; yet he is willing to associate us with himself. As the father suffers the tiny fingers of his son to grasp the basket, that his little heart may please itself by fancying that he helps carry it, and to learn early the luxury of doing good, so God, who spake, and the work of creation was done, who commanded, and the heavens, and the earth, and all the host of them stood fast, permits us to have part in the great work of the world's redemption. And we are to draw back, are we? We will clutch a little longer this gold, which of itself is as worthless as the stones of the street, — which depends for its value solely upon what it can do for us! We shall make a poor investment. We can, if we will, convert our money into stocks, and bonds, and mortgages, and houses, and carpets, and pictures, and laces, and plate, and jewels, and we shall receive such consideration as these will bring — when they are bought at the price of manhood; and then we shall die, and they will all fall off from us, and we shall go, naked souls, into the next world, and who knoweth what shall be after us under the sun? Or, on the other hand, we can turn our money into loyalty, and trust, and truth, and righteousness, and self-sacrifice, and magnanimity, and devotion to a just cause, succor to the oppressed, strength to the weak, a cup of cold water to Christ's little ones, and so our money becomes for ever and ever a part of ourselves, and the best and noblest part, from which neither death, nor life, nor angels, nor principalities, nor powers, nor things present, nor things to come, nor height, nor depth, nor any other creature, shall be able to separate us. O, blessed are the rich in these days, who can bring all the firstlings of their flock for a sin-offering, and blessed are the poor also, for a pair of turtle-doves and two young pigeons may be brought forward unto the Lord, — nay, even the tenth part of an ephah of fine flour shall be an acceptable sacrifice. Do we know that such an opportunity will ever again be offered us to speed our wealth or our poverty on an errand so grand? Let us not sink below the height of the hour.

And there is another advantage which, at such a juncture as this, taxation has above any and every other method of raising a revenue. They are round-about. This is direct. The disadvantage of a fair compared with a contribution-box is, that in the first you get something which is reckoned an equivalent for your money, — only a flimsy toy, perhaps, but enough to conduct away all the pleasure which the downright giving of your money would have afforded you. You have neither the satisfaction which arises from a "good bargain," nor the glow which springs from the gratification of a benevolent desire. So, even if we could put down the rebellion by increasing our imports, and by other expedients of that nature, we should miss half the pleasure. We should not be giving money to our country, we should only be paying high prices for tea and sugar. But with direct taxation, there would be no go-between to rob us of all our benevolences by way of commission. We should stand face to face with the object of our solicitude and our love. Our hearts would be warmed with the consciousness of actual contact. We should take joyfully the spoiling of our goods, knowing that we were laying up treasure in heaven and on earth for ourselves and for the generations that are to come.

If there are any with whom these considerations have no weight, they may perhaps be influenced by another. When the nation shall give its voice in favor of taxation, there is no appeal. You will have to pay "whether or no." It is only whether you will do it jubilantly, reckoning your cross a crown, counting it all joy to spend and be spent in so glorious a service, and so receive back full measure, pressed down, shaken together, and running over; or whether you will hold back, have your will throttled, your pride humbled, your purse taken by storm, and get nothing for it after all.

It remains now for the people to choose what they will do. We can rise up against taxation, save our money, and lose the day, lose the age, lose God's grand "occasion floating by," but what shall be the profit of such a gain?

"Gained — the infamy of fame,
Gained — a dastard's deathless name,
Gained — eternity of shame.

"Lost — desert of manly worth,
Lost — the right we had by birth,
Lost — lost — freedom for the earth."

And it may be that such a withholding will tend to the very poverty that we dread, the only poverty which our ignoble souls can feel. "Wisdom for a man's self," says Bacon, "is, in many branches thereof, a depraved thing. But that which is specially to be noted is, that those which are lovers of themselves without a rival are many times unfortunate; and whereas they have all their time sacrificed to themselves, they become in the end themselves sacrificed to the inconstancy of fortune, whose wings they thought by their self-wisdom to have pinioned."

God forbid that any of us should, standing, as we soon shall stand, on the outer shore of the world, and looking back over the land which was before us a land of golden promise, see it lying behind us a land of bitterness and desolation, — or hear ringing in our ears a voice whose tones would find its echo in our own hearts: "Mene, Mene, Tekel, Upharsin; God hath numbered thy kingdom, and finished it. Thou art weighed in the balance, and art found wanting."

I see but one reasonable objection to taxation. "We are willing," it may be said, "to pour out of our abundance, or of our poverty, to put down the rebellion; but we are not willing even to dole out our hard earnings to enrich dishonest contractors, lazy clerks, grasping sutlers, wasteful Congress-men, and the whole herd of unclean beasts who feed and fatten at the public crib." But, in the first place, if we are going to wait for purity before we provide power, we may as well give up the whole matter at once. To suppose that the affairs of this nation are to be carried on exclusively by disinterested patriots, is to obey Dogberry's injunction. We may lament the fact, but it must be recognized as a fact, and as a fact disposed of, that the world's work is, to a remarkable extent, done with unwashen hands. It would be a happy day for us that should see every man in our government a Washington, but that day will not dawn this many a year, and meanwhile we must do the best we can with our present material. Wheresoever the carcass is, there will the eagles be gathered together. Wherever there is a possibility of making money without work, or wherever salary is disproportioned to service, there the morally lame and the mentally lazy will inevitably congregate. Wherever a business is so vast that it must be managed by large masses of men, with the certainty of ample remuneration, with the contingency of perquisites, and a presumption of impunity for unfaithfulness arising from the very magnitude of the work and the numbers of the workmen, there, until the Millennium, the great unemployed, the unlucky, the indolent, the shabby-genteel, the unpractical and the impracticable, Micawberian waiters for something to turn up, lounging heirs for whom the dead men's shoes are not yet emptied, and unjust stewards who cannot dig, and are ashamed to beg, but not afraid to steal, will come up like a young lion from the swellings of Jordan, with a paw for every contract, and a claw for every clerkship, and a maw for every salary that can be wrenched or wormed from the powers that be. Even with the best intentions on the part of those with whom rests the responsibility of selection, some ring-streaked and spotted souls will smuggle in and usurp the places that should be filled only by those who walk in white. Some dishonest and unscrupulous men will rankle there, — men who will feather their own nests, though they pluck their country callow to effect it; — harpies that pollute what they cannot devour, — gulping down the very shew-bread from off the altar, — thrusting their three-pronged flesh-hooks even into the caldrons of sacrifice, and bringing thereby shame and dismay upon the whole priesthood.

But let it not be forgotten that this is not a feature peculiar to our government. Such men there are in all countries, a disgrace to their age and to the race. Probably our ratio of rascalage is not larger than that of any other nation. Probably it is smaller than most. This is surely consolatory.

Then, also, it is evident that, after all, it is comparatively a small part of our whole expenditure that is thus wasted, though it be large in the aggregate; and in the working of all machinery, allowance must be made for friction.

Thus much, supposing the evil to be irremediable; but it is not. There is no need of all this venality. The fact of its past existence furnishes no argument for its present toleration, and if the imminence of taxation shall rouse us to overthrow it, taxation will be no disguised blessing. It is the duty of every man to file a complaint, and to follow it up. Let him insist that taxation and purification and retrenchment go hand in hand. When the burden of taxation falls, let the burden of corruption be lifted, and all burden will disappear. To which end, let every man take hold of the lever that is nearest to himself. If each one would turn on the water of cleansing to his own corner of this Augean stable, the work would soon be done; and then, and meanwhile, let him keep a sharp lookout — careful, but not captious, watchful, not meddlesome — that the republic receive no harm at the hands of those servants whom his voice and vote helped to set in place. Tocqueville sagaciously says, that a government will be just as corrupt as the nation will let it be; and if the virtuous sit quietly at home, and do nothing to preserve or reinstate public purity, they are unfaithful to their duty, and have no right to cast the first stone.

As for retrenchment, there are a thousand ways in which something can be accomplished, and much will be accomplished if we all put our shoulders to the wheel. Congress is showing a faint disposition to walk in the right path, and the disposition should by all means be encouraged and strengthened. The franking system exhibits symptoms of rapid demise, and there are many other systems there, that will bear looking into, or rather that will not bear it, and should die the death. The office hours of the clerks of the departments are, I think, from nine A. M. to three P. M., and it is a current saying among them, that it is nine till it is ten, and three as soon as it becomes two; and if the public work can be done with such application, or want of application, surely it can be done by fewer clerks, who should render exact service; and the lowest salaries are $1,200 per annum. The salaries of our higher officers are not munificent compared with the income of the chief magistrates of other nations. The President is perhaps the worst-paid man in the country, but no salary can be any offset to the discharge of duties so onerous, and though I do not think "we the people" have the shadow of a right to ask for its reduction, yet, in this crisis, it seems to me that the moral effect of a voluntary surrender of a part of it would be so happy, that it would amply compensate for any self-denial that might be involved. (I trust, however, that Mr. Lincoln will not feel constrained by my suggestion. I certainly shall not press it to his embarrassment.) But what we want is that President, Congress, and people shall give a long pull, a strong pull, and a pull altogether, to get the nation out of the mire. Money, muscle, and mind are what we need. The muscle is on hand, the mind and money are in the country, and must be produced. Money we can all, or almost all, save and spare; for nearly all of us live a great way above our necessities. I do not advocate penuriousness. I believe in fine houses, fine estates, fine horses, and fine clothes. I believe it is everybody's duty to live as elegantly as he can, consistently with his other duties. I do not believe that the God who made everything beautiful in its season, who painted the wing of the butterfly, and burnished the scales of the beetle, and tinted the petals of the rose, and pencilled the outlines of the hills, who ordered his temple to be made of the purest gold, the most precious wood, the most costly scarlet, — who everywhere delights to lavish magnificence, — I cannot believe that this Being is most appropriately worshipped by an uncouth and homespun life. But there is a beauty higher than speaks to the eye, and beautiful things are beautiful only as they converge to this higher beauty. There is nothing more stately than the human body, and he who disfigures it by abuse or neglect, is guilty of sin; but more beautiful than Apollo is the soldier, lying face forward on the battle-field, grimed with powder, torn with shell, smeared with blood, — since for a sacred cause he dared to die. So we may not only innocently, but laudably, adorn our houses with the treasures of art and the wonders of skill, surrounding ourselves with whatever speaks to the eye or the ear of loveliness and grace; but when, in order to do this, we sacrifice the soul to which they all minister, we rob God. We misuse his bounty. We utterly mistake the meaning of his gifts. They have failed to do their work for us. Instead of drawing us up higher, they have thrust us down lower. We are sensual, when we ought to be spiritual. We value means more than ends. We take the hints and signs of beauty for beauty itself. We put the incidents of life for its essence. And what shall it profit us though we gain the whole world and lose our inward worth? When, on the other hand, we sacrifice these adventitious graces and glories that the soul which they grace and glorify may live, — that virtue and truth and justice may not want a man to stand before the Lord forever, — we show a just sense of the relative value of things, and approve ourselves worthy to be the depositary of liberty for the world.

So it irks me to hear such assertions as that a member of Congress, or any other man, cannot live in Washington, or any other city, on less than three thousand dollars a year. Cannot live? Have we not classical authority for saying that men can not only live, but cultivate the muses, on a little oatmeal? In land where corn is ten cents a bushel, and coal fifteen, is it to be said that a man must die of cold or hunger unless he has three thousand dollars a year? It is absurd. He may not be able to give French dinners and champagne suppers, and japonica parties, and to maintain a style of corresponding expenditure; but let him diminish his expenses. Let him put a knife to his throat if he be a man given to such appetites. When his country is struggling for life, is it any discredit to him to live narrowly for her sake? Is it not rather a credit? Does he not thereby give a pledge of his sincerity and his love? What was generous living becomes heartless extravagance. What would be meanness is heroism. Was Washington ashamed to exhibit before the minister of the great and gay French court "that plain and simple manner of living which accords with the real interest and policy of men struggling under every difficulty for the attainment of the most inestimable blessing of life, *liberty*"? Did Luzerne, dining off the shoulder of bacon, the almost imperceptible greens, and the contingent apple-pie, conceive a low idea of the cause whose champion could thus, for its sake, deny himself the luxuries which fortune had laid at his feet? And if, when the public good demands a reduction of any salary, its recipient profess himself unable to live on less, let him consider whether his life is absolutely essential to the nation.

> "I trust we have within our realme
> Five hundred as good as hee."

Of course, retrenchment should be accomplished

wisely and justly, not injudiciously and indiscriminately. There is that withholdeth more than is meet, but it tendeth to poverty. Let the people insist that abuses shall be abolished, mistakes rectified, extravagance discouraged, dishonesty punished. Let them be scrupulously honorable and careful and economical in all their private measures, effectually frowning down whosoever, in public or private, loveth and maketh a lie, and then welcome taxation! welcome self-denial! welcome poverty, and hardship, and suffering, and death, if, peradventure, the Lord will establish upon us the work of our hands.

Civil war cannot be so fatal to a nation as many have painted it. Cruel and bloody, indeed, must be the fight when brothers fall to blows; but England has thriven on such warfare. Her soil has been drenched again and again with the blood of her children. More than thirty years the white roses met the red in deadly conflict. It was eighteen years from the battle of Edgehill to the coronation of Charles the Second, and to-day, in all the arts of peace and war, England stands foremost among the nations. When mad clouds clash in the summer sky, there is fierce strife, — the flash of death-dealing lightnings and the terrific cannonade of the thunder, — but the earth looks up all the fresher, the air sweeps round it all the clearer afterwards. So we will hope that the storm shall be as a savor of life unto life. The bolts must fall, yet our moral atmosphere shall be purged of its miasms, and our beloved land bloom with a yet unknown freshness, in the light of the Sun of Righteousness.

"Glory to God in the highest, and on earth peace, good-will toward men," sang the host of heaven pouring through the pearly gates of the Celestial City, and floating over the hill-tops of Judæa to proclaim to a ransomed earth the glad tidings of her redemption, — the birth of the Son of God.

But when the fulness of time had come, and the child that was born in the city of David had grown into his manhood, and great multitudes followed him, what words fell on the listening ears of his disciples, whom he was commissioning to go to the lost sheep of the house of Israel? "Think not that I am come to send peace on earth; I came not to send peace, but a sword."

Was then the song of the angels but a song of sirens, or did the Saviour Christ repent or despair of his Divine mission, and in anger resolve to cut down the rebellious people whose hearts were unsoftened to his love? Not so. James, a servant of God, and of the Lord Jesus Christ, has bridged the chasm, and in one short sentence showed us how the stern declaration of Christ consorts with the resounding jubilance of the heavenly hosts: "First pure, then peaceable."

So the clash and clangor of arms that suddenly

cleft the usual din of our busy streets, and rent the silences of our remote hills, and ruffled the quietness of our Puritan Sabbath, was the Gospel — the good spell, the good story — of peace, rendered in a different, harsher, but not less emphatic language than that used by the angels. The sword cuts, through the dense forest and the tangled undergrowth, a highway for the Prince of Peace; the "feverish lips" of cannon thunder out the preparation for the Gospel of peace, and mighty men of war herald the millennial year.

Never has our country seen a more glorious day than that which dawned but now, blood-red in the east, but radiant with white brilliance in the high noon which surely follows. It is the day which the Lord hath made; we will rejoice and be glad in it. It is the day which prophets and kings desired to see, but have not seen. It is a day so pregnant with grand possibilities, that it were better for a man that a millstone were hanged about his neck, and that he were drowned in the depths of the sea, than that he should, by an ill-timed forbearance, or a culpable negligence, or an unmanly timidity, or a criminal love of peace, turn back its near-approaching chariot, and veil it again in the shades of a once-dispelled night. Thrice and four times accursed shall he be who cries peace when there is no peace! We feared, as we entered into the cloud, but we have heard a voice from out the cloud, saying, "This is my beloved Son," and though we can see those divine lineaments but darkly, we fear no longer. The cup which our Father has given us, shall we not drink of it? There may be bitter drops, but we know that love has mingled it, and life lies in the draught.

Many a lover of his country has sought to allay the fierce excitement and prevent its culmination in blows, not for his own sake, not for his country's sake alone, but for the sake of the world; some with the blush of shame, some with the tear of pity, some with the sigh of regret. "What will the world say?" has been often asked, and oftener thought. What will the despotisms say, to whom we have been hitherto a reproach and a terror? Where shall the struggling peoples look when the star that has shone upon them for a hope and a guide goes out in darkness? But take courage. The star has not yet gone out in darkness, and has no thought of going. Those who sorrow, and those who exult over our downfall, are alike premature, for we are not down yet by a great deal. On the contrary, we have been gradually, but continually, coming up higher, advancing, with many retrograde steps it is true, but with steady, average progress, to an elevation whence, looking down on the smiling valleys that lie behind, and the grim abysses that yawn before, we can yet, for the right's sake, with blanched cheek it may be, but with unfaltering step, "march right on, content and bold." We could not always have done it. Not every people can do it now.

As for the world, it cannot judge us. It is not in a position to judge us. It has had no precedent. England, which knows more about us than any other nation, — which has become familiarized by constant intercourse and a common language, and endeared by similar aims, family quarrels, and the strong tie of blood, — even England cannot form a clear and accurate conception of our position. It is the most difficult thing in the world for her to gain a tolerable knowledge of our geography, much less of our political and social institutions, their bearings and necessities. When intelligent English travellers go home and write books about America, in which they put Boston and Georgia side by side in the same class, either as both cities or both States, how can the rank and file of civilization be thought capable of judging what the reefs are on which we have struck? It is undoubtedly true that a very large majority of those who are watching the progress of our struggle from abroad, watch it as the trial of Republicanism. If we go down, many brave hearts panting for freedom will throb heavily, and wicked eyes, watching over tyrannies, will gloat on our destruction; but it is not Republicanism, not even our Republicanism, that is on trial for life, as people will presently learn. If the nation should die to-day, (but it will not,) our experience of self-government, so far from being a failure, would be a signal success. It has given us near a century of freedom and happiness. Under it we have grown from a little one to be a great nation. It has been to us a blessing, and only a blessing. It has not only ministered to our material prosperity, but it has educated our people to a degree of self-respect and self-control, which, low as it seems at times and in places, disagreeable as it often is in its manifestations, is yet, in both quantity and quality, unparalleled among the nations. What other community would have held itself on the brink of civil war as we did? Two forces, — one drawing itself up in battle-array, the other quietly pursuing the avocations of peace, — one dishonestly appropriating to itself for hostile purposes the vast wealth which belongs to both, the other half unconscious, and half apathetic when conscious, and, even when aroused, contenting itself with remonstrance, and held in check, through its loyalty to law, by a power which it despised, — day after day, week after week, month after month, stood face to face and held their peace. It would seem as if a rash act, a palpable blunder, an innocent mistake, might at any moment hurl them into a bloody embrace; rash acts, blunders, and mistakes there were in lamentable profusion; feeling ran high; hearts swelled with indignation;

each felt that the other was trampling on his dearest rights, (at any rate each *said* so, and we know that *we* spoke truly,) and we flamed up to a white heat of passion ; but there was no outbreak. And shall it be said of such men that they are not fit to govern themselves ? They *have* governed themselves, and, by their coolness and patience and wisdom, have shown that they were eminently fit to govern themselves. If the Republic falls, nevermore to rise, let no despot's hand point to the place where it stood, as a warning to future republics. Nothing in its life will have become it like the leaving it. No circumstance of its life hitherto can so strongly prove the inherent strength and dignity, not of man simply, but of men, as this present struggle, even if it should be unto death. The long forbearance of the people that would not believe in treason and matricide ; the simultaneous and spontaneous uprising of a people when treason and matricide spoke out in words that could no longer be misunderstood; the sudden tempest of love and courage and sacred fury that swept through a people when it saw the ark of its liberties endangered, — all this shall go down to the future, and men shall rejoice and tyrants shall tremble at the memory of our Republic, even should it be only a memory.

No, the struggle which convulses the nation does not arise from evils which inhere in its system of government, and develop naturally from its workings. Our Republic is attacked from without, not from within. The rank vine which twines its tightening coils around her sturdy trunk and lusty limbs is no parasite, but a foul foreign growth. It has indeed struck its roots into the same soil, and spread out its tendrils to the same breezes, but the one is a vile and short-lived weed, and the other a tree of life, whose leaves are for the healing of the nations. The contest arises rather from the purity and power of Republicanism. A form of government less antagonistic to human bondage might longer hold on the even tenor of its way, but Republicanism is so founded on the dignity of man, the rights of man, the sacredness of man, that it cannot exist even with a vestige of despotism. It must have free course to run and be glorified, or it must stop running altogether. We have an anomalous civilization. On the one side freedom in its purest form, on the other, slavery in its purest; and the genius of the one is so diverse from that of the other, that the two cannot coexist. All the forces of the one spring upward to light and air. All the forces of the other drag downward to darkness and death. It was the inconsistencies between their own struggle for their rights and a refusal to grant the same rights to their Negroes, that led our fathers to banish slavery from New England. But slavery, banished from New England, throve in a sunnier clime, side by side with the freedom of the austere North. Now the harvest is ripe. Let the mowers whet their scythes, and the reapers put in their sickles, for one or the other shall surely fall. Multitudes, multitudes in the valley of decision. For the day of the Lord is near in the valley of decision.

Is this a day for a man to afflict his soul? to bow down his head as a bulrush, and to spread sackcloth and ashes under him?

Though "it was but a dream, yet it lightened my despair
When I thought that a war would arise in defence of the right,
That an iron tyranny now should bend or cease,
The glory of manhood stand on his ancient height,
Nor America's one sole god be the millionnaire.
No more shall commerce be all in all, and Peace
Pipe on her pastoral hillock a languid note.

"And as months ran on and rumor of battle grew,
'It is time, it is time, O passionate heart,' said I,
(For I cleaved to a cause that I felt to be pure and true,)
It is time, it is time! . . . . . I wake to the higher aims
Of a land that has lost for a little her lust of gold,
And love of a peace that was full of wrongs and shames,
Horrible, hateful, monstrous, not to be told;
And hail once more to the banner of battle unrolled!
Though many a light shall darken, and many shall weep
For those that are crushed in the clash of jarring claims,
Yet God's just wrath shall be wreaked on a giant liar;
And many a darkness into the light shall leap,
And shine in the sudden making of splendid names,
And noble thought be freer under the sun,
And the heart of a people beat with one desire;
For the peace that I deemed no peace is over and done.
By the deathful-grinning mouths of the fortress flames
The blood-red blossom of war with a heart of fire.

"Let it flame or fade, and the war roll down like a wind,
We have proved we have hearts in a cause, we are noble still,
And myself have awaked, as it seems, to the better mind;
It is better to fight for the good, than to rail at the ill;
I have felt with my native land, I am one with my kind,
I embrace the purpose of God, and the doom assigned."

In summing up the pros and cons of this war, the deterioration of the men who are engaged in it, and the general backsliding of society, are usually set down on the *per contra* side. It is taken for granted that morality and religion will suffer, both with those who go and with those who stay. And having thus put matters in train, and given everybody to understand what is expected of him, and that if he sins it won't be very much his fault, seeing it is the prescribed thing to do under the circumstances, it is very likely soldiers and society will answer our expectations, and duly deteriorate according to the statute for such case made and provided.

It seems to me, however, that all this is entirely unnecessary. I see no conclusive reason why our men should come back to us any worse men than they went away, or why they should find us any worse men than they left us. It seems to me, on the contrary, that this is the time of all times when we should expect, and lay our plans for, and strive to bring about, a great revival of religion, — such a revival as we have never yet felt or heard of, so that even a whole nation shall be born into the kingdom of heaven in a day.

It does not prove anything to the purpose, that wars always have been attended with and followed by demoralization. It is a long lane that has no turning. America is not a land of precedents. She is herself an unprecedented nation. She has never scrupled to turn over a leaf because it was new, and there is no reason why she should now. If wars always *have* been demoralizing, it is high time they should stop being so, and there never was a better occasion to change this thing than the present. There is nothing in the origin or aim of this war to demoralize any one. Nobody has to slur over his convictions, that his patriotism may go scot-free. Nobody is required to forget his conscience in his country. Nobody is forced to merge his Christianity in his citizenship. Conscience and patriotism, right and might, all march under the same banner, and fight on the same side. It is such a war, as has, perhaps, never been seen outside of "Paradise Lost." It is a rebellion of wicked weakness against righteous strength. It is slavery, ignorance, cruelty, barbarism, writhing under the iron tramp, and striking its fangs into the mailed heel, of freedom, knowledge, and universal human progress. Every man and boy who goes down to battle can go in the name of the Lord. It is no personal animosity, no sectional jealousy, no party pique, that should whet the sword, and clean the rifle, and nerve the arm. A great cause is endangered, a great principle is attacked. The heart of humanity is struck at, the battle is for the world.

And who are they that go down to the battle? Not, as a general thing, beardless boys, with habits and principles yet in the gristle; not the off-scouring of society mainly, though that undoubtedly drizzles in to a considerable extent; but men with mothers and wives and children at home, — men who have been educated in our free schools, who have worshipped God in our sanctuaries, who have voted in our town-houses, and taken newspapers, and paid taxes, and tilled farms, and built engines, and talked politics, and heard lectures, and given parties. They are men who have had their position and reputation in society and church; and because they have left mother, and child, and church, and shop, are they to begin forthwith to swear, and drink, and turn vagabond, robber, and *roué?* Is this the strength of our boasted free institutions? Have we been trained to a morality that must be laid aside with the civilian's dress, and is vice the prerogative of regimentals? Is our religion a two-year-old child, to fly at the sight of a uniform? Is our virtue so weak that it must be bandaged, and bolstered, and coddled with herb-tea and water-gruel, to keep the breath of life in it, and the moment it is let out into the rough-and-tumble of the world, it droops and dies? Then, verily, we may as well have no virtue at all, and we have made much ado about nothing. It has always been our boast and pride that we raised men. It seems now that we have turned out nothing but overgrown boys. Liberty, education, self-control, individual responsibility, are the birthright of American freemen, and the upshot of it is, that when they are put to the test they cannot stand it! Thrown upon their manhood for three months, or three years, they have not sail enough to keep going, nor ballast enough to keep steady! Then let our free institutions go by the board. If, after near a century of working, they can show no better result than this, away with them. Despotism could hardly do worse. Let the war go, too. Let Davis come, and Floyd, and slavery, and stealing, and the age of pewter and pinchbeck and all uncleanness. A few rods more or less deep in the slough of infamy will not make much difference. Let us write on the door-posts of our churches and our school-houses, "Mene, Mene, Tekel, Upharsin," and then lock the doors, and board up the windows, and begin new.

It is not so. I do not believe one word of it. The eighty years' trial has not proved such an abortion. The mountain has not labored to bring forth such a mouse. I would not so slander our institutions and the brave men who have gone forth to defend them. Our soldiers are not mere machines, working according to the hands of the conductor, though they are that; they are not miserable conscripts, drafted and dragged into a quarrel of which they have no knowledge, and in which they have no interest; they are no vain and empty braggarts, clutching after a vague, glittering, worthless glory. They are men, and soldiers because they are men. They are soldiers of their own free will and choice, — soldiers of opinion and sentiment and settled purpose. They are fighting because they have decided that it is right to fight. They understand what they are fighting for, and what they are fighting against, and when they are going to stop. For a specific purpose, for a limited time, and the better to gain their objects, they have wisely and freely delegated the partial control of their movements to certain leaders; but they are, every man of them, a sovereign, wrestling for a kingdom which is his by divine right, and which usurpers are trying to wrest from him by infernal wrong. He is fighting for his children, and his children's children, to the third and fourth generations. He stands in the van of a vast nation. Behind him is a great multitude, whom no man can number, — men and women and little children, with eager eyes fixed steadily on him, — silent souls of the coming ages, awaiting from his hands their doom, — home, hope, happiness, all that makes life desirable and heaven possible; — above him, the heavenly hosts bending over the battlements of the Celestial City, and hell from beneath moved to meet him at his coming. Is this a day for a man to relax his hold on truth and righteousness?

Is this a situation that should tempt men to sloth and wickedness and riot? Are these the men that shall be found wanting when weighed in such a balance?

"I am shamed through all my nature," when I hear this talk of demoralization. Let us not for a moment admit the possibility of it. Let us not pave the way to vice by announcing that we expect it, and don't let us expect it. Let us not put up sign-boards and finger-posts to ruin, and map out the country for travellers? Let no soldier — let no Massachusetts soldier especially — fancy that his State will make a mock at sin. She will be lenient and tender and forgiving and considerate, but not indifferent. If he forgets or forswears his manhood, he is no son of hers. She does not nourish and bring up recreants. Let him remember that every profane and obscene word loosens the bond of love and sympathy between him and her, and diminishes his claim to her respect. If he steals, or lies, or drinks himself drunk, or in any way approves himself a villain, he disgraces her. He shames the mother who bore him, and is by so much a bastard, and not a son. Let him not think that, because he has bared his breast to bullet and bayonet, he shall cover the multitude of his sins. She will give him praise for bravery, but she will by no means clear him of guilt. Brute courage shall not save his soul from death, and the time is past when it might save his memory from shame.

Watchful, if loving eyes are upon him. North or South, in cottage or tent, Massachusetts expects every man to do his duty. If he is a traitor to that, let him not suppose that his death will bring any loss. However afflictive it may be to his family, however disastrous to himself, his State cannot mourn him. She has no tears for such as he. Sombre hearse and nodding plume, prayer and dirge and funeral pomp, there may be, for, though her blood runs base in his veins, it is still her blood; but for the heart-felt sorrow, and sore regret, and bitter lamentation, that rise to heaven when "a good man meets his fate," there shall be a sense of relief and quiet acquiescence. The air is purer by so much as his foul breath polluted it.

I know that a great deal of scum has probably floated southward in the army; but, if reports approximate the truth, there must be a greater deal of good, pure sap underneath. Many of the unthinking and unprincipled are doubtless there, but there must be a great number of those who have always had the credit of sober thought and guiding principle; and it is the nature of matter that, when light and darkness meet, darkness must give way. A pretty pass things have come to, if a lamp excuses itself from shining because it is in a dark room! What is the good of having a lamp, if it can shine only in the daylight? True, light has its limit, but one little candle can throw its beams very far in a naughty world; and I should think, according to accounts, that there are church-members enough in the army to Christianize the world. Now let them show whether the great revival of 1857 did anything. Let them show whether praying and Christian profession mean anything. If they do, every one of these men should be a missionary. He should not only keep himself pure, but he should be a disinfectant. All around him the air should be sweet and the sky clear. Let his good works be manifest, that his Father in heaven may be glorified. Never, never had men such a charge to keep as have our Christian soldiers. They are emphatically the Church militant. They have laid aside every weight of business and affection and ease; let them lay aside the sins which easily beset them, and they may become apostles and martyrs. "*Dieu et mon droit*," "*Christo et Ecclesiæ*," — every watchword that has quivered on the lips of saint and hero, and is tremulous still with the love and faith and tears and blood that it has embodied, — may tremble on his lips, and find them not unworthy. If he fall, he falls from a greater height to a lower depth. Let him remember that New England is on trial in his person. Though every other soldier should grovel among beasts, his mother State bids him among the rest, in shape and gesture proudly eminent, stand like a tower. Though all others be faithless, let him be alone faithful. Whoever denies the Lord, she bids him not deny the Lord.

She sends forth her sons to be

> "A glorious company, the flower of men,
> To serve as model for the mighty world,
> And be the fair beginning of a time.
> She bids them lay their hands in hers, and swear
> To break the heathen and uphold the Christ,
> To ride abroad redressing human wrongs,
> To speak no slander, no, nor listen to it,
> To lead sweet lives in purest chastity,
> Not only to keep down the base in man,
> But teach high thought, and amiable words,
> And courtliness, and the desire of fame,
> And love of truth, and all that makes a man."

So fulfilling her behests, forever green shall be the laurel on his brow, or, if God so will it, the turf upon his grave.

All this our soldiers will do and be, God and ourselves helping them. I do not believe we shall injure or discourage them, by putting the standard too high. If they are the men we take them to be, they will rise to the emergency. They will justify the confidence we repose in them, and magnify their office.

What is our duty? First, insist on their having plenty of good food. Hunger is a great demoralizer. Secondly, insist on their having good clothes to wear. Rags are the ally of the Devil. Thirdly, provide them with good reading. It is the idle hands into which Satan puts mischief. This is more directly in our power than the first two. Those we can only attain by roundabout measures, by furnishing money which must go through a circuitous channel, and by sharply supervising the supervisors, at the risk of being often in the wrong ourselves, but with the certain result of inducing a more thorough attention than if we were indifferent. Government, however, supplies no ration of books, and the soldiers must look directly to the people. Let them not look in vain. Fourthly, we should stop prophesying evil concerning them. Prophecies often work their own fulfilment. Fifthly, we should be good ourselves, and this is of the first importance. If we are at any one time under any stronger bonds than at any other to do justly, to love mercy, and to walk humbly before God, it is now. If any exigency can call out repentance and faith and love, it is this. If any terrors of the law can persuade men, if any judgments can avail to turn our feet to the testimonies of the Lord, it is the terrors and the judgments that are abroad to-day. Our sin entered into the world, and the death of our beloved ones, who have been smitten down in the beautiful promise of their youth, in the glorious ripeness of their manhood, came by that sin. Sin, sins, are the remote and the immediate cause of these calamities. Some of the ramifications we can trace, others subdivide and disappear from our view, but not from God's. We pandered to iniquity. We have again and again clipped our birthright, and sold the fragments for messes of very watery pottage. We have lightly esteemed our heritage of freedom. We have made us idols of gold, and silver, and bank-stock, and Yankee ingenuity, and material progress. We have waxed fat, and kicked weak nations, and ranted against strong ones, and exalted our own to the heavens. We have strained out without much ado the few little gnats that strayed into our foreign wine, and have swallowed, without wincing, the herds of camels that swam in our home-brewed ale. We have protected our citizens abroad, not so much from the sacred motherhood of country, or a chivalrous and Christian magnanimity, as from a tumid pride; for where our citizens have received infinitely worse treatment within our own domains, we have held our peace. Our reputation before the world was not at stake; it was only a family matter, so we hushed it up. As a people we have minded our personal affairs to the neglect of national. We have betrayed the trust which God reposed in us. We have been false to the blood of our fathers shed in battle. We have ignominiously suffered the nation's weal to be managed by unworthy hands. Becoming disgusted with the trickery, and venality, and selfishness, and sordidness of politics, we have given politics over to knaves, till the very word politician has become a term of contumely. Instead of going into the den, and clearing it out, we have stood off, and, like Pilate, washed our hands, as if to forego action was to forego responsibility. And here we are. Slacking sail, sleeping at the helm, neglecting our soundings, we find ourselves among the breakers. Sowing to the wind, we reap the whirlwind. The chastisement of our guilty peace is upon us. Now let us change all this. Patriotism demands that every man, and woman, cleanse his soul from sin. A nation is no nobler than its individuals. Every man who cheats, or slanders, or steals, adds to the aggregate guilt of the nation, helps to put it beyond the pale of God's protection, and is so far a traitor. Every voter who neglects to vote helps to put his country into evil hands, by not exerting his utmost to put it into good hands, and is so far a traitor, for

> " On life's current he who drifts
> Is one with him who rows or sails."

Let every man see to it that the sin of the nation lies no longer at his door, that his iniquities shall not draw down the wrath of God upon it. Let every man, by his own upright dealings, by his own unblemished manhood, show convincingly that he is on the side of God and his country. This is the way in which things ought to work, and this will effectually dispose of demoralization at home.

The events of the last few months have carried us forward by centuries. It is like one of those great convulsions that mark the geologic ages. After each upheaval, the earth clothed herself with new creations, each higher than the last. She never went back on one day to the rude organizations which were the glory of the preceding day. So we, owing to this great fissure in our prosperity, this great change in our moral atmosphere, have to adjust ourselves to new conditions. We shall press towards the mark for the prize of a higher calling. We owe to God grander lives, holier hearts, than we owed him last year.

O the glory of this new-born freedom! O this splendid rebound from servile acquiescence! To have thrown off the intolerable burden! To cower no longer before an overshadowing evil! To rise up disenthralled! The green withes that bound us snapped asunder at one blast of earnest resolution, and we walk joyfully, unfettered. The thing which we greatly feared is come upon us, and lo it is bursting with good. That fearful looking for is over. The terrible evils, war, secession, disunion, that have been impending so long, are here, and it is a joy to meet them face to face like a man. We know now what their grim features are like, what their boasted power is. We can grapple with them now in unrelaxing death-gripe, and we feel an added strength with every effort. The very struggle has a stern delight. The very consciousness of fighting for the long-oppressed righteousness is an inspiration. If by any sacrifice we can atone for the past, if any efforts can make restitution, they shall not be wanting. God accept the penance and forgive the sin.

Here then we stand on vantage-ground to do battle with sin. We have the prestige of victory. Our consciences are aroused. Our moral sensibilities have partially recovered tone. Now strike while the iron is hot. Now for great awakenings, revivals, not of emotions merely, but of religion, morality, and virtue. Let Christians bestir themselves, and the day is theirs. God's occasions are floating by. As we have dealt with one sin, so let us deal with every sin, — meet it, throttle it, away with it.

It must be so. It will be so if Christians do their duty. With nations, as with individuals, the cross leads to the crown. Suffering is Heaven's agent. It is coming out of great tribulation that we shall wash our robes and make them white in the blood of the Lamb. This sickness is not unto death. It is to eternal life, if we will have it so. Trouble is perhaps an indispensable agent in the formation of character, and we ought to come out of this trouble like gold seven times tried. We ought to be a greater and a wiser nation, a nobler and an honester people, better men, better Christians. We ought to develop those heroic virtues which spring only in troublous times. We shall do it if Christians will be strong, and quit themselves like men.

We have every encouragement to effort. All

hearts are stirred and softened. The air is full of the voice of prayer. Christian mothers pray now as they never prayed before, and mothers that never prayed before pray now. The tens of thousands gone from us went from homes. They were husbands, brothers, sons, the centres of happy circles, the light of tender eyes. Love filled their knapsacks, and bade them farewell. Love could even make their hearts strong with words of good cheer; but love cannot turn aside the swift lead or the flashing steel. God alone is great. He is love's last, as he should be love's first resort. When love can do no more, love turns to God with earnest prayers and tears. Every son in the field can be wrapped around with an atmosphere of prayer. Every mother will pray for her son, and because there are some there who have no mothers to pray for them, let every mother pray for all the motherless, and because every man who fights for our country belongs to us all, let all pray for all. Let no soldier be able to say or to feel, "No man cares for my soul or body." Let the lines between God and us be kept constantly open. Pray that our soldiers and our citizens may be true to their cause, may be kept from evil ways, may wax valiant in fight, invincible in virtue. And this praying spirit should not be suffered to run to waste. Let it, from an emotion, be hardened into a principle, a habit. Let it be penetrative and aggressive.

Let all sorrowful hearts be gently led to Christ, if they do not know the way thither. Let the tender promises of his Gospel fall like dew upon desolate souls. Let our churches and our prayer-meetings be places where grief can find consolation, where love shall find sympathy; ignorance, instruction; loneliness, society; discouragement, hope; repentance, assistance; and the feeblest germ of good, that dew and rain and sunshine which shall make it spring up and bear fruit an hundred-fold.

Let us be mindful of the bodily and spiritual welfare of those who are gone out from us, and let them constantly feel that we are mindful of it, that no forgetfulness or negligence of ours give them excuse, or occasion, or temptation to falter. Let us be equally mindful of those at home, remembering that we are all children of a common Father. Let us keep ourselves pure. Let us pray without ceasing. Let us do with our might, and this affliction shall work out for us a far more exceeding and eternal weight of glory. We shall go on from strength to strength, till in all, and through all, and over all, the Lord God omnipotent reigneth. Hallelujah!

It should continually be kept in mind for our consolation, that this war is a consequence, and not a cause. It is the conclusion, not the commencement of a series. It is accepted, not initiated. It is recuperative, not destructive. I do not, of course, mean to say that, in the Divine plan, it may not work largely as a cause; I speak of the fact as it presents itself to us. Florence Nightingale says that all disease is more or less a reparative process, an effort of nature to remedy a process of poisoning, or of decay, which has taken place weeks, months, sometimes years beforehand, unnoticed. So this war is but the subsequent of disease. We may not survive, but it is not the war that will kill us, but what has preceded the war. The disease was in our blood. War is but the reaction of our sound humanity against it. So long as we went on peacefully, we were heaping up wrath against the day of wrath. The war is only saying to the disease, "Thus far shalt thou go, and no farther."

They, therefore, who lament it as barbaric, heathen, a relic of paganism, are not wise. It is all that. War is always that. An appeal to force is always the resort of savage, immature natures. But the war does not make us savages. It only reveals the fact that we are savages, — a thing which it behooves us to know. The war is not a going back. We were back before. We have never been forward. It is true, we thought we were. We fondly believed ourselves in the van of civilization and Christianity, and it may have been so; but civilization and Christianity were not so far advanced as we thought. This war shows us where we were, and we cry out as if it had put us there. On the contrary, it has not only not retarded us, but it has given us a good lift forward. When we come out of it, if we come out at all, we shall be a great deal farther on than we ever were before. There will be deterioration in detail, but we shall be on higher ground, with firmer feet, clearer vision, stouter hearts, wiser heads. Agriculture, manufacture, and commerce may be crippled, but life will be purified and energized. We shall be greatly improved by being distilled.

What we have to fear in this war is not rebel batteries, or foreign bulletins, but God's sovereignty. Providence is on the side of the heaviest battalions only when the heaviest battalions are on the side of Providence. Nothing has yet been revealed in the ranks of our opponents, actual or possible, which should dishearten us. So far as anything we have to fight against is concerned, I do not see that we need anticipate anything but ultimate, and perhaps not very distant success. But what I fear is, that more is meant than meets the ear, or eye, or pulse of the great body of the people. I tremble when — and only when — I remember that God is just. The woe that I dread does not threaten us from the South, nor from over the sea, but from the justice, the inexorableness, of God. He is a sovereign. His broken laws must be appeased. Who can stand in the day of his anger? I fear lest we have sinned so deeply, that he will hurl against us the thunderbolts of his wrath, till we be utterly consumed.

It is not only the sins of the past, but of the present, that rise up in judgment against us. It is not only slavery, and the vices which it engenders and occasions, for which we must give account, but an unclean spirit, whose name is Legion, who is preying upon our integrity. We have abused the good gifts of Heaven. We have accounted the blood of our covenant an unholy thing, and have done despite to the spirit of grace. Liberty has grown to license on our hands. Loyalty has given place to treachery. Our democracy is rampant and reckless. Our free press is blatant and bloody. Our free speech seems sometimes to have grown idiotic. Our enterprise runs mad. Proofs multiply daily. The course pursued by some of our newspapers is almost enough to make one sigh for a single hour of good, thorough Austrian despotism. Love of country, fear of death, honor, prudence, delicacy, sense, seem to be swallowed up in the desire to see, or to hear, or to tell some new thing. Nothing is too gross for our greedy ears. Dinner-table talk is spread out with Boswellian minuteness on a daily newspaper, and the proprietor thinks it is a feather in his cap. Some fly of a Congressman chances to hear a Cabinet conversation, and, with an itch for immortality, hops straightway into the House of Representatives, and twitters it all out. An exposed place turns up near Washington, through which a hostile army might safely and speedily march to our hurt, and anon a dolt turns up alongside to proclaim it. It is no matter that the information may enlighten rebel brains as well as ours. He who can tell a piece of news is the man for the times, even if we smart for it afterwards. If anybody can, no matter how, find out anything, no matter what, his first duty is to run and tell of it, no matter to whom. The possession of news seems to give a factitious importance. He who can worm himself into the inside of anything, and then turn it wrong side out, is a hero. It would seem as if holding one's tongue were a deadly sin. The gossiping propensities of village sewing-societies have long been the theme of sarcastic comment; but sewing-societies and female tea-drinkings are deaf mutes, compared with the great Gab Club into which American society seems to have resolved itself.

The war has also developed an equal inability or disinclination in our people to mind their own business, and let other people's alone. Civil fingers do not pry into the military arcanum quite as much as they did before the 21st of July, 1861. Then we were carrying on the war swimmingly, knowing a great deal more about it than General Scott, marching down to Richmond with drums beating and colors flying, sweeping the South from Washington to New Orleans, when, of a sudden, Bull Run brought us all up standing. We rubbed our eyes, and concluded that some things could *not* be done as well as others, cleared ourselves by laying the blame vigorously on everybody else, and have since been more modest and reticent. But the evil, abated, is not destroyed. Officers swell and strut in sudden importance at Washington hotels, and their men lie drunk in the streets. A quartermaster sends provisions to troops, and of thirty commissioned officers not one is to be found in camp. Congressional busybodies, instead of stopping at home on Sunday, and saying their prayers, must needs tramp down to see the fight. It may or may not have been necessary to fight the battle on Sunday, but it certainly was not necessary for civilians to leave their churches, and stand agape while it was going on. It is pleasant to reflect that at least one of them atoned for his folly in the prisons of Virginia.

The petty schemes and petty ambitions which are constantly transpiring in our own ranks are far more alarming than anything which has yet transpired in the rebel ranks. It was to be hoped that, in such an emergency, all merely personal interests would be forgotten in the general good; that every man would put his shoulder to the nearest wheel; that fitness would be the only recommendation to place, and propriety the only inducement to measures. But political chicanery cannot be given up; so there is bickering about rank, and parleying on old party distinctions; and, while the country is on trial for life, men dare talk on the bearing which such and such a movement will have on the next Presidency!

There is another thing on which I look with horror, as calculated to bring on us swift destruction, and indicating that we deserve it. I mean the indulgence of what is called the war spirit. The war spirit is utterly hateful. Just so far as it acquires dominion over us, it will drag us down to death. We may count it all joy that we are reckoned worthy to resist unto blood striving against sin. We should count it all joy that God has given us spirit and strength to rise up at last against the iniquity which has overshadowed us so long. We should feel a righteous satisfaction in the struggle, so far as it is a struggle of right against wrong; but coarse exultation, ghastly jesting, lust of revenge, pride of conquest, gloating over the anticipated punishment of the rebels, — this is of the Devil, devilish. I see prints in the shop windows which seem to me like the handwriting on the wall. I see little boys dressed in Zouave costume, and brandishing tiny swords, and I am sick at heart. We are throwing a meretricious glare around the war, and concealing its true issues. We ought not to veil from ourselves the fact that it is solemn, terrible, momentous. We cannot comprehend the grandeur of the interests involved, but we can gird ourselves to present duty, lay aside every weight and the sins which so easily beset us, and press forward. Levity is the result of ignorance or bravado. What I want is, that we should be awake to the emergency. We should put down the war-spirit, and put up the Christ-spirit. It is a question, not of the strength of the people, but the virtue of the people, which is their strength. Are there ten righteous men to save the city? I believe there are, notwithstanding unfavorable indications. The scum comes first to the surface, but there must be a mass of pure liquid below, which will make itself felt. The unanimity of the people is astonishing. Their spirit of self-sacrifice is noble, and not to be mistaken. Only when we have bestowed our goods, and given our bodies to be burned, let us not withhold that other gift without which this will profit us nothing. While doing our utmost, we should pray our utmost, for we are in the hands of God, and not in the hands of man. We must sanctify ourselves, if we would keep the sacred fire burning. We should humble ourselves before God, repent of and turn from our sins, purify our motives, and count all sacrifices nothing, if at last, tried seven times in the fire, we may stand before Him, accepted in the beloved.

No one lesson is more clearly taught by passing events, than the danger of tampering with iniquity. Our fathers knew and felt and acknowledged that slavery was wrong. Its glaring inconsistency with the principles for which they had fought, and on which they proposed to found a great nation, was as obvious to them as it is to the Garrison Abolitionists. They would gladly have exterminated it at once; but there was strong opposition, and, in view of its expected speedy natural death, they decided not to throw it summarily over the ship's side, but to roll it gently down an inclined plane — just as surely into the sea. Instead of making it go at once, they stood upon the order of its going. They compromised with the sum of all villanies. They admitted it into the Constitution, not by name, but by a well-understood euphuism. They meant no harm. They meant only good. They conceived themselves to be acting wisely and rightly. Nothing was further from their thoughts than the subsequent sudden rise and increase of slavery. They supposed that, though they had not killed it outright, they had but smoothed its pathway to the tomb. What was the result? The demoralization of the country for years, the rebellion and treason that now stalk abroad unashamed, the blood shed in Baltimore and in many a battle since, the earthquake shock that quivers through all the land, — these make answer to-day, "Sin, when it is finished, bringeth forth death." It was a little sin, — only a little yielding to wrong, for a little while, — but it has brought forth death.

Not that we should reproach our fathers for incorporating into our national existence one baleful element; but that we are to take warning from them. They had not our precedent and our lesson. They saw only as a mustard-seed this evil which we see as a broad-spreading tree. It was so small a compromise that doubtless it seemed to them scarcely any compromise at all. But we have seen how the little worm has gnawed at the life of a nation, and carried sorrow and a fearful looking for into thousands of families. Their motives were doubtless upright, but God's laws in action are modified only by each other. A mother's tenderest love ruins her child by mismanagement just as thoroughly as if it were the intensest hate. Isabella of Spain, a pure and lovely woman, a most just and gracious monarch, cherished in her inmost heart the welfare of her people; yet she fastened upon their necks the heavy yoke of the Inquisition, under which they have groaned, being burdened, now these four hundred years. God did not hinder her from laying the axe at the root of her kingdom, because she verily thought she was doing him and it service. It may be said that the original concessions were necessary; that the war of the Revolution, with all its sacrifices and sufferings, would have been in vain without some such compromise; that the States would have refused to become United States, and so the nation would have been strangled at its birth, — nay, would not have been born at all.

Here we pass from the known into the unknown. We do not know that anything of the sort would have happened; and if it had happened, we do not know that it was not the very best thing that could have happened. We might have failed to be a great power, but God is able of the very stones to raise up powers unto himself. "It is necessary for me to go, it is not necessary for me to live," was Pompey's reply to the weeping friends who would have held him back from fate. It is necessary to do right; it is not necessary to be a nation. What might have happened had liberty been brought out from the struggle with no blot on her escutcheon, we do not know. She came out with one damning spot thereon, and what has happened we do know. Sin, finished, has brought forth death, and the end is not yet.

No. Wrong is wrong forevermore. The corrupt tree brings forth corrupt fruit, however carefully planted and constantly watered. Purity of motive may avail the actor before God, but not the act in his world. Consequences follow relentlessly on the heels of causes. A fact once a fact is forever beyond our reach. What may come of it we do not know, and it is not our province to ascertain. We are responsible only for the fact. Of course, I speak only of actions that have a moral quality. There are many courses of conduct which have, of themselves, no moral quality, and their eligibility depends entirely on the probable consequences; but when two ways are open, one of which is right, and the other a little wrong, we are to choose the right, notwithstanding the evils which threaten to follow. The choice is ours, the consequences God's. We see the evils behind the right; we do not see the evils behind the wrong; but the inexorable logic of God's laws will ultimately reveal them. It may seem to you that the wrong is but for a moment, and its effects imperceptible; but some fact of which you never dreamed may be travelling towards you with swift, unerring feet, and its spear-touch shall change your dwarf into a giant. Your little sin shall receive an impulse that will drive it on continually, perpetuating, enlarging, and multiplying itself. The men of the Revolution could not see an idea which lay hidden in Whitney's brain, but at the appointed hour it came forth, and changed the face and fate of slavery. The moment you do a wrong thing, no matter though your motives be pure, no matter even though you are unconscious of the wrong, that moment you have put yourself out of the line of God's righteous sequences; you have disturbed relations, destroyed balance, broken law, and you know not where you are, nor whither you are drifting. But do the right thing, and, though you may not see the way far before you, you may surely know that you are in harmony with God, you are parallel with the line of his laws. You are precisely where you ought to be, and who is he that shall harm you, if ye be followers of that which is good?

But this "logic of events" has two sides. It is powerful for good as for evil. An act done with bad intentions may result in good, just as truly as act done with good intentions may result in evil. Let this be our hope to-day. A most wicked war is waged by the South for the support and extension of slavery. Glory to God in the highest, and on earth peace, if it shall result in the abolition of slavery. Our fathers did not take up arms for independence, but they achieved it before they laid them down. We did not enter upon this war for the purpose of abolishing slavery, but every day strengthens the probability that that will be the issue. It is not the end which the government has in view, but it may be the end which God has in view. Destiny marches on, and if slavery stands in the way, slavery must go down. There would, indeed, be a sublime, a divine justice, in destroying this overshadowing wrong by the very instruments relied on for its indefinite increase. It was begun with set purpose of wickedness, but let not him that girdeth on his harness boast himself as he that putteth it off. Once begun, the war and its issues passed out of the hands of its beginners forever. It will go on according to its own irresistible laws. The voice that evoked is powerless to lay it. The hideous monster may become the terror and the destruction of its creators. Nor, if this is indeed in the decrees of God, can men at the North, any more than mobs at the South, prevent it. The Northern mind is gradually becoming familiarized with the thought, and the more we look at it the more desirable it seems. The Republicans spoke truly in affirming that they did not design to meddle with slavery in the slave States; but twenty, fifty, a hundred years of change have come since then, and different premises require different conclusions. Slavery has meddled with them. Slavery has reached out its leprous hand to strike at them, and to pollute the fair heritage they would leave to their children; and it is to be decided now how best to "crush the wretch." It is a difficult and a dangerous problem, but it will be solved. Just how the bands of the oppressed are to be loosened we do not see; nor how the victims of oppression, freed from its fetters, shall be freed from its horrors, its vices and ignorance and barbarism; but the same God that has used this nation to enslave them, and shall use it to free them, — making us, free agents as we are in our small spheres, blind tools to work his will in his infinite sphere, — can surely make and point out a way to preserve, protect, and enlighten his down-trodden little ones. We must hurry slowly. We need not borrow trouble. When the time comes, we shall have come too. Our present duty is to secure and maintain the integrity of the nation. God will strengthen and fit us for any work that may result from the prosecution of this work,

Confident I am, that where one man, a year ago, considered the speedy extinction of slavery feasible and desirable, one thousand watch, and wait, and pray for it now.

Let the war go on, then. If we are not engaged in a righteous cause, may the Lord send us defeat after defeat, disappointment after disappointment, till we weary of fighting against him, and return repentant to his ways. I know no such ethics as "My country, right or wrong!" save, as has been admirably said, when right, to be kept right, — when wrong, to be put right. If we are, as I verily believe, armed with the sword of the Lord, let us go on, if God please, till every inch of our soil is free, — free to slaves, free to freemen. Let the Black Hole be cleansed, and thrown open to the day. Let there be no corner of our vast domain where man shall not be held sacred, where his opinions may not find free utterance, and his person entire safety. The South says she may be crushed, but she cannot be conquered. Very well. Let her be crushed, then. Just as she pleases about that. The hurt of the daughter of my people is no surface wound, to be gently bathed and tenderly bandaged. It is a deep-seated sore, sending down its malignant influences to the dividing asunder of soul and spirit, making the whole head sick and the whole heart faint. If nothing will avail but the surgeon's knife, let the surgeon's knife cut sharp, quick, and deep. It is better to enter into life maimed, than to die unscathed. Let us be sealed unto God, even though we be baptized with the baptism of fire. The North is not to be saved from the South. The South is to be saved from herself. Her own loyal sons are to be saved from the foes of her own household. Her children are to be saved from the vice that creeps in upon their hearthstones, and corrupts their blood, and poisons their manhood, and darkens their womanhood. The whole country is to be saved from the traitors that defile while they attack it. Every blow struck is struck for the South as much as for the North. We strike *at* the rebels and the rebellion of the South, and *for* the South. The only victory we want is over her worst enemies. North and South will alike, though not equally, suffer. We look for no easy conquest. We are prepared to meet the energy of despair. We anticipate a mortal combat, but the South must be redeemed. She must be brought out from the Valley of the Shadow of Death. Most gladly would we give every son of hers the right hand of fellowship, and bid him good luck in the name of the Lord; but if the wrong can be wiped out only by wiping out the men who cherish it, and the men who defend it, God's will be done. The land shall rest and enjoy her Sabbaths. As long as it lieth desolate, it shall rest. It is better that a state should be a desolation than an abomination. Men and women and children, the innocent and the guilty must suffer alike; but it hath been so aforetime. It is the immutable law of God, that the penalty of guilt shall not be monopolized by its perpetrators; but the South grinds in the prison-house, and the redemption of her soul is precious. Not revenge, nor hatred, nor pride, but the tenderest love and the largest benevolence demand the sacrifice. The dumb mouths of her fettered children, black and white, the generations that wait in the grand and awful future, the here and the hereafter, all demand this at our hands. The justice and truth in our own hearts demand it with so imperative a voice, that it were

> "better to have fought and lost,
> Than never to have fought at all."

Let us make the case our own. Is there a man, woman, or child in Massachusetts, who would not rather our beloved State (God bless her!) should sink into the ocean depths forever, with her freight of a million souls, than that she should be given up to slavery? And should we spare any sacrifice to save others from a doom which is so fearful to ourselves?

Let us come up to the height of this great argument. Let us be strong, and quit ourselves like men.

I have seen and heard deprecations of slavery discussions at the present crisis. "This war," it is said, "is not a war for the abolition of slavery, but for the existence of the government." "Antislavery harangues will only alienate some who are now the stanch allies of the government." "Many will become disaffected, if the war is made to turn slavery-ward." "One thing at a time." In all of which there is some truth; but, ever since I can remember, balancing of powers, parties, and principles has been in vogue, and this is what we have come to. Here, an able leader, a world-renowned statesman, cannot be our candidate for the Presidency, because his election will drive the South into secession. There, a measure must be dropped, because it will alienate certain localities. Such and such a territory must be acquired, at the price of blood, to conciliate such an interest. Such and such a question must not be debated, because it will inflame passions. So we have tacked and shifted and beaten, and here we are plump in the middle of the very whirlpool which our prudence was to avoid. With all our reticence, we are precisely in the position which we were reticent in order to keep out of. Now let us try another plan awhile. Let us say what we think, and be straightforward, and not so far-sighted for consequences, and see where that will land us. If there are any persons attached to this government by such a spider's web that they will fall off if slavery is brought in, let them fall. Doubtless the government can stand it, if they can. A patriotism that, at this late day, will suffer itself to be cut loose from its country by slavery discussions, is not a thing to be depended on. Patriotism, to be good for much, must be made of sterner stuff.

Moreover, what is true in the remarks I have quoted applies solely to the government. Nobody wants Mr. Lincoln to issue a proclamation announcing the object of the war to be the abolition of slavery. It would not be true. The war is, indeed, a war of self-defence, not of slavery extinction; but this self-defence may come to demand the extinction of slavery as a "military necessity." Until then, government has no right to act in the matter. "One thing at a time," certainly. The one thing on hand now is the war, which is to be carried vigorously on to a successful termination. But it is to be carried on by the government; and the readers and writers of books and of newspapers generally, the speakers and hearers in popular assemblies, the hosts and guests in drawing-rooms, the knots at the exchanges and the village post-offices, are not the government. Down below the government lies the people; and while the government, at the bidding of the people, its creator and master, is crushing rebellion, and uprooting treason, and protecting loyalty, and vindicating its own life, "we, the people," may legally and reasonably take counsel together that the republic nevermore receive harm from the hand that strikes at it now. This is alike our duty and our right. Having provided the sinews of war, we have nothing further to do with it but watch and wait and pray. It is not in our power or our province to direct its processes. Our interference would be intermeddling. We order its existence, but we delegate its details to other hands. Yet we hold the power. We are responsible to God, and we shall be held to strict account by posterity, for the direction which that power takes. When this people wills to put away the accursed thing, the accursed thing will go. While the armies are fighting, we should plan. When they come back to us garlanded with laurel, we should go out to meet them, not only with grateful welcome, but with the death-warrant in our hands of the wretch whose wrath they have bearded, whose cunning they have foiled, and whose power they have broken.

Has not the accursed thing filled up the measure of its iniquities? Read the roll of crimes. It is written in blood. What woe it has wrought to that unhappy race which has writhed under its grinding heel, we only a little know. Into the secrets of that prison-house we cannot penetrate. Over that bridge of sighs we may not pass. Ever and anon a miasmatic blast sweeps past our startled ears. A sob, a wail, a shriek, a moan, floats up the heavy air. A lurid light flames out, a sickly sunshine, pale, and blue, and ghastly, flickers for a moment on the sluggish bog, but the silence and darkness come back. Only the All-seeing Eye discerns. God forgive us that we have been too insensate of our lowly brother's woe, too unmindful of his weal. God overrule his long sorrow to his longer joy, as we believe He has already begun to do, and turn away from us the fierceness of His anger.

But what the grim Grendel has wrought for our own race we better know. All these years he had been working evil under the sun. Bench, and bar, and hall, and pulpit, and counting-room, and field, and fireside, have been tainted with his presence. He has tampered with public and private honesty. He has debased, degraded, and brutalized American freemen, marring their birthright. He has turned their beautiful garden into a wilderness. The ignorance that disgraces, the vice that demoralizes, the barrenness that lays waste the South, are all his work. He has made our nation a stumbling-block, a hissing, and a byword to the nations. He has introduced discord and brawling, insolence, rapacity, and murder, into our national councils. The bitter hatred that fires the South against the North is all his doing. The financial derangement that weighs so heavily and perplexes so fearfully, that plows furrows in young brows, and baffles the wisdom of old experience, and scatters the fruits of life-long toil, and imbitters homes with anxieties for the loved, — all are of him. But the destruction of property, the stagnation of business, the pressure of want, are the least evils of Slavery. He has despoiled us of our honor. He has poisoned our fountains. He has polluted our holy things. The widespread treachery that has desolated us like a plague, and made us feel as if the solid ground were failing beneath our feet, had its root and rise in him. The broken oaths, the piled-up perjuries that have at once exasperated and saddened us, lie at his door. What shall a man give in exchange for his soul? What woe can fall upon a nation like the disgrace of her children? What is the price of a mother's blush for her son's shame?

Slavery has done more. His hands are red and reeking. O my country! The voice of your children's blood crieth unto you from the Everglades of Florida and the lowlands of Texas. It was Slavery that led them and left them there to die. It is Slavery that arms brother against brother to-day. Young wives are widows, young children are fatherless, old men go mourning to the grave, matron and maiden are desolate, because Slavery has laid the delight of their eyes in the dust. From once fair Maryland and royal Virginia — old and blighted and effete before their time under the simoom of Slavery — pale, still forms are borne back to us, that went out overflowing with sweet life. The youngest, the bravest, and the best have fallen. Love and liberty and law, whatever is most beautiful, most cherished, most sacred, this Slavery demands.

The tears of mothers, the silent anguish of white-haired fathers, the fears and foreboding and heart-ache that sit by uncounted firesides, mark where his footsteps have been.

Now let us make an end; for why should we be destroyed, we and our children? When we scotch the snake, why not kill him, and have done with it? We may disable him for a time; but so long as there is life left in him, there is an accursed thing in the midst of thee. O Israel, thou canst not stand before thine enemies until ye take away the accursed thing from among you. We may crush the rebellion, and reinstate peace, but if we leave slavery where it was, if we simply restore the *statu quo*, it will be sowing to the wind, and our children will have to reap another whirlwind, only more violent than that which is sweeping over us. Just as long as slavery is a part of our institutions, just so long is there a rotten pillar in our temple, which may at any moment give way, and bring us to confusion and destruction. To restore peace, leaving slavery as it was, is to put a ship on her course when she has been lightened by the spasmodic efforts of "all hands at the pumps," without stopping the hole through which the water rushed in. It is to weed a garden by cutting off the witch-grass with a hoe. It is to allay boiling and steam by pouring on cold water. We want not only the hold emptied, but the leak stopped. We want not only treason cut off, but its roots dug up. We want not only the steam checked, but the fire put out, so that there may be no more steam made. We do not want every generation or every century to be convulsed as we have been. Let us make a full end. If we stop short of that, all our work will have to be done over again at some time. There is an irrepressible conflict between freedom and slavery. There will be an irrepressible agitation so long as they both live. We never can have peace with this element of discord. We cannot serve God and mammon. One or the other must be dethroned. We are not left in doubt as to which it shall be. Eighty years of trial have revealed the true aspect and tendencies of Slavery. Arraigned at the bar of civilization and Christianity, the verdict is, "Guilty!" In her has been found the blood of prophets and of saints. She is become the habitation of devils, and the hold of every foul spirit, and a cage of every unclean and hateful bird. All nations have drunk of the wine of the wrath of her fornication; and I hear a voice from heaven saying, Come out of her, my people, that ye be not partakers of her sins, and that ye receive not of her plagues; for her sins have reached unto heaven, and God hath remembered her iniquities. Reward her even as she rewarded you, and double unto her double according to her works: in the cup which she hath filled, fill to her double.

I know that even slavery has its sunny side.

Kindness, benevolence, affection, devotion, self-sacrifice, are not wanting there. Instruments of love as well as instruments of cruelty are in that habitation. Man is better as well as worse than his system. But a luxurious vegetation springs up from the deadly Pontine Marshes. It was a *goodly* Babylonish garment, a splendidly massive golden wedge, shekels of fine silver, that wrought folly in Israel. But for all their gold and goodliness, they were none the less an accursed thing. Moreover, the virtues that exist in slavery do not spring from it, but in spite of it. Slavery does not cherish them. It only cannot kill them. The destruction of slavery would not be the destruction, but the cultivation, of every good thing that is found in it. Its abolition will be the abolition of what is hideous, an abomination to God and man. Every pleasant relation, every opportunity for the exercise of every virtue, will remain. Every grace that makes slavery less repulsive will make freedom more beautiful. Every gem that adorns the brow of slavery shall be transferred, to shine with renewed and increasing lustre in the diadem of freedom. Nothing will be permanently lost, but that whose loss is infinite gain.

I know that slavery cannot be destroyed without inconvenience, and perhaps positive suffering, on the part of many who are guiltless of its sin; but it cannot be retained without immeasurably greater. It is not a question between an evil and a good, but between an evil and an evil. It was a great deal of trouble to stop in the enemy's country, take Israel by tribes, the tribes by families, the families by households, the household man by man, till Achan was taken. It was a sad thing to bring Achan, and his sons, and his daughters, and his oxen, and his asses, and his sheep, and his tent, and all that he had, into the valley of Achor, and stone him with stones, and burn him with fire; but it was a greater trouble, and a sadder thing, to see Israel fleeing before their enemies, and the hearts of the people becoming as water, and the face of the Lord turned upon them in anger. It is hard to lose a right eye; but if thy right eye offend thee, pluck it out, and cast it from thee. It is not only no loss, it is *profitable* for thee that one of thy members should perish, and not that thy whole body should be cast into hell. In the extirpation of the accursed thing, loyal hearts may be alienated, undeserved indignation may be aroused, unoffending persons may suffer, but in the face of great events "the individual withers, and the world is more and more." The evil will be temporary, the good everlasting. So far as we can, we will help our brothers bear the burden, but the burden must be imposed. For their sakes and for our own, for the nation's sake and for posterity's sake, we must take this weight on our shoulders. The scenes of the last few years, culminating in the horrors of the last few months, must never be repeated. It would be unspeakable cowardice, and weakness, and selfishness, for us, with our experience of its effects, to hand this accursed thing down to trouble future Israels. No opposition from any quarter must be allowed to overbear our will to be free. All manner of opposition from those whose affections or whose selfishness is interested must be expected, and met, and put aside. Slavery has glorified herself, and lived deliciously; and it is natural that the kings of the earth who have committed fornication and lived deliciously with her shall bewail her, and lament for her, when they shall see the smoke of her burning. And the merchants of the earth shall weep and mourn over her; for no man buyeth their merchandise any more. When the fruits that her soul lusted after are departed from her, and all things which were dainty and goodly are departed from her, and she shall find them no more at all, it is not strange if the merchants of these things which were made rich by her shall stand afar off, for the fear of her torment, weeping and wailing, saying, Alas, alas! for in one hour so great riches has come to naught. And every shipmaster, and as many as trade by sea, shall stand afar off, and cast dust on their heads, and cry, weeping and wailing, Alas, alas! for in one hour is she made desolate. But rejoice over her, thou heaven, and ye holy apostles and prophets; for God hath avenged you on her.

The constitutionality of slavery has been the stumbling-block to conscientious and practical minds. Recognizing fully its undesirableness both in a moral and economical point of view, they have felt that they had neither the right nor the power to lay their hands upon it. The only weapon they could bring to bear against it was influence. This discrepancy between conscience and the Constitution has been fruitful of conflicts between well-disposed citizens. One extreme has gone so far as to set aside the Constitution because it recognized slavery. They called it a covenant with death and an agreement with hell. The other extreme accepted slavery against their own moral sense, because it was found in the Constitution, and they considered themselves bound by that for better, for worse. Accepting its benefits, they felt constrained to accept its drawbacks. I must confess that the Constitution never troubled me in the least. It is to be interpreted either by the letter or by the spirit. If by the letter, there is no recognition of slavery. The word "slave" or "slavery" does not once occur. It talks of "persons held to service," &c. It says such persons "shall be delivered up on claim of the party to whom such service or labor may be due." Certainly. By all means. Common honesty requires it. If a teacher is engaged to teach a year in Mississippi, and falls homesick, and is so weak as to run home instead of staying there and braving it out, stern justice should shut its eyes to his weakness and force him to return and finish his school. If a Northern blacksmith refuses to put on Southern horses the shoes which Southern money has paid for, and rushes to his mother State for help, let her not shield the culprit, but set him *vi et armis* before his forge and anvil. If a clergyman stealthily and feloniously leave his parish before his time is out, bearing with him both salary and sermons, O carry him back to old Virginia, and make him preach his barrelful. Law and equity alike demand it, and all well-educated people will say, Amen! But what service is due between two parties whose only contract is force on the one side and fear on the other? Who can show the papers wherein God made over his ownership of his children to any man or men? If any slave-hunter can show to the slave-harborer a quitclaim deed from God of Sambo or Andy, let Sambo and Andy be given up, but not till then. When service can be proved to be due, let service be exacted, but let not past service exacted be the proof of future service due. That would be to make wickedness self-generative. That would make the fact of plunder the justification of plunder. That would turn Christ's "If any man take away thy coat, let him have thy cloak also," into "If thou *canst* take away any man's coat, it establishes thy claim to his cloak also," and would make a true thief's motto of "Whatever is is right."

If it is the spirit of the Constitution that is to be observed, we are all in delightful harmony again. The spirit of the Constitution contemplates the speedy removal of slavery, not its increase or perpetuity. The framers of the Constitution did not design to cherish it into vigor and power, but to break its fall. The safeguards they threw around it were not to save it, but to make it die easy! Those who are its firmest supporters admit this. The so-called Vice-President of the Southern Confederacy admits that the fathers were antislavery. They could not conceive that a nation which had just struck the fetters from its own limbs should rivet them on the limbs of another nation. They could not conceive that liberty should be worsted in a nation which had just come off conqueror in its name. Their fear was lest liberty should degenerate into license. They saw that there might be danger lest, in their enthusiasm for universal liberty, they might trample on rights. So far as I remember, there are but three allusions to slavery in the Constitution. None of these ordain slavery. All three are rather protective. No unprejudiced reader can, I think, deny that they are designed as breakwaters against the rapidly and powerfully advancing tide of antislavery. The framers of the Constitution evidently believed they saw the signs of slavery's speedy overthrow. They seem, indeed, to have feared lest it should be overthrown before the country could be disentangled from it, and so both fall together. Slavery must fall, but they would let it down softly, and give everybody time to stand from under. The Constitution was so framed that emancipation would make not even a verbal change necessary. The spirit of the Constitution is essentially antislavery.

So then we are at one both as to the letter and the spirit, though we get there in a roundabout way, — somewhat as light travels in that instrument by which itinerant showmen enable the astonished to read through a brick. By an arrangement of mirrors, the rays of light are so reflected that the image to be seen, instead of going straight to the eye, turns four angles, but comes right side up at last. (Opticians will pardon a confusion of popular and scientific language in this illustration. Most of my readers are not opticians, and will not know that everything is not just as it should be.)

If this should seem a Jesuitical and tortuous mode of reasoning, I will simply say, that, although I do not think so, I will not press the argument, because I do not need it. For slavery neither by name nor nature is ordained in the Constitution. It is recognized as a fact, but it is not established as a law. Now the recognition of a fact does not establish a law. It was a fact that there were persons in the country at the time who were not free, and, though the fact could be glossed over, it could not be entirely ignored; but its acknowledgment neither justifies nor perpetuates it. To say that a man is not free, is a very different thing from saying that he shall not be free.

"Slaves for want of legislation are not quite like slaves by law." So long as slavery hid its noisome head in the Dismal Swamps of the South, I will admit that there may have been "reason on both sides," but the secessionists have changed all that. Slavery, under their lead, has abandoned its stirring, silent, watchful passivity, and struck openly. Even as a transient thing, the fathers opposed slavery, but with an opposition which its expected speedy death made feeble. Supposing that it would be confined to the very limited locality where it then existed, and that it would shortly perish before a rapidly advancing energy, education, and Christianity, they contented themselves with rocking the cradle of its declining years and preparing for it decent burial. But even granting that they legislated with its perpetuity in view, they legislated only for an institution, not for a mortal foe. Since their time, slavery has reared its huge form in open hostility. It has striven to strike down the pillars of state, unconscious that its own ruin would be involved therein. It has attempted the life of the nation. It has assaulted with intent to kill. It is guilty of murder in the first degree. Whatever constitutional right it had to live, its wicked course has forfeited. It has no more lien upon life than the murderer. Just as well might he lift his blood-stained hands, and plead against his gallows sentence the acknowledged right of all men to life, liberty, and the pursuit of happiness, as slavery point to the Constitution for protection. A woman promises to obey her husband, but if he goes mad and bids her fling herself from the garret window, does her marriage vow bind her to do it? A man takes a pet kitten to please a departing friend, and promises to cherish it all his life as a memento. But the kitten turns out to be a tiger, and puts the man's life and the lives of his children in jeopardy; does his promise bind him? The slavery which our fathers saw was a playful, if rather snappish kitten, compared to the ferocious tiger into which the accursed thing has grown. Now lifting its fiery eyes from rending our children's flesh, and licking its bloody chaps, and growling its beastly wrath, shall it find safety in the Constitution? Heaven forbid! Rather take the beast, and with him the false prophets who deceived them that had the mark of the beast, and them that worshipped his image, and cast them into a bottomless pit of reprobation, abhorrence, and infamy, in whose lowest deep a lower deep still threatening to devour them opens wide.

I am sick at heart when I hear the word *compromise.* The rumors which have sometimes darkened the air seem to have had no foundation; yet, because habit becomes a second nature, I cannot hear them without a thrill of dread. I could almost wish the word even blotted from our language. Doubtless there is such a thing as a just and righteous compromise, — a relinquishment of individual benefits for the general good, — a yielding of desires for the sake of peace, — a sacrifice of prejudices, tastes, sentiments, interests, in deference to the weakness of others. But the compromises with which Americans are most familiar are such as to whelm the word in odium. We have not so much compromised as submitted. We have deferred to threats till we have earned the reputation of cowards. We have incurred the contempt, even, of those for whose sake we have given up our principles. We have sacrificed everything to peace, and — Heaven be praised! — we have not got it. Besides being cowards, we have been fools. We have been deaf to the voice of history, which has always thundered in our ears that no nation ever purchased a satisfactory peace. Rome bought off her foes with gold. We have bought off ours with honor, and the result is one. Every evil spirit so exorcised has returned, bringing with him seven other spirits more wicked than himself. But the lesson went unlearned. One after another of our great men has passed through the fire to Moloch, and the cry is still, They come. Compromise is the rock on which our lives, our fortunes, and our sacred honor have been stranded, and men dare to speak of it still. We have seen both its wickedness and its folly. It has outraged our moral sense, and has not accomplished anything; yet there are men who cling to it. Firmness in the outset might have prevented the evil, and certainly could not have made it any worse than it is now. If, when slavery threatened disunion, we had but stood our ground, this quarrel might never have arisen, or, if it arose, it might have been speedily allayed. Every time we have staved it off by compromises, we have been giving it ampler

"room and verge enough,
The characters of hell to trace."

With every respite, the accursed thing has taken breath, enlarged its lair, sharpened its claws, and waxed fat. With every day, the arena of the contest has been widened, its results multiplied, and its intensity and bitterness increased. It may indeed be, that, in the end, this postponement may be seen to have resulted in good. It may be that God will overrule the severity of the struggle to the welfare of the combatants. It may be that, if the question had been sooner and more easily settled, treason would not have been so utterly abolished as we trust it now will be. It may have been allowed to attain its present enormity, that men may awake fully to its character and consequences, and trample it under foot forever. But, although it is well enough for us to console ourselves with this reflection, the thing being done, it is no justification to the authors, and no guide for the future. It is always right to make the best of a bad position, but it is never right to put ourselves in a bad position because we *can* make the best of it. Judas betrayed our Saviour to the cross, and the world was redeemed, but no thanks to Judas. However much God may overrule our sins to carry on his own wise purposes, we are not justified in continuing in our sins. Our business is to make *straight* in the desert a highway for our God, — to let our eyes look right on, and our eyelids straight before us. If God can use evil for good, how much more can he use good for good!

As for compromise, it is not to be so much as named among us. Compromise! Compromise with traitors! Compromise with men who have incurred the unutterable guilt of lifting their hand against their own mother! What fellowship hath righteousness with unrighteousness? What communion hath light with darkness? What concord hath Christ with Belial?

It is said that these vague reports are sent out as "feelers." Let them be feelers! Let them feel the indignation and abhorrence and utter loathing of an outraged people, from whom virtue is not yet clean gone forever; and, when they have felt this long enough and strong enough, let them draw back into their dens and make report.

There is probably less danger of a compromise now than there will be after the war shall have been finished. The indignity offered to our flag roused the patriotism and chivalry of the people, and they are not likely to sheathe the sword till the insult is avenged. The measure of their long-suffering is the measure of their indignation. I think they are more awake to the importance of crushing this rebellion than they are to the importance of eradicating its cause. I fear that, when the war is over, a mistaken magnanimity towards the vanquished, an eagerness to show to the South that we are not their enemies, the lack of a full and clear comprehension of the magnitude of the issues involved and the bearing thereon of the continuance of slavery, will induce them to deal with it leniently, and give it a new lease of life. I fear that slavery now, as after the Revolutionary war, dreading immediate destruction, will clamor or sue for new or renewed guaranties, and that the people, with a false generosity, will grant them, and so let the occasion for righting themselves pass by. Slavery will lie bleeding and helpless at their feet, and pity for a fallen foe will make them overlook the enormity of his crimes and the malignity of his nature. But slavery, in little or in great, loyal or rebellious, tyrant or suppliant, is always and everywhere accursed, and we cannot stand till we take away the accursed thing from among us. Cruel in power, subtle in weakness, its malign purpose is ever the same. Whether by a direct or a winding way, it goes to one mark. It preys and feeds and gloats on the souls of men. Enslaved and enslaver are alike its victims. It is of the Devil, and the lusts of its father it will do. Armed to the teeth to rob us of our birthright, and speaking great, swelling words of vanity, it is no more dangerous than fawning at our feet and begging for guaranties. Guaranty! Yes, give it one more. Guarantee to it a swift death and a shameful burial. It certainly seems to me that if, after our experience, we let things go on just as they did before, we shall richly deserve to be oppressed and despoiled evermore. It is not enough to restrict slavery. All our restrictions will scarcely bring it into smaller compass than it occupied eighty years ago. But from that acorn sprang to-day. Experience has proved that simple restrictions are not enough. We must not only bind it with cords, but the cords must be continually tightened to the death. We should not only adopt measures that look to its extinction, but measures that are to bring about its extinction. Never, never again, must our beloved land receive such a stab as that from which she is now bleeding. In what manner her redemption is to be accomplished — whether by a skilful untwisting or a sharp and sudden cleaving of the Gordian knot — we are neither able nor called upon yet to decide; but let it be done. It is no hostility to the South that shall rid her fair borders of the accursed thing, nor any true friendship for the South that shall retain it there. Fire, and earthquake, and a great and strong wind, may accompany and retard its removal, but they are of the Devil, and will pass away. And after them shall come the still, small voice of the Lord, to approve and soothe and bless, and then shall we have that peace whose basis is righteousness, and whose effect is quietness and assurance forever.

So far I had written weeks ago. Now, as I take up my pen once more on this sad summer evening, there falls upon my ear the inarticulate roar from a fearful battle-field, — the melancholy moan of wounded men; and the shadow of a million hearts rests heavily on mine. Be pitiful, O God!

But the clangor of battle, the deathful embrace of brothers, the wail of passion and pain and anguish, are the works and words of the accursed thing. O thou accursed thing! The Lord send upon thee cursing, vexation, and rebuke in all that thou settest thine hand unto for to do, until thou be destroyed, and until thou perish quickly. The Lord make the pestilence cleave unto thee, until he hath consumed thee from off the land. The Lord smite thee with a consumption, and with a fever, and with an inflammation, and with an extreme burning, and with the sword, and with blasting, and with mildew, that they pursue thee till thou perish. The Lord cause thee to be smitten before thine enemies, that thou go out one way against them, and flee seven ways before them. The Lord smite thee with madness, and blindness, and astonishment of heart, that thou grope at noonday, and be only oppressed, and spoiled evermore, and no man shall save thee.

O my people! I call heaven and earth to record this day against you, that God hath set before you life and death, blessing and cursing; therefore choose life, that both thou and thy seed may live. That thou mayest love the Lord thy God, and that thou mayest obey his voice, and that thou mayest cleave unto him, (for he is thy life and the length of thy days,) that thou mayest dwell in the land which the Lord sware unto thy fathers to give them.

Alas! sadder than any moan from battle-field, sadder than any mother's lament, comes to me the voice of a people that will not be wise, — the voice and vote of a people that thrusts out the Negro from its borders, ignores his rights, his claims, his weakness, and says to the Most High God, "Am I my brother's keeper?"

What we have most to fear in this war is not iron rams nor infernal machines, but the stupidity and wickedness of our own selves. It is this which prolongs, and must prolong, the war more than anything which the rebels can bring into the field, or sail or sink in the water. Such a paragraph as the following, from the *New York Times*, is full of shot and shell: —

"A prominent gentleman, and a Republican office-holder, who has just returned from Cincinnati and other Western points, reports a general development of an intense anti-Abolition sentiment in all quarters of the West, since the Wendell Phillips riot in Cincinnati. This feeling, he reports, is based on the popular repugnance to 'Negro equality,' toward which the Abolitionists are supposed to be tending, — no white man being so poor in his own esteem as not to feel himself 'better than a Nigger.'"

We have no right to expect peace, we should have no desire for peace, so long as such a frame of mind remains. If a year of war has done no more for us than this, if a year of war leaves us still in such bonds of iniquity, a thirty-years' war will hardly more than free us, and I pray that the war may never cease till we *are* free. I should esteem as the greatest curse with which this nation could be accursed, the coming of a peace when there is no peace. We welcomed this war with a solemn joy, because we believed its crimson hand would scatter broadcast over our country the seeds of a new life. We believed that the day of the Lord was nigh, when he would either wrench up the evil or wrench up the nation. We cannot think the last. We cannot yet read a handwriting on the wall, "God hath numbered thy kingdom, and finished it"; nor can we believe that he has shaken this nation from centre to circumference only to let us settle on our lees once more, with our taste remaining in us, and our scent not changed. Surely there is a future for us only waiting our eye and touch. And if in the nation the paltry and pitiful idea couched in the closing paragraph which I have quoted still obtains, we shall have no peace yet, though Donelson has slain his thousands, and Pittsburg his ten thousands. That miserable paganism must be scourged out of us. We must be driven by ten, and ten times ten plagues, if need be, to recognize that God hath made of one blood all the nations of the earth. The hire of our laborers, which has been kept back by fraud, crieth, and that cry has entered into the ears of the Lord of Sabaoth. In his hand there is a cup, and the wine is red; and we, in such case, the most wicked upon the face of the earth, shall wring out and drink the dregs thereof, if we shut our ears to that exceeding bitter cry. In the thunders of the cannonade that roll from shore to shore, I hear the voice of the Lord: "Understand, ye brutish among the people, and ye fools, when will ye be wise?" Every stalwart form that sinks down upon the battle-field, or wastes away in the hospital, is a messenger from God, saying unto us, "Turn ye, turn ye, for why will ye die?" Let the land be sown thicker yet with graves. Let the bolts of Divine wrath descend swift and ceaseless, till through all the land there shall not be a house in which there is not one dead, rather than the hurt of the daughter of my people should be slightly healed. If the sword should be sheathed before slavery receives its death-blow, — before its vile image falls face downward on the threshold, — before our respect and deference and tenderness for it are obliterated, and its name and memory uprooted, cast out, and trodden under foot of men, — I should believe that God had *reserved* us to a day of fiercer wrath and more signal destruction. I should believe that he had given us this last golden opportunity to rid ourselves of an incubus, a shame, a crime, and that we, failing to embrace it, had incurred the terrible doom, "He is joined to his idols, let him alone."

So it seems to me that we are not yet ready for peace, even if peace were ready for us. We shall not be ready for it so long as we go a-whoring after caste, and color, and other false gods. The war has not yet done for us what we hoped, and prayed, and worked for such a war to do. It has broken up our idols, but it has not extirpated idolatry from our hearts. If it should cease to-day, I greatly fear that we should go wallowing in the mire again to-morrow. We are not yet, as a people, brought straight up to an out-and-out abhorrence of slavery for its own sake. We have not yet been set long enough face to face with its barbarism. We have not yet been lashed close enough cheek to cheek with its body of death. Its slime and stench have not gone deep enough into the secret place where our souls abide, and turned them sick with loathing. We execrate the derangement and devastation which it has wrought in our own homes, but we are not half awake to the horrible crimes which it has committed against the wretched race that has so long ground in its prison-house of despair. It lifts its head from bending over their prostrate forms, lifts its hand dripping with our brother's blood, and turns its glowering gaze on us, and leaves its baleful finger-prints on our door-posts, and we spring up shuddering, to thrust it back; but a simple folk, whose only power to resist was patience to endure, a mirthful people, made pathetic and apathetic through woe, an affectionate people, borne down, and held down, even, by their affections, hold out chained hands, dumb hands, beseechingly to us. Not only because we will not be slaves, but because they shall be free, should our swords leap from the scabbard, and our cannon belch forth death. Down into the valley of the shadow where they have walked so long, that sword-shine has gleamed, that cannon-roar has echoed, and carried light and hope for their darkness and dole. It belongs to us to keep keen blades and strong arms till hope has become fruition. It is not enough that we fight to preserve our government. We must fight to purify it. We should fight not only for our own lives, but for the lives of these little ones. We must not only break the heathen, but uphold the Christ. God will certainly not forget these poor who have cried day and night unto him. I tell you that he will avenge them speedily, and if he does not avenge them by us, he will avenge them on us. If we do not fight for God, we shall fight against him, and if haply we be found to fight against God, we shall surely be on the losing side.

We do ill when we merge the moral aspects of this war in its political aspects. We must act politically, but we should think morally. And only when our politics are moral can they be truly politic. Good morals may not always be good politics, but bad morals can never be. We cannot free slaves because we think they ought to be free, but we can think they ought to be free. We can bring our opinions abreast of our powers, and shoot our desires and designs world-wide beyond them. We can press, with our public spirit, and our public opinion, and our private deeds, close up behind the slowly advancing ranks of our soldiers and our law-makers, and receive with open hands the panting fugitives who came to them slaves, and whom they pass over to us men. These outraged people have demands upon us, though they do not know it. They are grateful to us, though we only discharge a late duty. We can and should recognize their claims. We should pay, not give. Liberty is their due. Education is their birthright. Withheld, it has not been forfeited. More than this, we should urge on our soldiers and law-makers to greater deeds. Our thoughts should be continually in advance of them, though our acts can only follow in their wake. Let this idle, brutal, and madly stupid talk of fanaticism, and abolition, and emancipation cease. Emancipation is the touchstone of this nation. By this sign shall it be known whether we work the works of God or of the Devil. The government that we are fighting to uphold is not the old hulk, dismantled, water-logged, rolling, helpless, becalmed, on slavery's dead sea of Sargossa, but a new, strong, oaken-ribbed, iron-clad man-of-war, with her steam up, her portholes open, her banner streaming, bearing down with her whole fire, and force, and speed, and strength, upon that mystery of iniquity; and her sealed orders are to loose the bonds of the oppressor, and to let the oppressed go free.

What do these men want, — these denouncers of fanaticism? That slavery should be let alone? It will not be let alone. It shall not be let alone. There is no such thing written in the book of fate.

20

All the agitation that has been deprecated and denounced for the last thirty, forty, fifty years is but a ripple in a wine-glass compared with the rage and madness, the sweep and swirl of the heaving, seething, boiling ocean-billows that such a settlement of the slave-question would stir up. The infernal dragon has sown his teeth in every valley, on every hill, by every water-course of the North, and for every tooth springs up a man, and every man a Garrison. For every spirit laid by such exorcism shall come seven other spirits seventy times more rabid with antislavery virus than the first. Men talk about saving the country by putting down Abolitionism. Have they been asleep for these last thirteen months? Do they think the American people is the same people now that it was then? Do they think the old spectre of dissolution is going to haunt us again, and the old farce of Union-saving to be played over? Are they going to raise storms about the ears of Abolitionists, as in the good old times?

Yet there is danger just here. Though thou shouldst bray a fool in a mortar among wheat, with a pestle, yet will not his foolishness depart from him. Folly that is persistent, vigilant, determined, is more than a match for wisdom that is careless, lazy, and diffusive. Weary of conflict, longing for peace, we shall be very apt to declare in a general way that slavery has received its death-blow from the war, and so relax our efforts and let things work. But a great wrong like slavery, that appeals to indolence, and avarice, and lust, and pride, and every evil passion and possibility of the human heart, will stand a good many death-blows without dying. It has received hard knocks, but if the war stops now, what is there to prevent slavery from girding up her loins and starting afresh? It is not safe to let things work unless you have put them in good working order. It spoils the fabric and ruins the machinery. You must make things work right, or they will work wrong.

We need not clamor for the immediate abolition of slavery. But by all this most costly blood that we have poured out on a thrice accursed soil, we have a right to demand that no settlement of this controversy shall be final, which does not provide security for the future as well as indemnity for the past. No settlement which merely holds out inducements to abolition — which merely contemplates the possibilities of emancipation, and provides for its contingencies — is enough. Our fathers settled it so, and here we are. We want a plan laid, landmarks set up, boundary-lines defined, and a hand on the wall, visible through all the world, writing before the doomed gaze of slavery, "Thus far shalt thou go, and NO FARTHER! God hath numbered thy kingdom, and FINISHED it!" We want a paved highway through every State, from Maine to Texas, on which Wendell Phillips and

Lloyd Garrison and Beecher and Sumner and Lovejoy may go secure, lecturing, as they go, to all who choose to hear them. We want the scourging of women, the stealing of children, the crushing of men, the stifling of free speech, all the raving and ravening of the mother of harlots and abominations, to cease. A year of agony that shall have done this is a year of the right hand of the Most High. A thousand years that shall have failed to do it are but as the small dust of the balance.

What matters it though we do not yet know what shall be done with these freedmen of the republic. The best way to find out what future duty will be, is to do present duty. Present duty is to free the slaves as fast as possible, and educate them as fast as they are free, and keep our eyes open all the while. If we do not do this, we are more guilty than the slaveholders. They did but accept slavery thrust upon them. We shall reject liberty thrust upon us. God provided himself a lamb when he would receive sacrifice. "Who shall roll us away the stone from the door of the sepulchre?" asked the mournful women, for the stone was very great. But when they came to the sepulchre, lo! the angel of the Lord had already descended from heaven, and rolled away the stone. So let us go with sweet spices, not to embalm a dead, but to anoint a risen Lord, in the person of these his little ones. Never fear but that we shall not only find the stone rolled back, but where we looked to see a stark corse and garments of the grave, we shall stand face to face with an angel, whose countenance shall be like lightning, and his raiment white as snow; and so this sepulchre of death shall be the temple of the Lord of life.

Cambridge: Stereotyped and Printed by Welch, Bigelow, & Co.

www.ingramcontent.com/pod-product-compliance
Lightning Source LLC
LaVergne TN
LVHW020933110826
845150LV00004B/850